FROM NEWMAN
TO NEW WOMAN

UCD WOMEN REMEMBER

Edited by Anne Macdona

**NEW
ISLAND**

Editorial Board of UCD Women Graduates' Association

Acknowledgements

Nothing worthwhile happens without hard work, and this undertaking required just that from the committee working on the project. One of our committee members, Sally Corcoran, is deserving of special credit for her work in promoting the project, and thanks are due to all of the other members who also worked so diligently with it. The committee would also like to extend their deep gratitude to our editor, Anne Macdona, who was so patient with our many demands.

The Editorial Board wishes particularly to acknowledge the assistance given to it by Katie Kahn-Carl, Maire O'Neill, Louise Richardson, and Audrey Woods.

Thanks are also due to the UCD Achives Department for kind permission to use archive material.

FROM NEWMAN
TO NEW WOMAN

UCD WOMEN REMEMBER

Edited by Anne Macdona

**NEW
ISLAND**

FROM NEWMAN TO NEW WOMAN
UCD Women Remember
First published November 2001 by
New Island, 2 Brookside
Dundrum Road, Dublin 14

Editorial matter copyright © UCD Women Graduates' Association
© The copyright for each contribution in this volume remains with the
original copyright holder

ISBN: 1 902602 67 6

British Library Cataloguing in Publication Data
A catalogue record for this book is available from the British Library

*The publishers have made every reasonable effort to contact the copyright holders of
the material contained herein. If any involuntary infringement of copyright has
occurred, sincere apologies are offered and the owners of such copyright are
requested to contact the publishers.*

The Arts Council
An Chomhairle Ealaíon

New Island receives financial assistance from The Arts Council
(An Chomhairle Ealaíon), Dublin, Ireland.

Cover design: Slick Fish Design, Dublin
Printed in Ireland by Colour Books Ltd.

CONTENTS

UCDWGA President's Foreword   *i*
Women in University Education in Ireland:
   The Historical Background   *iii*
Mary Hayden: The First President of the WGA   *xii*
Women Graduates' Association: Beginnings   *xviii*
Editor's Note   *xxv*

Contributions
   1906–1920   *p1*
   Mary Semple: *Frances Kennedy: What's in a Name?*   1
   Kate O'Brien: *UCD As I Forget It (1916–19)*   2
   Catherine McDowell: *Margaret Dearey (Ginnety),*
      A Daughter Remembers   10

   The 1930s   *p11*
   Mary Semple: *Going Hatching*   13
   Bridget O'Brien (Carroll): *In Dublin's Fair City*   14
   Doris O'Brien Cassidy: *Society Girl*   21
   Lorna Reynolds: *Hereditary Martyrs*   22
   Monica Nevin: *Tribunals — Even Then*   25
   Peig Roche: *Coffee, Cream Buns and Civil War*   31
   Cliodhna O'Neill: *Caitlin Uí Neill (Ní Chaoimh), Trailblazing*   36
   May O'Meara (Carroll): *A Trip in Time*   38
   Máire Redmond: *Lightening the Mood*   41

   The 1940s   *p42*
   Breda Ryan (O'Brien): *Parking? No Problem!*   45
   Marie O'Neill: *Doing Two Things at Once*   47
   Nellie Beary O'Cleirigh: *Looking Back*   50
   Marie Fennell: *The Age of Innocence*   54
   Carmel Duggan: *Seats for Sale!*   56
   Teddy Burke: *The Coldest Winter*   58

Sister Kathleen Sullivan: *Observing the Silence* 61
Máire Gibbons: *Standing Room Only* 63
Maedbh Ní Concubhair: *A Scoop* 65

The 1950s *p67*

Joan Trodden Keefe: *Course Work Optional* 70
Anne Kernan: *A Bygone Era* 73
Mary Fahey Mc Keogh: *One Hundred and Seventy-Two
    Women Grads* 75
M. A. F. Carley: *The Idea of a University* 77
Susan McKenna Lawlor: *The Road to Damascus
    through Merrion Square* 79
Eda Sagarra: *Jobs for the Girls* 83
Sarah H. J. Poyntz: *Who Am I and What Am I Doing Here?* 90
Katie Kahn-Carl: *Out of Africa* 92
Lelia Doolan: *Dramsoc* 95
Clare Mc Donough (Connolly): *No Trousers Please, We're Ladies* 99
Rosaleen Linehan: *First Good Revue* 102
Teresita Durkan: *From* Goldenbridge: A View from Valparaiso 106
Eithne Bennett: *Ellen Power* 108
Helen Burke (Binchy): *Not Just Ivory Towers* 112
Sister Eveline Loreto McLoughlin: *Seasons in the Sun* 117
Paula Loughlin (Doyle): *Girls Do Honours Now* 121
Maeve Binchy: *Another Circle of Friends* 125
Gemma Hussey: *Was it a University?* 130

The 1960s *p133*

Eleonore Tuohy (Johnson): *No Registration Necessary* 136
Barbara Prendergast: *On Your Bike!* 140
Nicola Jennings: *Starting Out* 143
Ita Daly: *Skies Always Blue* 146
Sally Corcoran: *Three Ages of College* 149
Sister Vera Mc Grath: *Infinite Possibilities* 152
Deirdre Carroll: *Changing Times* 153
Una Claffey: *Gentle Revolution* 156
Marie Egan-Buffet: *Passion Will Out* 159

Olivia O'Leary: *Dangerous Enthusiasts* 161
Dolores MacKenna: *A Rich Landscape* 165
Perdita Quinlan (Gusken): *Coming in from the Cold* 168
Áine Gallagher: *The Terrace Years* 169

The 1970s *p172*
Éilís Ní Dhuibhne: *Reader, I Married Him* 175
Bernadette Glenn: *It's a Learning Thing, Man* 180
Catherine O' Callaghan: *If at First You Don't Succeed …* 184
Marie Altzinger: *Locker Room Romance* 185

The 1980s *p188*
Suzanne Egan: *Have J1, Will Travel* 191
Clare Eager: *Age is No Requirement for Maturity* 194
Susan Towers: *From Leg Warmers to Power Suits* 197
Doreen Finn: *Look Back in Envy* 200
Teresa Duggan: *A Daring Adventure* 203
Paula Hastings: *Meet You at the Blob* 205
Emma Donoghue: *A Free Space* 209
Ciara Considine: *Leap into the Unknown* 212

The 1990s *p216*
Anne Cassin: *Soldiering On* 219
Anne Simpson: *Growing Up* 222
Anne Mc Gettrick: *Following in my Mother's Footsteps* 225
Catherine Rossiter: *Party Time in the Goldfish Bowl* 227
Lynn McGrane: *Not Always a Bed of Roses* 229
Ruth McNamara: *Small World* 232
Katie Long: *A Fine Madness* 234
Emer Horan: *Of Mice and Men* 237

UCD Women Graduates' Association: Now *241*
UCDWGA Chronology of Activities and Events *243*
UCDWGA Presidents, Vice-Presidents, Secretaries,
    and Treasurers *245*

The UCD Women Graduates' Association gratefully acknowledges the financial support of University College Dublin and A&L Goodbody Solicitors towards this project.

Foreword

There was a hit song in the middle of the last century entitled 'Memories are Made of This'. This book is made of memories: memories of the experiences of women who attended University College Dublin during the twentieth century; many happy reminiscences, some less happy, but each one encapsulating the writer's own unique recollection of her student days.

In 1998, when there was a global focus on the approaching end of the millennium, the UCD Women Graduates' Association decided to assemble a compendium that would reflect women graduates' perspective on UCD during the last century. It was, of course, the first century during which a new social category, 'Irish women graduates', had emerged. It was due to the efforts of many of our founders that the advantage of university education in Ireland was secured for women. You will read more about that in the brief history of the Association that forms part of this book.

Women graduates from all faculties and time-spans were invited to contribute to this compendium. All of the contributions received have been lodged in the UCD Archives. It was decided that an anthology would be produced from edited material to celebrate the centenary, in 2002, of the founding of the Women Graduates' Association. The contributors are not all necessarily well-known, although many names will be familiar. The contributions are simply from women who responded to an invitation that was extended to all women graduates. That invitation still stands. The Association would be delighted to receive contributions for the archives on an ongoing basis.

For the present volume, we owe a debt of gratitude to our contributors, all of those women who took the time, in the midst of very busy lives, to sit down and write their recollections. Our work was more than rewarded by the enjoyment we got from reading their reminiscences and being transported as we read them into other times, other locations, but always, in essence, UCD. We hope that you will share the same experience.

Eithne White
UCDWGA President 2000–2002

Women in University Education in Ireland: The Historical Background

University education for women in Ireland began with the establishment of the Royal University of Ireland (RUI) in 1879. The Queen's Colleges in Galway, Cork and Belfast quickly followed suit, with all facilities in those colleges available to women by 1895. Dublin University – or Trinity, as it was popularly known – was closed to females until 1904.

The experiences of females in third-level education can be gleaned from college magazines. *St Stephen's* (of the Catholic University, later UCD) gives a hint of such experiences in a regular piece entitled 'Girl Graduates' Chat'. (The title was later changed to 'From the Ladies' Colleges', following charges that the original title was frivolous and suggested 'childish babble'.)* The contributors were primarily students from St Mary's Dominican College, Alexandra College, and Loreto College, Stephen's Green, all of whom were studying for RUI degrees. They exchanged gossip and described efforts to obtain employment for university graduates. Lively debates in Irish were reported from St Mary's, with Agnes O'Farrelly, a future Professor of Irish at UCD, to the fore.† Students who excelled at examinations were singled out for praise. Miss Ada English was congratulated on her success in medical examinations, as was Agnes Perry on becoming the first woman to gain honours in the M.A. in Mathematics.‡ *St Stephen's* noted with delight that female medical students were 'well known' and excited 'little or no extraordinary attention in moving through

---

* *St Stephen's* Feb. 1904, p. 44.
† *St Stephen's* June 1903, p. 258.
‡ *St Stephen's* June 1903, p. 266; *St Stephen's* Nov. 1905, p. 179. Agnes Perry was the sister of Alice Perry B.E., who became the first female engineer in Ireland in 1906.

Dublin social circles'. However, it was felt that in certain homes, where daughters were 'trained to no method of earning their bread', university students were 'received with ill-concealed envy and jealousy'.*

Alexandra College Magazine likewise gives an insight into the activities of that college. Like *St Stephen's*, it regularly praised its illustrious graduates. Regular reports from societies (such as the Literary Society), as well as games activities (particularly hockey) featured. The magazine also devoted space to possible openings for women, and talks were given on topics such as 'Journalism as a Profession for Women', and 'Women as Poor Law Guardians'.†️ Opportunities for women in the colonies were also alluded to, and the Debating Society debated the topic, 'Should Women Enter the Professions?' Nineteen supported the motion and six were against. The debate aroused great enthusiasm according to the secretary.‡️ An indication of the manner in which the debate over women's work had progressed, partly in response to World War I, is evident from a motion discussed in 1917. The topic by then was 'That every Woman should receive Professional Training'.§️ Readers of *Alexandra College Magazine* could keep in touch with international events in the educational field through the reports on the International Federation of University Women. Past pupils also recounted their experiences of other educational institutions, such as Danish High Schools. Student publications alerted graduates to opportunities in the jobs market, as well as providing news of social activities.

---

* *St Stephen's* Feb. 1904, p. 44. One of the reports from *St Stephen's* indicates the manner in which nationalism and suffragism became intertwined, particularly in the Catholic University. One female student threw a heavy volume of Byron at the Union Jack flag above the lecturer, and shouted '*Vivent les femmes!*' *St Stephen's* June 1904, p. 89.

† *Alexandra College Magazine* Dec. 1899, pp. 427–33, 440–44.

‡ *Alexandra College Magazine* June 1908, pp. 39, 59.

§ *Alexandra College Magazine* June 1917, p. 64.

It is worth bearing in mind that, for most females, third-level education until the early 1910s was by way of the Ladies' Colleges. Graduate numbers between 1891 and 1900 were as follows: Victoria College Belfast, 95; Alexandra College Dublin, 84; Loreto College Dublin, 20; Queen's College Belfast, 19; St Mary's Dominican College Dublin, 17; Magee College Derry, 17; Queen's College Cork, 2; Queen's College Galway, 1.

Many of the aforementioned institutions were single-sex environments. Mary Hayden, while presenting evidence in 1902 to the Robertson Commission on University Education, proposed that co-education would alleviate many of the disparities suffered by women at third level. This was achieved with the establishment of the National University of Ireland in 1908.* A contemporary of Hayden's, Mary Macken, remembered her time at Loreto College, Stephen's Green, where tuition in Latin and Science was difficult to obtain. P.A.E. Dowling helped the First Arts students with the compulsory Mathematics and Science. Macken also noted the excellent teaching in Latin and Logic of Sr Mary Eucharia, who gave her a letter of introduction to Monsignor Macken, one of the trustees of the Catholic University.

Mary Macken here alerts us to the need for students to have a 'sponsor' who would see that they were catered for. Catholic connections were fully utilized by religious orders in placing their students at universities abroad for language study. When Sr Eucharia went to Cambridge as Superior, Mary Macken went with her and studied at Newnham, one of the women's colleges at Cambridge University.† These links were vital to the development of professional and social networks for women, and should not be

---

* Macken, Mary, 'Women in the University and College: A Struggle Within a Struggle' in Tierney, Michael (ed.), *Struggle With Fortune, a Miscellany for the Centenary of the Catholic University of Ireland* (Dublin, 1954) pp. 142–65. [For a short biography of Mary Hayden, see pp. xii–xvii below.]

† Macken, 'Women in the University and the College', pp. 153–54.

underestimated. Male students were at an academic advantage in that the Royal University appointed Fellows to teach on their courses, whereas women were more likely to be taught by non-graduates. Hence, the pursuit of qualifications abroad was essential.

Trinity officially opened its doors to women in 1904. Alexandra College undoubtedly viewed the opening of Trinity in an ambivalent manner. Many, particularly Isabella Mulvany, the headmistress at Alexandra School, thought it would benefit females in their pursuit of suitable employment; Henrietta White, the principal of Alexandra College, thought it would adversely affect student numbers at her institution. In the long run, hers was an accurate assessment. Nonetheless, for a quarter of a century before Trinity was available, Alexandra provided the vital qualifications for a professional career.

By 1934, there were 242 females (16%) and 1,484 males in Trinity. The presence of Oxbridge female students who came to Trinity to graduate since they could not graduate from their home universities, may also have opened intellectual doors for Irish women. The writer Mary Colum describes the visitors: 'intellectual dragons, they knew all sorts of things like biology and modern science such as our more literary training discounted'.[*] As regards college activities, the 'Ex-Science Association' (an association for students who had graduated with a Science degree) was the first college society to accept women as ordinary members, and their exclusion from the Classical Society was all the more puzzling given that they were taking Classics courses, and winning prizes.[†]

In a work focusing on American women, Barbara Miller Solomon suggests that female collegians 'came from a range of

---

[*] Colum, Mary, *Life and the Dream* (Dublin, 1966) p. 82.
[†] Purser, Olive, *Women in Dublin University 1904–1954* (Dublin, 1954) pp. 8, 14.

families within the broad and expanding middle class'.[*] From the evidence available on Irish university women, there is nothing to contradict the view that Ireland was any different. Education was expensive, and scholarships scarce. True, some students resourcefully worked their way through college, but these appear to have been exceptions. Family support was often crucial. Just as interested staff sought opportunities for their students, extended family members were also vital in providing support systems for female students. It was not unusual for women to be aged twenty before commencing a university degree. Some worked before they entered college. Lengthy college careers, such as medical degrees, occasionally necessitated work, possibly teaching, before preparing for a second profession. Several medical graduates took a B.A. degree, a Higher Diploma in Education, or a Music degree before they opted for a medical career.

As noted above, the Ladies' Colleges were at a disadvantage in the RUI as they did not have the benefits of university Fellows on the staff. However, university graduates taught in some of the Ladies' Colleges. When the first RUI degrees were awarded in 1884, five of the nine female graduates were teaching at Alexandra.[†] Not surprisingly, there was a strong link between these educated women and their efforts as activists in the Central Association of Irish Schoolmistresses, to improve female access to higher education. In March 1891, for example, the CAISM discussed the possibility of establishing a course in the RUI to train teachers. This group of educated women was heavily involved in opening Trinity to women, and making the Junior Fellowships of the RUI available to them also.

---

[*] Miller Solomon, Barbara, *In the Company of Educated Women: A History of Women and Higher Education in America* (New Haven, 1985) p. 64.

[†] O'Connor, Anne, and Parkes, Susan, *Gladly Learn and Gladly Teach: A History of Alexandra College and School, Dublin 1866–1966* (Dublin, 1983) p. 44.

Northern women, particularly those in Belfast, could attend Victoria College Belfast, Methodist College Belfast, or St Dominic's. Alternatively, they could sit the RUI exams through private study. This was preferable for Catholics in particular, since Queen's College Belfast (after 1908, Queen's University Belfast) was perceived as a Presbyterian institution. There were only 208 male and female Catholics in QUB in 1920. In 1947, Catholics constituted only 20% (400) of the student population.[*] Magee College in Derry admitted women students in 1883. Eight matriculated female students entered, including Mary Kennedy, who subsequently went to Girton in Cambridge and was placed first in the Natural Science Tripos. Unlike Queen's in Belfast, where women were eligible for all prizes from 1895, the Magee females were immediately eligible for all prizes. With the establishment of the NUI, Magee was linked with Trinity. Some Magee students excelled in the Trinity examinations, and the females were particularly prominent in languages.[†]

The Royal College of Science also provided aspiring professional women with qualifications. Their register of students indicates that women who were taking Science courses at the RUI used the facilities of the College of Science for practicals and specific courses. Some students were registered as 'teachership in training' and most had their fees paid, possibly by the Department of Agriculture and Technical Instruction. The register for 1905 to 1926 (when the College was transferred to UCD, and became the university's Science Faculty) indicates that over 40 female students were awarded Royal College of Science diplomas. Many of these

---

[*] Rafferty, Oliver, *Catholicism in Ulster 1603–1983: An Interpretative History* (Dublin, 1994) p. 175.

[†] Holmes, R.F.G., *Magee 1865–1965: The Evolution of the Magee Colleges* (Belfast, 1965) pp. 46, 70, 75.

described themselves as teachers in training or National School teachers.[*]

There was also scope for occasional students to study at the Royal College of Science. In 1881, Isabella Mulvany registered for Practical Physics, as did ten students from Alexandra, probably at her prompting. However, they did not complete the course. Amelia Grogan, who later became a medical doctor, completed several courses in 1887. Emily Dickson, the first female Fellow of the Royal College of Surgeons, was awarded the second prize in Botany in 1890.[†] Katherine Maguire, who graduated from the RUI with a First class Honours medical degree in 1891, passed examinations in Botany and Zoology in 1887.[‡]

It is interesting to note that women were admitted to the Cecilia Street Medical School (subsequently the UCD Medical School) before they were admitted to lectures at the Catholic University. The RUI recognized Royal College of Science courses as part of one's medical training.[§] These opportunities were vital for women who were starved of Science courses at second level. The possibilities for women in Science contrast favourably with continental developments. It was not until 1920 that women in Germany were granted official permission to obtain a doctorate, while Rosalind Clarke, for example, who pursued an academic career in Chemistry at UCG, was awarded a D.Sc. in 1914 by that university.[**] At second level, the numbers of women taking Science had improved, no doubt because they were benefiting from trained

---

[*] RCS Student Registers UCDA B64 1905–25.

[†] RCS Student Registers UCDA B65 Register of Occasional and Non-Associate Students 1867–1906; 1879 nos. 50–61; 1887 no.1, 1889 no. 22.

[‡] RCS Student Registers UCDA B65 Register of Occasional and Non-Associate Students 1886–87 no. 32.

[§] Hogan, Mary, *U.C.D. Women Graduates' Association 1902–82* (Dublin, 1982) p. 10.

[**] UCG Calendar 1930; interview with Christy Townley (who worked in UCG between 1936 and 1982; he was librarian from 1960 to 1982), July 1995.

Science teachers. By 1921, 31% of those taking Science at second level were female.[*]

By 1930, women were well established in Irish universities. In one of the smallest of Irish universities, University College Galway, which had 263 students in 1926, there was an equal number of male and female students by 1930.[†] In University College Cork, for the 1917–18 academic year, there were 113 (20%) female students of a total of 566.[‡] How do these figures compare internationally? In 1925, 11% of German university students were female; in Italy, women constituted 17% of university students. Meanwhile in France, the figure was 20%, whereas in Finland, one third of university students were female. Ireland was on a par with Finland, as by 1925, 30% of all Irish university students were female.[§] The Irish figures therefore compare well with other Western European countries.

Higher education, it was believed, would allow women to lead 'a richer, freer life and made fuller personal development possible, freeing women from mere eccentricity, political faddism, philanthropic hysteria and busy-body shallow restlessness.'[**] This was an inaccurate assessment. Ironically, it was the experience of college life that propelled many women into political activity and philanthropic professions. University education provided women with opportunities. They had the chance to excel at examinations,

---

[*] O'Donoughue, Thomas, 'The Irish Secondary School: Curriculum and Curricular Policy in Ireland 1921–1962' (Ph.D., UCD, 1988) p. 250.

[†] Townley, Christy, 'UCG: A Short History – The Early Years' in *Cois Coiribe* 1993 p. 26.

[‡] Murphy, John A., *The College: A History of Queen's University College Cork, 1845–1995* (Cork, 1995) p. 130.

[§] Flora, Peter, *State, Economy and Society in Western Europe 1815–1975. A Data Handbook. Vol. 1. The Growth of Mass Democracies and Welfare States* (Frankfurt, 1983) pp. 574, 575, 589, 596, 601.

[**] Quoted in Bhreathnach, E., 'A History of the Movement for Women's Higher Education in Dublin, 1860–1912' (M.A. UCD, 1981) p. 146.

therein finding the motivation to seek professional occupations. University careers also aided the development of female networks that furthered professional careers. Moreover, the presence of female role models stimulated aspiring professional women. Records indicate that, having received a university education, female graduates were indeed more likely to pursue professional careers.

What had changed for UCD women by the end of the twentieth century? An essay of this brevity could not even attempt to chart the changes and, more importantly, the absence of change. Perhaps the following statistic will provide food for thought: in 1998, there were 64 sports scholarship students in UCD. Four of them were women.[*]

Ad Astra and *Comhthrom na Féinne* – *To the Stars* and *Fair Play* – are the Latin and Irish phrases on the crest of University College Dublin. Their university years, for some women, provided an opportunity to reach for the stars, but for many others there was very little fair play.

Margaret Ó hÓgartaigh

---

[*] Sport scholarship statistics courtesy of Dr Tony O'Neill. One female athlete who was consistently refused a scholarship competed in the Olympic Games in Atlanta. She graduated with an Honours degree.

Mary Hayden:
First President of the Women Graduates'
Association

No account of women in UCD in the twentieth century would be complete without a portrait of Mary Hayden, first president of the Women Graduates' Association and a leading campaigner for women's rights. The names Mary Hayden and George Moonan may still evoke some memories of the textbook, *A Short History of the Irish People*, which was used by Leaving Certificate History students until the early 1960s. The section of the book covering the period from 1520 onwards was, apart from an occasional chapter on Gaelic literature, entirely the work of Mary Hayden. Published in 1921, the *History* was, as the authors acknowledged, written from a frankly national standpoint, and was intended to provide for the new State about to be established an acceptable account of its history.

Mary Hayden was the first Professor of Modern Irish History in University College Dublin and held the chair from its establishment in 1911 until her retirement in 1938 at the age of seventy-six. During her years as Professor she wrote no other books, but published on historical subjects many articles and book reviews in *Studies* and on occasion in the *Journal of the Royal Society of Antiquaries of Ireland* and *Irish Historical Studies*. Though aged well over forty when she obtained her first university post – the Lectureship in Modern Irish History in 1909, which was indeed her first permanent job – she had been engaged in teaching for her entire adult life. She had taught in the Dominican School at Eccles Street, St Mary's College, and Alexandra College, where she had herself been a student, and she had also taken private pupils.

Born in Dublin, Mary Hayden had a comfortable middle-class upbringing; her father, Thomas Hayden, was a medical practitioner and Professor of Anatomy in the Catholic University School of Medicine. Her mother died when she was eleven and her father some eight years later, leaving Mary to develop the self-reliance and the spirit of independence that seem to have been inherent in her character. The young Mary was a keen, quite serious reader and there seems to have been no question but that she would pursue her education through secondary level – not then an automatic choice for many girls – and attempt the public examinations only recently established and, most significantly, open equally to girls as well as to boys with the passing of the Intermediate Education Act 1878 and the establishment of the Royal University of Ireland under the University Education (Ireland) Act 1879. Passing the Matriculation examination of the Royal University in 1882 and the first woman to win the three-year scholarship of the University, Mary was now launched on an academic career and was awarded the B.A. Honours degree in Modern Languages in 1885, the second year of women graduates of the Royal University. Two years later she achieved a First class M.A. degree.

The Royal University was not a teaching university, but it did appoint Fellows whose duties were to conduct the examinations and to teach in certain colleges where students were preparing for the examinations and degrees of the University. The Fellows in Dublin, however, were appointed principally to the Catholic University – then managed by the Jesuit fathers – where women students were not admitted. No Fellow was ever appointed to teach in any of the colleges attended by women. In Dublin, women students attended Alexandra College and, after 1886 and 1893 respectively, the Dominican St Mary's and the Loreto Institute. Students could also prepare for the University examinations by private tuition, which the women sometimes combined with attendance at college. Although the women students achieved results of high standard in the Royal University examinations, their exclusion from the lectures by the Fellows – the examiners – was a cause of concern and grievance to them.

In 1895 for the first time, two women, Mary Hayden and Katherine Murphy, won Royal University Junior Fellowships. The awards included examining duties, but the two women Fellows did not receive the usual teaching appointment. The notion of women lecturing to men in the Catholic University was not yet an acceptable one, particularly to its President, Father William Delany. Unlike the Junior Fellowships, which were awarded on the results of an examination, Senior Fellowship awards were made by the University Senate on consideration of the qualifications of candidates whose names were proposed to it. Though highly qualified, Mary Hayden failed on two occasions to secure a Senior Fellowship, a fact referred to several times by various speakers, including Mary herself, in evidence to the Royal Commission on University Education in Ireland (the Robertson Commission). Mary Hayden, a founding member and Vice-President of the Irish Association of Women Graduates and Candidate Graduates, presenting evidence to the Commission on behalf of St Mary's College, made a compelling case for equality of access to university education for women and men.

So effectively did the IAWGCG present its case that the Commission in its final report in 1903 accepted the recommendations of the Association, describing them as in accord with the views of those 'best acquainted with the requirements of Ireland in regard to the higher education of women'. The Irish Universities Act of 1908 was welcomed by the IAWGCG, providing as it did that all courses, examinations, prizes, distinctions, and offices should be open equally to men and women. Furthermore, the accompanying charters nominated both Mary Hayden and Agnes O'Farrelly as members of the first

Governing Body of University College Dublin, and Mary Hayden also as a member of the first Senate of the National University of Ireland.

Some members of the Association now saw no need for its continuing existence, but the majority, including Mary Hayden, believed that it should play an important role in advancing the interests of women graduates in employment opportunities and admission to the professions, and in the general encouragement of women in their university education. Mary Hayden was appointed President in 1913 of what in the following year became the National University of Ireland Women Graduates' Association (Dublin University and Queen's University Belfast also establishing separate associations). Not only did she hold that office until 1942 – in effect, for the rest of her life – but she continued as an active member, regularly presiding at general and committee meetings, and urging the Association to interest itself in issues relevant to women's education, women in public life, and the equality of women in the workplace and in society.

It is possible that the obstacles, or to say the least the discouraging circumstances, with which Mary Hayden and her contemporaries had to contend in order to obtain their university degrees, were of considerable influence in developing their views on social and public affairs. Mary Hayden and Hanna Sheehy Skeffington are frequently mentioned in this context. Both were founding members of the IAWGCG and both were early supporters of the movement for women's suffrage. Unlike Hanna, Mary did not favour the militant tactics adopted by some in the years 1912–14, but she would not condemn those who believed militancy necessary for the achievement of votes for women. Notably, Mary made a public protest about Hanna's dismissal from her teaching job following her release from imprisonment for breaking windows on public buildings in Dublin. Shortly before that militant demonstration, Mary Hayden had presided at a mass meeting in Dublin to demand that the Home Rule Bill, then under consideration at Westminster, should include provision for women to vote for members of the Irish Parliament when established. She frequently addressed meetings, signed petitions and wrote to the newspapers on the issue until 1918 when the parliamentary franchise was first granted to women.

The Women Graduates' Association does not appear to have taken part in the suffrage campaign, but the contrary is the case in the 1930s in another issue of importance to women – the Constitution of 1937, in the draft of which several provisions were seen to imply threats to the status of women and to be a reversal of the guarantee of equality for women which was contained in the Constitution of 1922. The NUWGA immediately organized a meeting, at which Mary Hayden presided, to seek amendments to the draft provisions. This was the start of a short but vigorous, sometimes even strident, campaign in May/June 1937 led by the NUWGA which, when adequate amendments to the terms of the Constitution were not forthcoming before its adoption by the Dáil, proceeded then to campaign for rejection of the entire Constitution in the referendum to be held on July 1. Although Mary Hayden was now aged seventy-five, she was involved in the thick of the campaign of meetings, deputations to de Valera and other Dáil members, articles and letters to the newspapers. On this issue, as in the earlier suffrage movement, Mary Hayden was one of those who urged a nonpolitical approach to the question of women's rights. In the event, the referendum resulted in a majority in favour of the Constitution, but it appears that the intensity of the women's opposition came as a surprise to many, including de Valera, who devoted considerable attention to refuting the arguments advanced by the women critics.

Before the end of that same year, Mary Hayden was again presiding at a meeting organized by the NUWGA, this time to establish a non-party organization to promote and protect the political, social and economic status of women, the Women's Social and Political League. Though strongly critical of the contentious articles of the Constitution and of other restrictive legislation that preceded it, she seemed to take an optimistic view in the long term; when addressing the annual dinner of the NUWGA in December 1937, she spoke of unlimited opportunities for women of the future. In that speech she saw women not as rivals of men in public life but working with them for the general good of humanity and the advancement of social and economic issues throughout the world. She herself truly has a place in the history of education, of women, of University College Dublin, and of the Women Graduates' Association.

Joyce Padbury

The Women Graduates' Association: Beginnings

Gentlemen,

We desire for all women in Ireland the full advantages of university education and that the same teaching, privileges, prizes, honours and degrees shall be open to them as to men students.

Opening of a letter from Miss Agnes O'Farrelly to the Royal Commission on University Education in Ireland, 1902 (Plate 1)

Today we tend to take the participation of women in university life for granted. Knowledge is part of our national heritage, one to which all citizens are entitled to have access. Education is recognized as a keystone of women's meaningful participation in democratic society. But it was not always so.

Women graduates of the Royal University at the beginning of this century appear to have been very aware of the privileged position that they had attained and of the responsibilities that their status as graduates conferred. These women had succeeded within an inherently unjust system, which since 1879 had permitted women to take university examinations and to obtain degrees, but which had prevented them from attending lectures or having access to tutorials.

The prospect of women's participation in higher education was viewed with distaste and suspicion. The possibility of women speaking in public was considered an abomination, and their physical presence at lectures a distracting influence that would trivialize such events and constitute a threat to the virtue of male students. The suggestion that women students might attend lectures at Trinity College accompanied by chaperones was rejected on the basis that it could not be left to the discretion of the porters to adjudicate which of two women entering the College was the chaperone.

The changes to the educational system described above by Margaret Ó hÓgartaigh and Joyce Padbury (pp. iii–xvii) resulted in a body of educated, articulate women impatient for reform. Many women perceived how access to higher education could counteract the economic and social dependence that rendered them vulnerable to arranged marriages and to unrewarding and badly paid employment. They also recognized their entitlements and expressed their desire to share the benefits of higher culture.

The establishment in 1901 of a Royal Commission on University Education (the Robertson Commission) was identified by these pioneering women as an ideal opportunity to promote change. The Commission established a sub-committee of eight women graduates, among whom were Mary Hayden and Hanna Sheehy Skeffington. In response to a questionnaire, 277 of the 282 women graduates who replied registered their support for the establishment of an Association of Women Graduates. The Irish Association of Women Graduates and Candidate Graduates, which first met in the Gresham Hotel on 14 March 1902, resulted from a process of consultation, and within a few months had over two hundred members.

The Association aimed to improve communication and mutual action. One of the movement's main objectives was 'to promote the interests of women in any scheme of University Education in Ireland and to secure that all the advantages of such education shall be open to women equally with men'.[1] The Association also

---

[1] *Freeman's Journal* 15/3/1902.

sought to create a placement service that could act as a clearing-house between applicants and employers, thereby attempting to ensure that women's newly acquired skills and qualifications would be matched by opportunities in the workplace.

The first combined achievements of the women graduates were certainly positive indicators for the future. In a climate that regarded university education for women as either an unnecessary luxury, a vehicle for producing social disruption, or a waste of resources, the evidence meticulously compiled by the Association and submitted in written and oral form to the Robertson Commission was effective: the Irish Universities Act 1908 required that women and men be treated equally in relation to entry examinations, prizes, fellowships, and eligibility to apply for any position in the College.

The significance of such an achievement can be appreciated when set alongside some of the pronouncements of representatives of the Universities, the Church, and the State at that time. In 1895 the Bishop of Limerick at a Prize Day speech in Laurel Hill boasted: 'We have no girl graduates, nor even Intermediate students but we are working away on the old Catholic rules and principles and I am not aware that we have lost anything thereby.'[2] In 1913 the Bishop of Ross in his Lenten Pastoral refers to the efforts of womankind to escape dependence on man, aping his dress and copying his social habits. 'Many women,' he says, 'bitten by the Higher Education craze, openly and aggressively assert their own superiority, and, reversing God's order, attempt to exercise dominion over men.'[3]

The ambivalent attitudes concerning women and higher education can also be observed from the series of six photographs of female graduates and the accompanying caption in Plate 2

---

[2] *Freeman's Journal* 14/7/1895.
[3] Letter in the *Irish Citizen* 1913, quoted in Rosemary Cullen-Owens 1984, p. 69.

below. De jure equality had been won; de facto equality was to be a more long drawn out and complicated matter, one with which women graduates struggle still.

Throughout the first decades of the century many associations were established that helped to promote the interests of women and in which women graduates became involved. The fight for women's suffrage and the struggle for Home Rule were major concerns. The struggle to obtain the vote for women was successful in that in 1918 a qualified franchise was granted linked to age (over 30 years), property, and other factors, including university graduation.

The right to work, which includes access to, and conditions of employment, has concerned women graduates from the foundation of the Association. As mentioned above, one of the functions that the Association envisaged for itself was the facilitation of links between employers and graduates seeking employment. The Association sought improvement in the position of women in secondary teaching, the opening up of more Civil Service jobs to women, and the appointment of women as Inspectors under the Board of Primary and Intermediate Education.

Negotiations over a three-year period were unsuccessful. However, a challenge was made by the Irish Women's Citizens and Local Government Association, led by Mary Hayden (President of National University Women Graduates' Association), questioning the legality of an advertisement in the *Irish Times* of 25 October 1924, which offered jobs in the Department of Agriculture for a Superintendent and a junior Marketing Inspector. Both jobs were offered to men only. The challenge was followed by the withdrawal of the advertisement and the introduction of the Civil Service (Amendment) Act into Parliament in 1925, an act that sought to legitimate appointments to men only. It was at this point that the Women Graduates' Association entered the campaign against a bill that would exclude women from jobs for generations to come. The Association put pressure on the University representatives in the Dáil to have the bill withdrawn or at least defeated. The bill passed through the Dáil but was defeated in the Seanad by twenty votes to nine. Another successful campaign had been waged.

In challenging the Conditions of Employment Bill 1935, the National Council of Women of Ireland, and women graduates including Mary Hayden, recognized that although the ostensible purpose of the Bill was to improve working conditions by imposing a maximum of 48 hours per working week, this was a form of 'window dressing' to disguise the implications of the provisions for women. Section 16 allowed the Minister for Industry and Commerce to prohibit employment of female workers in certain industries. In those industries where women could be employed, employers were forbidden to take on more women than men. The Bill was recognized as a clear attempt to alleviate economic depression by removing women from the workplace and giving their jobs to men; it also gave unlimited power to the Minister. Mary Hayden participated as President of NCWI at a mass meeting of women held in the Mansion House in protest against the Bill, but despite enthusiastic opposition, it was passed.

The attitude implicit in this legislation was a foretaste of things to come. It was in protest about the 1937 Constitution that women graduates played their most challenging and revolutionary role. Many capable and strong-minded women there were who, having caught a whiff of freedom in the revolutionary decades, were not willing to become second-class citizens for any man. These women consistently referred to the 1916 Proclamation of the Republic and its position regarding equality between men and women. They noted that certain articles of the Constitution could leave the door open for reactionary legislation against women in many areas, and they deplored as sinister and retrogressive the omission of the principle of equal rights and opportunities enunciated in the Proclamation and confirmed in Article 3 of the Constitution of Saorstat Éireann 1922. Five articles in particular discriminated against women. Two of these – Articles 9 and 16 – were amended following protest. Plate 3 is a facsimile of a letter detailing the concerns that remained regarding the unamended Articles 40, 41 and 45.

Mary Hayden and the other NUWGA members had been the only women to battle right to the end. Cumann na mBan and Irish Women Workers' Union had pulled out when the amendments were announced. To women graduates, however, the Constitution was not just an attack on one aspect of women's lives, but an attack on every aspect, and a threat to their future status and treatment in Irish society. If at the highest level women were restricted, what hope was there of equal treatment and respect at any level?

As a result of their uncompromising attitudes to the curtailment of freedom of women implicit in the sections of the Irish Constitution virtually confining women to the home, Mary Hayden and fellow campaigners were heralded as enemies of the State, and for supporting women's right to work, enemies of the Church. Refusal to allow women to be confined to the home was interpreted as a move towards disruption of the family unit. The objections of the campaigners resulted in a vicious attack on them in the *Irish Press* in December 1937, an extract from which can be seen in Plate 4.

In 1859 the *Dublin University Magazine* expressed the wish that women would be nobly and purely educated so that they would think well and think strongly, and then 'the more they know the more silent and humble will they become, for all real knowledge has the stillness of the ocean which is gained from depth'.

Mary Horkan
University Women of Europe President 1994–2000

Editor's Note

I have to confess that until I became involved in the editing of the present anthology I knew very little about the UCD Women Graduates' Association. The work on the material involved visits to the UCD Archives, which houses a collection of documents relating to the Association from its earliest days. To see there the handwritten and typed evidence of so many battles fought on my behalf was a humbling experience. To read the many recollections offered here – particularly in light of those battles – is fascinating, at times depressing, and more often than one would wish, frustrating. The frustration stems from the fact that even now, a century later, women still have to prove that they are capable, in the face of assumptions to the contrary.

It became obvious almost immediately that the most sensible way to present this collection was in chronological order, and this is what has been done. The contributions have been divided, as nearly as possible, into decades. Each decade has been prefaced with a short introduction that sets the contributions loosely in the wider context of the cultural and political climate of the day. It was felt that even such thinly drawn sketches might be of use, both to those readers who had not lived through the years in question, and also in a strange kind of way, to those who had; there is sometimes a sense in these writings – and often this is picked up on by the contributors themselves – that life in College and life in the Big World are not at all the same thing. Some realized this while they were still in their undergraduate years; more often, however, the realization dawned in hindsight.

In the body of reminiscences presented here, certain 'general patterns' may be discerned. The taking of tea and coffee is an apparently noteworthy feature of student life no matter which decade one explores, though there is a gradual progression from cream buns in the DBC to pints in the bar as time goes by. On a more serious note, there is a sense that among the earliest graduates there was a very definite feeling of excitement and of privilege at being at university at all. In those earlier decades, of course, the fight for women to be allowed access to university education was still fresh in the memory. Later students take this privilege for granted as women, but have other battles to fight. Not everything is rosy at all times, even in the Iveagh Gardens, but the note of criticism, if sounded at all, is muted until the 1960s, a pivotal decade in many ways.

To say more at this point would be to pre-empt what is hoped will be an interesting and a pleasant reading experience. The voices in this anthology have been left to speak for themselves, with very little editorial intrusion. The only limitation imposed on prospective contributors to the volume was one of length: 1,000 words was the suggested upper guideline. 'Your memories may be happy or unhappy, positive or negative, funny or sad, but we would like *your* thoughts and experiences of College', the original invitation stated. The pieces received in answer are as diverse as that rubric allows. The tone varies from one piece to another; most are informal, some even 'chatty'. The focus ranges from a close-up of a single day or incident to the panorama of three years of undergraduate study and beyond. Some start or finish abruptly, as memories themselves often do.

The open letter to prospective contributors to the present volume expressed the conviction that each contributor's experience of UCD would be 'of interest to others'. This may have been matched, at least in some measure, by an equally strong conviction on the part of many of those reading the letter that their experience of college would not be of the slightest interest to anyone but their nearest and dearest. If this is so, it is a pity. The 'everyday' memories included here – a snowball on the ear; the smell of boiled cabbage; a cheated TV meter – are threads as necessary to the reconstruction of the tapestry of life in UCD as experienced by women over the past century as are those memories of great and historical events on the larger political and academic stages.

A century that saw so much change deserves to have recorded even its 'everyday' memories. The word is in inverted commas for a reason. To smell boiled cabbage in Newman House may not seem like a big thing. To be allowed the privilege of doing so undoubtedly is.

Anne Macdona

Mary Semple

Frances Kennedy:
What's in a Name

In 1906, my mother, Frances Kennedy, sat her arts degree in the Royal University. In those days there were separate examination rooms for men and women and Frances went to the correct location only to find that she was not on the list of women students. There was quite a to-do, and when the powers-that-were checked the Men's List they found that she had been listed as 'Francis Kennedy' and that a place had been reserved for her with the men. There was no space in the women's room; Frances said that she did not mind where she sat to take her examination and offered to sit at the allotted desk. After considerable kerfuffle she was allowed to do so, but screens were placed around the desk to isolate her from the male candidates ...

Kate O'Brien

UCD As I Forget It (1916-19)

This article first appeared in *University Review* (Organ of the Graduate Association of NUI), 1962 vol. 3, no. 2 and is reprinted here by kind permission of Cork University Press.

Proust has taught us that the memories we sit down to, that we select and seek, are false. Perhaps we might have suspected that, those of us who were reading Turgenev when Proust's first volumes were coming out. The past blows up when it will, and cannot be commanded; but the tonic sharpness of its accidental visitations is a gift, a restitution to age for which no one would know how to pray, but which must not go unthanked. And house-moving can stir a lively dust, bright motes throwing shafts of backward light; so all this healthy fussing out of UCD to Belfield and the suburbs turns some of us towards unsought remembrances.

A. McWeeney protested in print when someone faultily placed the old Aula Maxima of University College in his father's house, no. 84 St Stephen's Green; and indeed Aula Maxima was a part of no. 85. There was 82, at the eastern end of the Georgian row, where girl students left umbrellas on their passage to the garden; Mrs. Greene lived at 83. The little Byzantine doorway of Newman's church jutted beyond 86. Even on glacial Sunday mornings the distance was small from it to no. 77's slummy side-door, past Lord Iveagh's. The smell of breakfast from that servants' hall still hangs around External Affairs. Coffee-toast-and-kidney incense — we breathed it sadly before we went back through that side-door.

From 82 to 86 is a small bit of pavement, a slice of dilapidated masonry. But in its last hundred years it has been crowded and worked upon; has suffered many histories. Ghosts walk about it often, and slowly — living ghosts anyway, and sometimes they can summon the dead.

John Henry Newman, one of the Founding Fathers of that institution now called UCD, but which has had many names — a founding father of the Catholic University, also its brilliant, difficult and self-dismissing servant, gave generations of us a prose style. Surely it is essential now to change the textbooks of First Arts English? For one can grow old still trying not to echo that clarion-writing, throughout a long life in flight from 'I look to a land both old and young …' and the ensuing paragraph — inescapable. That, however, is merely a writer's problem, technical. Newman said for our founders some plain, true things. He seems to me to have sighted a final classification of truth when he wrote that 'There is no crying demand for a Catholic Euclid or a Catholic Newton'. Any intelligent ten-year-old can see the exactitude of that — nor will he lose sight of it when he has become an undergraduate.

I remember once pushing my way into some debate or lecture in 86 — through an excessive crowd of beetle-black, scrubby-faced boys from All Hallows, and having to crush against the hieratic touch-me-not robes of young daughters of Saint Louis; and saying something sharp as to all this medievalism to a boon companion from Tralee, Joe Power, of cool and flying wit. She smiled around on the black and rosary-beaded mob. 'Newman said,' said she, in her civilised, clear voice, 'Newman said that a university is neither a convent nor a seminary …'

Being a coward, I was momentarily sorry I had spoken. But the point that was good about the untidy UCD of our time was that such things were said out loud — and that, signs and appearances all against it, the rough-and-tumble place was not a convent or a seminary. It was a seemingly ill-directed, or if you like non-directed place of learning — but it was open. You could find books and wits there. We were not, as Newman had feared, 'refused the masters of human thought'. We rubbed shoulders with ignorance indeed in those extraordinary lecture-halls down the garden; but there was learning and eccentricity about, and an excellent kind of indifference in government — so that whoever wanted to, just up from the country, could run free and wild enough into at least the first sweet shallows of the humanistic studies.

For there was always, across the Green, the National Library. When I sit in that Reading Room now in age, as often it is my pleasure to, I look up sometimes to the silly encirclement of naked *amoretti* or whatever they are, a décor surely eccentric, devised in the 1870s for our good and gravely intentioned library — I look up at them and at the dictionaries and biographies just below them — and try to remember forcedly, against the Proustian instruction, what this silent place used to mean when it was new to me, a gate and a revelation.

And I cannot remember. All I can do is apprehend that indeed I was young under this round roof — and at peace, restlessly and in confusion at peace. I remember of course, in the ordinary sense, a few unimportant things: as, being shown de Valera where he stood — when can that have been? — by the Irish dictionaries. He wore some terribly ugly black gaiters — an anti-hero who said nothing to immediate curiosity. With generations I remember Father Dineen's messy bags of food. And there was a seminarist who used to hand me love-letters at the turnstile. But of the reality of long hours in that room, of reading Taine and Renan and Santayana, of being alarmed and enchanted, of silence and isolation and the catalogues leading on into mazes of questions, of cheeky librarians, of poets and friends and first readings of Joyce; of the weather beyond that window, of the love I had for the green lamps and the clacking bookrests — of drifting out and down the street with the amusing, great friends of that time — to the Café

Cairo, to the Grafton Picture House — through the Green in the rain or over noisy leaves — all of that I do not well remember, but only apprehend it — in a kind of desolation.

This is sharply remembered, however: that I met Violet Connolly on the bridge in the Green one bleak day of 1918 — February, March? — and she thrust a small blue book into my hand and said 'Read this'. And we stood in the wind and cold, the book fell open and I read: 'I caught this morning morning's minion, kingdom of daylight's dauphin, dapple-dawn-drawn Falcon, in his riding ...' Gerard Manley Hopkins was news that would not stale. And I associate the shapes of his verse, foolishly enough, with the hump of the bridge in Stephen's Green.

Back to the old worn steps; the ordeal of coming out of the Green at the gate that fronted 86. For the porch was filled all day with lounging male geniuses, and although one was not finally concerned with the opinions of one's hat, or legs, or intelligence that might be pronounced as one passed, by Eimar O'Duffy or long John Meagher or Paddy McGilligan or the gloomy Platonist from the west, Michael Tierney — still, one was young, and momentarily at their mercy.

But let us go in now — not past those mocking philosophers, but through a quieter door, at 82. Let us leave our umbrellas in the stuffy backroom, and face the terrible garden — on to which opened all the backdoors of UCD. Between the four old houses and the hideous tin huts we mostly — we of arts and classics anyhow — sought and found whatever we were likely to seek or find.

There was Earlsfort Terrace too — ugly place with an unventilated brashness solidly built into it, a building where one suspected cheap plumbing — as I still do when I walk its brutal corridors. Unfortunately, even in my day the directors of the English school preferred Earlsfort Terrace to the airy muddles of 82–86: but my spirit, for one, never settled in it. Robert

Donovan's long readings from *The Prelude* notwithstanding. So I hardly remember Earlsfort Terrace in relation to myself — and when I enter it now, like the Old Man of Baroda I think I perceive a bad odour. But in the wet garden the air was sooty and fresh — and I remember its bleak mornings as a part of myself.

Sometimes I am asked what lectures and lecturers were like in my time. And turning over my surprisingly clear recollections under the two headings, I begin with remembering that *twice* in the summer term of my first year the President sent for me, to tell me, with icy indifference, that my non-attendance at the lectures of Douglas Hyde and Agnes O'Farrelly might bar me from sitting for the First Arts examination in June. The first time that I stood thus on Dr Coffey's carpet, I cannot have believed his cool pronouncement. I had been spoilt at school, where no one had ever suggested that I could in any circumstances be barred from any academic trial that I proposed to myself. Further, I had been taught Irish quite magnificently by a remarkable, brilliant nun, and I found the First Arts honours lectures, or whatever they were, in Irish both infantile and tedious. I think I said almost that to Dr Coffey, but his small, white face did not respond to me — and anyway, I cannot have taken him seriously, because Mother Eucharia at Loreto Hall — who worshipped Dr Coffey — very nearly had a stroke when, a fortnight later, she told me I must see the President *again*.

The same pronouncement. The same cold voice. But this time I took in the simple fact that I had to be present at every First Arts Irish lecture for the following four weeks — that was sixteen lectures — and if I did not do so I would not sit for First Arts.

I attended the sixteen lectures — and did well in First Arts. God knows why — because on a lovely summer day, the eve of our logic examination — Dan Binchy and Frank McCabe together, on a bench in Stephen's Green, took me through the whole text of Palestrina in an exhaustive grind, and sadly, because they wished me nothing but well, decided that my chances for the morrow were poor. I flew home in logic nevertheless, and can still spot a fallacy. But hardly thanks to our distinguished instructor, Father Shine. Does anyone recall with me those First Arts logic lectures, in the old Physics Theatre at 86, at nine a.m. on Monday and Thursday mornings? Of the hundreds of youths, rowdy and unwashed, and mostly in the crumpled black of the seminaries, of those hundreds and the twenty or so sleepy girls who sat below them, who now, in lost eastern mission, in desolate Donegal townland or in South Dublin kitchenette, remembers the soft, bored mutterings of that weary, attenuated scholar? Not I, anyway — though I can hear an irritable buzz of words, and see the exasperation of the faraway, high-up eyebrows. And I remember the moods of those mornings, the stuffiness and the chalk-dust, the wind outside — and the scramble to get one's *adsum* onto the sheet of paper that used to flutter down to us from those extraordinary, inhuman hands.

The second year the lectures, in themselves and not just as local atmosphere, began to capture attention. For one thing we were thinned out from crowds to a few, had said goodbye to Father Shine's ice-cold mornings, and to the kindergarten of Agnes O'Farrelly. And there was no more reading of Livy from Kelly's Key, for Mr Tierney. '*Dum haec geruntur …*'

At the risk of shocking readers of this learned journal* by the foolishness of my memories, I must indulge my recollection of a good laugh. During one of Father George O'Neill's lectures on Anglo-Saxon names, a solemn girl from England, fat and rather grand, interrupted the extremely irritable and shy little Jesuit in order to inform us all in crystal voice, that certain English friends of hers called Ramsbottom pronounced their surname (as far as I can get it phonetically now) *Ray-ams-bot-tome.*

---

* *University Review*

There was an astonished silence. Father O'Neill's little withered pink face grew purple; and the entire class — about fifteen of us, and largely made up of very well-controlled and holy young men out of Rathfarnham Castle — broke into enchanted and unmeasured laughter. It truly was a moment of blazing comedy to remember forever.

Father O'Neill thought for a while that he had in me an Irish Alice Meynell, a shepherdess of sheep. He gave me prizes for poems and was very kind. But my witty, unkind fellow-students were much kinder, on the long view — and anyway I always knew myself that the only poet I could ever be would be a thoroughly bad one. From Austin Clarke, shy, unhappy, I suspect, in his first job — from that rapidly muttering, fresh-minded and always-in-flight young lecturer, the attentive — of which on my own terms I became one — could get light, and direction. He said striking things, when one could hear them. He was amusing and rude about essays — but once he actually said out loud in class that in one of mine he found 'the outward sign of inward grace'. I have not forgotten either my pleasure or my astonishment.

Yet — still on myself! — I cannot look back to the lectures of my time in UCD without saying that I took adult education, exact direction, from Professor Roger Chauviré. I sat at his lectures — mostly in the old tin huts behind 86 — for only two terms. He came to Dublin late in 1918, immediately after the November Armistice — and I took my degree in September, 1919. But I account myself lucky that I was there for his beginnings, which were brilliant beyond exact explanation. Wit, clarity, reason, system, tolerance and gaiety — all these were the ground material of his addresses. He took literature into cold daylight; he cut it out clearly as an exact and exacting skill, a form of lovely science. Listening to Chauviré on French writing of the seventeenth and eighteenth centuries I grew up. And to sit and reflect in Stephen's Green during those last two terms — to consider in French light

Racine and Madame de Lafayette — or Ronsard or de Vigny as the chances of programme might be — was to have summer in one's head, and to be quite coolly dazzled.

And perhaps it is in summer that lastly one remembers the South side of that Green, and those grey houses. For September blazed, I remember, in 1919 — and anxiety intensified the light and heat in which one lived. Yet there was within a grey sense of farewell. Loreto and its clanging, horrid side-door; the Literary and Historical, the wind in Leeson Street, the savageries of *The National Student*. Discomfort, wild wit and sweet friendships — a time was ended; a door was about to close. 'Never mind,' said Kathleen Cunningham, 'in Grafton Street there is still lemonade' — a very silly joke from those last weeks.

The ghosts, our own among them, the memories were assembling before their time. 'This thinking was a dusk of doubt and self-mistrust ... and he met the eyes of others with unanswering eyes for he felt that the spirit of beauty had folded him round like a mantle and that in reverie at least he had been acquainted with nobility. But, when this brief pride of silence upheld him no longer, he was glad to find himself still in the midst of common lives, passing on his way amid the squalor and noise and sloth of the city fearlessly and with light heart.'

Joyce was glad to be a student 'in the midst of common lives'. So were many, I think, who had the slap-dash freedom of 86.

Catherine McDowell

Margaret Dearey (Ginnety): A Daughter Remembers

My mother was born in Dromisken, Co. Louth in 1897 and educated locally and in Dominican College Cabra from 1911 to 1915, when she went to UCD to study arts. During her time in UCD she stayed in Dominican Hall on St Stephen's Green. She recalled Countess Markievicz being pointed out to her whilst walking through the Green; although she was in UCD at the same time as Kate O'Brien, she could not recall knowing her.

She studied French, German, and English, but remembered that Mary Hayden, who taught history at the time, was, because of her long, flowing tresses, referred to as the 'Hairy Maiden'.

Thomas MacDonagh lectured her in English, and my mother remembered that before the Easter break in 1916, some of the students put three candles on the desk and lit them; she could not recall why they did this, but when MacDonagh arrived, he blew them out, remarking, 'Three candles — not lucky'. He was, as we know, executed some weeks later for his part in the Easter rebellion.

My mother graduated B.A. in 1918 and completed a H.Dip. in 1920, after which she went to Plumstead (now part of Greater London) where she taught in the Convent de Notre Dame until 1923.

The 1930s

The picture of life in UCD in the period 1930–1940 as painted by the contributions from that decade is reasonably consistent. There are common reminiscences: the flowering of writers in that generation of students, memories of outstanding professors, and the important role of the L&H. In 1930 the Irish state was not even ten years old and, as Lorna Reynolds writes, many of the students then in UCD 'were the sons and daughters, or the nephews and nieces of the men of 1916'. De Valera re-entered the Dáil in 1932 and Fianna Fáil won the following election. Many academics who had held seats in the Dáil returned to the university to resume their positions. Among these were Michael Hayes, who had been Ceann Comhairle, and John Marcus O'Sullivan, formerly Minister of Education.

Tuberculosis was prevalent in that era. The Spanish Civil War was something else that brought us face to face with our own mortality at an age when ones feels immortal.

Arts students predominated in college, so it is not surprising to find few science graduates among the contributors. Máire Redmond and Mary Semple recall Rag Day, the highlight of the Michaelmas term. Hand-in-hand with college memories goes the remembrance of Dublin city of the time; the roads around Stephen's Green free of parked cars, the lilac and laburnum in bloom in the Spring as we walked through the park to Grafton Street, and in autumn, as Lorna Reynolds remembers, 'the twilight globes of light around Stephen's Green turning it into an enchanted place'.

College is as much about people, especially one's contemporaries, as about location. Those returning to study for a higher degree could feel lost when they failed to see familiar faces in the Main Hall. Our time in university was a happy interlude between school and our entry into the world of work. It must be said that work was scarce for graduates in the thirties. Those who wished to teach had, of necessity, to go to England, and some with good honours arts degrees were glad to accept temporary clerkships in the Civil Service. When one did obtain a post with a prospect of permanency one had to face retirement on marriage. As Peig Roche reminds us, the ban on married women in employment was not revoked until 1973.

Monica Nevin

1932   De Valera enters government for the first time.
1933   Hitler becomes Chancellor in Germany.
1935   Sale and importing of contraceptives is made illegal.
        Age of consent raised from 16 to 17.
1936   Civil War in Spain.
        First Aer Lingus flight between Dublin and Britain.
1937   Constitution of Ireland comes into force.
1938   Seanad Éireann meets for the first time.
        Douglas Hyde is President of Ireland.
1939   Franco's government in Spain recognized.
        Irish Free State neutrality in any imminent war declared.
        Beginning of World War II.
        Petrol rationing in the Free State.

Mary Semple

Going Hatching

A huge difference between UCD in the Thirties and today's university is class size. In the early years there were as few as six students in a class in many arts subjects, and when it came to doing orals you knew the professor and he knew you. Professor Mary Hayden held tutorials in a room on the top corridor in Earlsfort Terrace. It was a Victorian sitting room with curtains on the windows, a fire in the grate, and a little table with a plush cover and an aspidistra on it.

A feature of those days also was the long crocodile of bicycles ridden by clerics, which wended its way from Drumcondra to UCD. At least one professor dreaded meeting these particular students as they would take their hats off to him and he had to do the same to them, but for far longer in his case.

The expression 'going Hatching' meant that you were off to a little shop called the Hatch Dairy on Leeson Street, where milk was kept in a crock on the counter. A cheap lunch often availed of was a glass of milk and a cream bun.

The College Rags were a major event. These were held on a Saturday, as the drays to hold the various floats were collected from business firms that would not be using them on that day. Six to ten drays would parade through the city with tableaux on them. The medical students did a mock-up of an operating theatre with a recumbent figure and surgeons brandishing fearsome instruments. The floats, however, tended to hold up traffic in the city, a fact that led to the eventual abolition of such spectacles.

Bridget O'Brien (Carroll)

In Dublin's Fair City

This article first appeared in the UCD magazine, *Alma Mater*, Spring/Summer 1997, and is reprinted here by kind permission of the author.

From St Mary's Convent School, Nenagh, I went up in autumn 1934 to University College Dublin. Two of my classmates accompanied me. Our lodging was in Dominican Hall, 48 and 49 St Stephen's Green, two lovely Georgian houses now pulled down and replaced by modern red-brick.

The University at that time was housed in Earlsfort Terrace, the College of Science in Kildare Street and Number 86 St Stephen's Green. The latter had been the old Jesuit University which figures in James Joyce's *Portrait of the Artist as a Young Man*. Before becoming a Jesuit college it had been the home of the notorious Buck Whaley.

Belfield existed only as a sports ground. All arts lectures were at Earlsfort Terrace. Medical students, scientists and engineers did much of their work at the College of Science and had to trek backwards and forwards to Earlsfort Terrace between lectures and practicals. Their route took them via Dominican Hall and when not at lectures ourselves we could be in wait at a window to see the current objects of our affections go by.

Soon after I left university, Number 86 was cleaned up and renovated, losing its old individuality. A lot of our social life took place in 86. One afternoon a week there would be a céilí and one night a week a 'hop'. The grander College dances took place in the Council Chamber in the Terrace.

On Saturday nights the meetings of the Literary and Historical Society were held in the Physics Lab. The L&H was a training ground for generations of speakers. The quality of the debate was good and the heckling was brilliant. The rules about going out at night were very strict in Dominican Hall. In the first year one had to be in by 7 p.m. and subsequent years by 10 p.m. The 7 p.m. rule was waived for First Years to allow them to go to the L&H. Theatre leave was granted occasionally but was often used to go dancing. It was important to be well acquainted with the plot of the play one was supposed to be seeing as well as any changes in cast or anything else unexpected so as to be able to cope with Sister Dolores' 'innocent' questioning at breakfast next morning.

There were two entrances to Earlsfort Terrace. One was the main entrance, which led straight into the Main Hall. To the right of the Main Hall was a corridor which led to the Ladies' Reading Room and the Physics Laboratory; straight ahead was a staircase leading to the Council Chamber, and underneath this staircase was a corridor that led to the Library, past the dissecting room, a gruesome place full of 'stiffs'. To the left of the Main Hall was a long corridor that led to, amongst other things, the college restaurant.

Both the Library and restaurant were very interesting, as boyfriends, or at least putative boyfriends, could be seen there. A cup of coffee and a Club chocolate biscuit cost four old pence. This was an era of stable money and prices never changed. By the standards of today everything was very cheap. Dominican Hall cost £50 per annum and after the College fees were paid, students on a scholarship had £3 6s 8d (£3.33) per term over. Thus the College fees must have been £15 per annum. This meant that students living in Dublin, or any university city such as Cork or Galway, could get a university education for £15 per annum providing their parents were able and willing to keep them at home free. From our £3 6s 8d a term we had, in theory, to find money for books, fares, clothes, entertainment and any other expense which might arise, such as doctor or dentist.

It was essential to get some money from home, and it was a myth that anyone with really poor parents could get through university on a scholarship. There was no hope of us finding work on the long vacation as there is now. Our parents had to keep us in the vacations, which were almost six months in the year. The fare on the bus from Nenagh to Dublin was about 12s 6d. Artificial silk stockings could be bought for 1s 11d but did not last very long.

Students then could not dress from jumble sales or live in jeans as they do now. Entertainment was cheap, however. With a Students' Union card the current film at the Savoy Cinema could be seen for 1s 6d on a Sunday afternoon — in the dress circle at that. For 1s a hard but reasonable seat could be purchased at the Gate Theatre. Curiously enough, I never remember going to the Abbey. I do recall seeing and hearing Ramon Navarro at the Theatre Royal.

As far as I know, girls never visited Grogan's pub at the junction of the Green and Leeson Street, now gone. It was a great meeting place for the men. Opposite Grogan's was a dairy where one could purchase a glass of milk and a real cream bun, for, I think, two old pence. These were consumed at the white marble counter and kept our innards from rumbling during the 1–2 o'clock English lecture. Robert's Café in Grafton Street and the Monument Creamery served delicious pastries and at the Swiss Chalet in Merrion Row one could buy a large plate of excellent chips with tomato sauce for 4d.

To buy entertainment one would very occasionally sell or pawn something. There was not much worth pawning. Medical students pawned their *Gray's Anatomy* on a Friday in the hope of redeeming it on a Monday when their money from home came through. To this day, when in a disturbed frame of mind, I have nightmares of exams looming and my French or English books lying unread in George Webb's secondhand bookshop on the quays.

Then, as now, poverty was a relative term. I was finding it hard to get money to go to teashops or to buy stockings or for the fare to Paris (as part of my honours French course), but I had three good meals a day, a warm bed and was getting a university education at the taxpayers' expense. Many were not so lucky. This was Dublin in the 1930s, described by a foreign writer of the time as having the worst slums in Europe. I found this out for myself. It was the custom in Dominican Hall to send Second Year students — Second Year being a no-exam year — into the poorer parts of the city with vouchers for coal and food for the needy from the Society of St Vincent de Paul. One day I found myself with a companion in a slum less than a stone's throw from Merrion Square. The tenements themselves were run-down Georgian mansions, 'The bare bones of a fanlight / Over a hungry door'.

We found the house we were looking for. As we entered, and before we even had time to notice the bareness of the spacious hallway, we were met by a smell such as I have never been able to forget. I learned much later that it was a smell compounded of poverty and bugs and dirt and despair and death. We started up the wide, broken staircase, its bannisters long gone for firewood, and passed by a closed door through the keyhole of which protruded an ancient, gnarled finger endeavouring, no doubt, to open the knobless door. On the next landing we came to another doorway, half open. In the middle of the lofty room, which was completely bare of furnishings of any kind, stood a man holding in his arms a baby that was little more than a yellow bag of bones. I looked and turned and ran in horror, cowardly, craven. The finger was still fumbling at the keyhole. Outside I was sick. I was never sent on such an errand of mercy again.

Politically, we were naive, ignorant. Irish politics were still drawn along Treaty and anti-Treaty lines. A very small Labour Party existed but we knew little or nothing of the true meaning of socialism. At school and at home it had been drilled into us that

17

Communism was the ultimate evil. Then came the Spanish Civil War. Sides were taken. Des Bell led the Christian Front which supported Franco. They marched down O'Connell Street giving the Fascist salute. The Basques, despite being devout Catholics, were against Franco. Father Laborda, a Basque priest, had taken refuge in Ireland and was a supporter of what some would call the Republican, some the Communist, some the Government side. He had set up a small Basque museum at the back of the DBC [Dublin Bread Company] teashop in Merrion Row where my friends and I visited and talked to him. There was a left-wing movement of sorts in the University allied, perhaps, with the IRA of the time.

We knew little of this. The movement organized 'hops' to help Father Laborda's refugees and we would attend them. At one such hop I met and danced with Frank Ryan shortly before he went to Spain and his eventual death. We talked of Limerick and Nenagh and the Shannon. My politics were ill defined, uninformed. One felt that the theory of Communism was good. I did not relish the smell of Fascism that was coming out of Spain. Perhaps some instinct told me that one day I too would be at the receiving end of German bombs such as were then falling on Spanish cities. My friends and I listened to Father Laborda's stories of the Franco atrocities and we gave him our rather uncomprehending sympathy and support. Generally at UCD it was fashionable to belong to the Christian Front.

Our professors were a fascinating lot. Some were the stuff of recent history. Mary Hayden shuffled along in weird and wonderful clothes. I did not know then that she had been Patrick Pearse's closest woman friend. We knew her well as the author of our main history text book at school. Professor Agnes O'Farrelly ('Aggie'), who taught us Irish poetry, had been another of those early Gaelic-Leaguers. Professor Eoin MacNeill could often be seen, and Dr Douglas Hyde, though not on the staff at UCD at that time, came to help at Irish oral exams and was one of the examiners at my oral. Some of the professors were left over from the old Jesuit university.

My favourite professor was Louis Roche, then second in the French Department. After Professor Chauviré's retirement he got the Chair. Louis had a biting tongue but could be very kind. Many people were afraid of him. Chauviré lectured entirely in French, which was a little hard on those of us who had come up with no background of oral French. Darina Laracy was the most brilliant student in the class. She and the professor would engage in long discussions of the text, oblivious of the majority of the class who found it very difficult to follow. Darina married the celebrated Italian left-wing writer, Ignazio Silone, who died in 1978.

The honours French class was small, smaller than any of my other classes, so we all knew each other fairly well. It consisted of a handful of girls, a few nuns and clerics and two 'laymen'. One of the laymen was Tom Waldron/Tomás de Bhaldraithe, later Professor of Irish at UCD. At lectures we always sat in the same order — nuns in front, then girls, then clerics and behind them the boys, or the 'men' as I should call them. The latter would stamp their feet rhythmically while waiting for the lecturer. This activity is described by Joyce in *Portrait of the Artist* as letting off 'a few rounds of Kentish fire'.

If our professors were the stuff of history some of our fellow students were not far behind. There were so many de Valeras that there was one in every year — Vivion, Máirín, Eamon, Brian, Ruadhrí and Emer. I shall never forget my first meeting with Barbara MacDonagh in the Ladies' Reading Room. Thomas MacDonagh was perhaps the 1916 leader I most admired and most identified with. My headmistress at school, Mother Paul Leahy, had been lectured by him in English Literature at UCD, and she would often speak of him. Cathal Brugha had also been one of my heroes, and the Brugha sisters, Noinín and Nodlagh, were prominent in the Camogie Club. Tom O'Higgins, later Chief Justice, was in my English class.

In 1935 the UCD Dramatic Society had the honour of producing T.S. Eliot's *Murder in the Cathedral* for the first time. All over the place posters and placards appeared advertising the great event and snatches of strange, brooding choruses could be heard coming from behind closed doors when rehearsals were taking place. The producer was Liam Redmond who was married to Barbara MacDonagh, then a Second Arts student. The Dramatic Society was a very lively one. All the Societies were exciting and played a big part in our social life. Each had an inaugural meeting once a year at which sumptuous buffet meals were provided.

About 1936 the Kevin Barry Memorial Window was unveiled in the Council Chamber at UCD. I remember seeing Maud Gonne MacBride — an unmistakable figure in her French widow's weeds — crossing the Green, alone, on her way from the ceremony. Tears streamed down her face, and to cruel young eyes there seemed little trace of the soft beauty that the poet Yeats had sung. 'Old and grey' she was, and full of tears, if not 'of sleep'.

Doris O'Brien Cassidy

Society Girl

It is more than seventy years since I entered college in a wonderful atmosphere, no stress or strain. Our professors were excellent. Two stand out in my memory. The first that comes to mind is Professor Douglas Hyde who was later President of Ireland. I regret to have to say that I was only in his class for a very short period — my Irish was not up to standard! The other I remember is Professor Mary Hayden who always wore the academic gown, which was not worn by all professors.

There were various societies too numerous to mention — thirty-five in all I believe. Each organized its own functions. The L&H was possibly the best known, with many brilliant speakers. I recall Denis Devlin, Cearbhall Ó Dálaigh, Roger McHugh, Mary N. Wall, and Kevin Boylan (a Cistercian monk) as outstanding.

There were two walking clubs. The one I was in met on a Sunday morning at the Yellow House in Rathfarnham. We walked up the mountains towards Glencree where we stopped for a snack and a chat at a restaurant near the Hellfire Club. These walks were, as you can imagine, most enjoyable.

The Friday night hop in 86 was a delight. A different dance was one organized by Vivion de Valera, which took place on an afternoon in 86 and was called a 'Practice Céilí'. It was held to help people to learn Irish dances and I enjoyed it very much. The Dramatic Society and the Musical Society were wonderful and would need a book to themselves to describe their activities.

Another feature of college life was the Annexe where we went for a cup of coffee, etc. The lady in charge was very nice to all of us and did not seem to notice when we nibbled lumps of sugar.

Lorna Reynolds

Hereditary Martyrs

A lifetime ago — and yet how vivid in my memory are the years 1930–33 when I was an undergraduate in UCD. They were the most illuminating and formative years of my life. To begin with, the imposed discipline of schooldays was over; one learnt to discipline oneself as best suited one's system. If that meant reading late at night and not getting up at 6.30 in the morning, so what? No one was injured. Then one discovered Dublin, because one was free to wander around at all hours, hours when earlier, high school windows had excluded the delicate signs of the seasons. I still remember that October of 1930 as a golden month with high blue skies and the thinned leaves of the lime trees outlined against the blue, and the twilight globes of light around Stephen's Green turning it into an enchanted region. I remember also the following February when the motif of blue returned in the lengthening dusks of the evening. In that Dublin little buses stopped anywhere at the sign of an outstretched hand, and the great galleon-like trams took one from one side of the city to the other for a two-penny fare. I saw their magical reflections in the dark night-time Liffey, and they sailed against vermilion and lemon sunsets in the west. One never knew what mysterious snippets of conversation one might hear, sitting quietly on their hard seats. I remember hearing two young men talk of 'taking the mag out of her and beating her till she roared'. I thought they were talking about a girl and was petrified; as the conversation developed, however, it turned out that the subject was a motorbike.

The generation of students to which I belonged was called by a wit of the day — and there were many such around — the generation of the 'Hereditary Martyrs'. We were the sons and daughters, or nephews and nieces, of the men of 1916. Among my contemporaries were Donagh and Barbara MacDonagh; Nora O'Mahony, niece of Michael Collins; Colm Gavan Duffy, son of Judge Gavan Duffy; Betty Kettle, daughter of Tom Kettle. I was a niece of John Richard Redmond who had fought at the GPO.

But we had more immediate reasons for pride. Just ahead of us were Mervyn Wall, Denis Devlin, and Brian Coffey, the latter two of whom each published a book of poems in 1930. In my year were numbered Niall Sheridan and Brian O'Nolan (figuring then as Brother Barnabas and reporting on international gatherings in *The National Student*. He was at work, though we did not know it, on *At Swim-Two-Birds*). Mary Lavin was already nurturing the seeds of the short stories that she was to publish a few years later in *Tales from Bective Bridge*. She and I spent many an evening walking round and round St Stephen's Green discussing, not fine points of literary creation, but the social conditions of the Dublin of our day. Another contemporary was Cyril Cusack, whom I remember as prominent in the History Society rather than Dramsoc.

Famous figures from the past were among our instructors. Douglas Hyde lectured in Irish. At least he attempted to, but usually ended up singing to us, with the young men in the class keeping time with their boots. Miss Agnes O'Farrelly — inevitably called 'Aggie' — who lectured on Irish poetry, always arrived late still dressed in her outdoor clothes, even to her gloves. Her idea of lecturing was to read the Irish poem and translate it into English prose. For Irish history we had Mary Hayden, known already to us at school as the co-author, with George Moonan, of *A Short History of the Irish People*. The one outstanding lecturer of the time was Roger Chauviré, Professor of French. Those of us who were not taking French envied his students, who would never dream of missing a single lecture of his.

One way or another we all grew up in our undergraduate years. What I drew from them was the general idea that one might dedicate oneself to the life of learning, that it was as honourable as becoming a doctor, a lawyer, or a businessman. After I had acquired my B.A., I returned to work on an M.A. thesis, but I remember feeling desolate the first time I went into Earlsfort Terrace in 1934. All was changed, new faces, no one I knew. I felt like the speaker in Moore's 'The Light of Other Days':

> I feel like one who treads alone
> Some banquet-hall deserted,
> Whose lights are fled,
> Whose garlands dead,
> And all but he departed!

But that feeling was soon dissipated. Some old friends re-appeared, new ones were made, and one became immersed in a new phase of one's scholarly development. As it happened, I never left the academic world, but nothing remains as vivid in memory as my undergraduate years. *Et in arcadia ego*.

Monica Nevin

Tribunals — Even Then

When I entered University College in the early thirties the custom of wearing the short undergraduate gowns of Newman's day had only recently fallen into disuse and there were still one or two abandoned gowns to be found in the lockers in the basement of the college. That year there were about two thousand students studying for degrees and diplomas, about one third of whom were women.

It was not until recently that I realized the Earlsfort Terrace buildings were only then about twelve years old when I first set foot in them; the construction of the buildings begun in 1914 was completed in 1919. Earlsfort Terrace was the centre of administration and the seat of all the faculties, except those of Agriculture, which was in Glasnevin, and Science and Engineering, which was in Merrion Street. The offices of the President, Registrar, Secretary, and Bursar, and the Professors' Common Room were all on the ground floor; immediately above the Main Hall was the Council Chamber where the Governing Body met and where degrees were conferred.

Having enrolled in the Faculty of Arts with a view to taking a degree in modern languages, I became one of a vast company of undergraduates attending lectures in English and Irish. The number studying Irish in First Year was so great that it was necessary to divide the class in two, one half being allotted to Seamus Delargy, the other half to Myles Dillon, then lecturer in Comparative Philology. I had intended to take a degree in French and English and to drop Irish after First Year but I found Myles Dillon's classes stimulating and so was drawn to Celtic Studies. By my second year I was following classes in Old Irish and the other subjects in the Celtic Studies group though still attending lectures in French; in effect I was doing a double degree. However, towards the end of the year I reluctantly gave up French, thereby missing the legendary tea party that the lecturer in French, Mrs Mary Kate O'Kelly (one of the notable Ryan sisters, and wife of Sean T. O'Kelly), gave annually for her Third Year honours class.

The Faculty of Celtic Studies had links with Eugene O'Curry, who had been appointed Professor of Irish History and Archaeology in Newman's Catholic University, and it had links also with Kuno Meyer and the School of Irish Learning. We Celtic Studies undergraduates were tucked away in a small room on the first floor corridor in Earlsfort Terrace, called the Zimmer Library, which housed hundreds of books from the library of the German Professor Zimmer, a pioneer Celtic scholar. Here, the Professor of Old Irish, Osborn Bergin, lectured to us. There were four of us in my year; had it not been for meeting friends for coffee in the Annexe we would have had little contact during the day with our fellow students. Why the restaurant in the basement under the Main Hall was called the Annexe was a mystery. It was the social centre of College; hours were spent chatting and gossiping over cups of coffee. The benches covered in red plush that lined the walls of the Main Hall were the setting of budding romances.

College in the thirties had a number of aspiring writers, one of whom was Mary Lavin, at the time preparing an M.A. thesis on Jane Austen. I remember too Charlie Donnelly, a gentle delicate-looking boy who wrote poetry and who argued in a quiet earnest way about the current situation in Spain, a country then on the brink of civil war. Within a year or so Charlie Donnelly had gone to Spain to fight on the side of the Republicans. His tragic death in the war was a great shock to those who had known him. Donagh MacDonagh, son of Thomas MacDonagh, executed in 1916, was a friend of Charlie Donnelly and like him wrote poetry. My clearest recollection of Donagh was hearing him talk of a play that he hoped to write on the Deirdre saga. It must have been about fifteen years later that the play was finally written.

I was a member of the Dramatic Society but had come into college too late to see Cyril Cusack act in the Society. His performances were still talked about, however, and it was taken for granted that he would become a great actor. Normally, the Dramatic Society staged plays in one of the upstairs rooms of Newman House, but once a year a professional producer was engaged and the Abbey Theatre hired to present what was called the 'public production'. In my second year in college the play chosen for production in the Abbey was a translation of a Spanish comedy, the name of which I have long since forgotten. The fact that I had a part in it was all that mattered. John MacDonagh, uncle of Donagh, was the producer. We in the cast were excited to have an opportunity to tread the boards of the Abbey stage and to be able to greet friends in the greenroom after the performance.

The most prestigious society in College was the L&H, where on Saturday evenings aspiring lawyers and others who hoped to make their mark in life, tried out their debating skills. There were, indeed, many fine and compelling speakers among the members of the Society. The meetings took place in the old Physics Theatre of 86, the same Physics Theatre which features in James Joyce's *Portrait of the Artist*. (In my day it was still much the same as it would have been when Joyce was a student.) The auditorship of the L&H was a coveted honour. The auditor was elected by the members of the Society and there was keen competition for election to the post. I think it was in my first year in college that there was a furore over the alleged payment of a considerable number of membership subscriptions by one of the candidates who hoped to influence the way those whose subscriptions had been paid would vote. The President of the College, Dr Denis Coffey, appointed a committee or tribunal into the matter. The committee was headed by a young graduate lawyer, Tim

O'Hanrahan, who later became Attorney General, and the meetings were held in the evening in one of the large ground floor rooms of 86. The meetings were a Mecca for undergraduates — and indeed for some graduates — as the examination of witnesses gave rise to much lively exchange and witty repartee. I cannot remember the outcome of the inquiry but it was great fun while it lasted.

As I mentioned earlier, there were four students of Celtic Studies in my year and we were joined occasionally in the Zimmer Library by graduates doing research; one of these was Máirín Uí Dhálaigh, then working on her M.A. thesis under the direction of Professor Bergin. Osborn Bergin, one of the most distinguished Celtic scholars of all time, attracted graduates from abroad to study under him. To be in class with people older than oneself, some of whom were moreover already distinguished, was a great experience for us undergraduates. We were very much in awe of them and relieved not to be asked questions in their presence. Lecturing in the small room that was the Zimmer Library suited Bergin, who had a soft voice and was wont to talk down into his beard. Honours students of Modern Irish, who in those days were obliged to attend an introductory course in Old Irish, found difficulty in hearing Bergin, who lectured to them in one of the lecture theatres; in addition, they thought him unapproachable. In fact, he was a kind man but very shy. His lectures, based on his own research, communicated his critical assessment of the text being studied. We knew him to be a master of Old Irish philology. However, he transmitted to his students far more than the information he imparted in class, conveying also his evaluations and outlook. To this day when I find myself trying to justify an opinion I can imagine him asking, 'What evidence have you for that?' He commanded respect from us and at the same time made us feel that we could, if we used our talents, be of some importance. At a time in our lives when we were still unsure of ourselves that was very helpful.

There were hops every Friday evening at the Aula Maxima of 86. Over the years the linoleum covering the floor of the Aula Maxima had developed holes, leaving patches on which one could catch one's heel; the wise knew how to skirt these patches. Girls were usually good dancers, boys shuffled up and down the hall doing their best not to walk on their partners' toes. We foxtrotted to tunes like 'Love is the Sweetest Thing', waltzed to music from the film *Congress Dances*, and on rare occasions someone would attempt the tango. My elder sisters used to reminisce about a fancy-dress dance in 86 to which Bob Dudley Edwards went in a white tulle tutu, showing a great expanse of hairy leg and chest. Some of the College societies held formal dances annually in either the Gresham Hotel or the Metropole. It was quite a feather in a girl's cap to be asked to these formal dances. More routine social gatherings were the weekly meetings of the various societies; the cream buns for the teas came from either Mills or the DBC, both in Merrion Row. When we felt in need of a change from coffee in the Annexe we went through the Green to Roberts Café at the top of Grafton Street, where buns filled with a generous dollop of almond paste were our first choice and where we knew all the waitresses by name.

Most of my friends belonged to the Walking Club. It numbered a few graduates among its members. As there were lectures on a Saturday morning, Sunday was our only whole free day and the Walking Club functioned on a Sunday. We set off, usually from Rathfarnham, to walk across the Dublin hills, which in those days were sparsely populated; Stepaside, for example, had only a cluster of cottages. We might walk as far as Loch Bré, have tea in a cottage there and then walk back to Rathfarnham. I remember one Easter walking to the Sally Gap and then down to Enniskerry where we had tea before walking to Bray to catch the train home. Two graduates, Jim Meenan and Vivion de Valera, had cars and if they joined us for tea would offer lifts home to the weaklings among us.

The age span of the student body in the thirties was between seventeen years and twenty-two or twenty-three; there were mature students in evening commerce classes but none in the daytime, unless one included 'chronic medicals'. In those days one could repeat examinations year after year, provided of course one's parents were willing to pay the fees. We were carefree, cocooned in our own world, unaware of the shadow being cast over Europe by Fascism. We had no inkling that in a few short years we would be facing the cataclysm of World War II.

Peig Roche

Coffee, Cream Buns and Civil War

In the early thirties when I enrolled in University College, then housed in that fine neo-classic building in Earlsfort Terrace, I was unaware that as a woman my right to be there was fought for and won by two stalwarts, Mary Hayden and Agnes O'Farrelly, one a Professor of History and the other a Professor of Irish.

In my first year in college I attended Agnes O'Farrelly's lectures. She was a great enthusiast for all things Irish, not only the language, but the culture generally. She came to lectures dressed in tweeds and always wore a hat. Her devotion to the Camogie Club will be remembered by generations of UCD players. She never missed the College events or the inter-collegiate contests for the Ashbourne Cup. Lord Ashbourne, the donor of the cup, was a friend of hers, a striking figure in saffron kilts who often visited her in her cottage in Cloughaneely in Donegal where she kept open house.

A contemporary and good friend of Hayden and O'Farrelly was Douglas Hyde, who founded the Gaelic League. I had the good fortune to have him as a lecturer in First Year. From his area in the West of Ireland rich in song and folklore, he collected songs and translated them. He recited or chanted these songs while we stamped our feat to the rhythm of the metre. We all looked forward to his lectures. He seemed an elderly man then of genial disposition. He came to the lecture hatted and well clad in tweeds and colourful mufflers, which he would unwind to the rhythm of the songs, or so it seemed. He became the first President of Ireland in 1938.

Coming from the confines of a convent boarding school in the midlands as I did, I felt a wonderful sense of liberation in becoming a university student in the heart of our capital city. Strolling through the Green in its autumnal glory, and sipping coffee in Roberts Café in Grafton Street with one's newly made friends, was sheer delight. The Main Hall was the meeting place for all on their way to or from the lecture rooms; the university being small in numbers it could accommodate the diversity of students, urban and rural, in the many faculties. There was a great buzz of conversation as affairs of all kinds, mind and heart, were discussed. In the wintertime, for those of us who were in digs, the heat generated either from bodies or matters debated was welcome. If one was lucky to get near a radiator one would get the chance to dry out on a wet day (and these were many), or if one had money there was the comfort in the restaurant of hot coffee and cream buns.

Brian O'Nolan was a lively debater at the L&H, held in what was then called the Old Physics Theatre in 86. Later, when it was restored, Dr Murphy kindly allowed women graduates to have luncheons there, and as we sipped our pre-luncheon sherry some might recall the noisy sessions there on the landing in the days of the L&H, created by those who, not having gained admission, shouted protests at those inside.

The Cumann Gaedhealach was a society I occasionally attended in my undergraduate years. Máirín Nic Dhiarmaida and Cearbhall Ó Dálaigh were prominent members. Máirín was a student in Celtic Studies then and later worked in the Royal Irish Academy compiling the dictionary of Old Irish. It was a college romance that ended in a happy marriage. Cearbhall became the fifth President of Ireland.

I got accommodation in digs in Rathmines and later in Ranelagh. Women students from the provinces usually stayed in the Halls of Residence in Stephen's Green run by the Dominican and Loreto Nuns. In addition to accommodation, these halls — or 'colleges' as they were known before the foundation of the NUI and its constituent college, UCD — provided education to degree standard, since this was not available to women in the Catholic University in 86. They had splendid teachers — two remarkable nuns, Mother Gonzalis, Dominican, and Mother Eucharia, Loreto, and lay teachers of both sexes, but of course they missed 'the play and inter-play of energy and ideas that are the stuff of university life for the student'.

Many remarkable women passed through those halls: Helena Walsh (Concannon); Evelyn Nicholls (deemed the Beatrice of Pearse's vision); Mary (Maguire) Colum; the Ryan sisters, later wives of Mulcahy, McCullough, and O'Malley of Galway; Kate O'Brien, the brilliant novelist who writes of coming there in 1918, 'while Dublin was still smoking from Easter week'; the Sheehy sisters, Mary (who later married Tom Kettle), Hannah (who married Frank Skeffington), and Kathleen, the mother of Conor Cruise O'Brien.

There was a break in my early college career. I developed TB, the fate of many in their teens and early twenties at the time. There was no wonder drug, not until streptomycin came in the Fifties. Some went to sanatoria in Davos in Switzerland. A few of my college contemporaries died. I rested at home in the West where with the care of a devoted family I regained health and resumed my studies after a lapse of four years. My friends had departed. I was like *Oisín in ndiaidh na Féinne*.

As before, we congregated in the Main Hall. The Civil War in Spain was the topic of the day. There was a *pro fide* group and an anti-Communist effort. A medical student, the brother of a friend, took time off to fight on Franco's side. Oddly enough when he qualified as a doctor he joined the British Army (a strange volte-face), fought for the Allies in North Africa and was awarded an M.C., later becoming a Major. Frank Ryan, who fought in Spain with the anti-Fascists, was the icon of most students and was a hero when he died later in Germany from exhaustion.

I began my college career with the intention of studying for a B.A. and B.Comm. On my return after such a long lapse I continued with both; the hope of an honours degree in arts I had to forsake for a pass course concentrating on commerce. Barney Shiels was the Professor of Commerce. His book on the subject was not gripping but it was compulsory reading, and since his lectures were mainly based on the book and my response to the book was poor, I found it difficult to get involved. He was a good-natured man, kind and understanding with students.

In contrast, George O'Brien's lectures were always stimulating; he was an intellectual giant, but for all that a shy man. Political Economy was his subject. He explained in simple terms the 'real cost' and the 'money cost' of a cup of coffee, drawing attention to the economic significance of the pretty and pleasant waitress. They all seemed of that ilk to George.

As one who was living in digs where not only heat but also light and privacy were in short supply, I must mention here pleasant times of research and study in the National Library. During breaks from study I would repair downstairs with a few friends to the vestibule for those disputations that students revel in, and we might continue them as we made our way homewards, perhaps having coffee en route if we had the price of it.

The subjects for the B.Comm degree other than commerce were accountancy, banking and finance, statistics, and national economics. What a formidable array. I wonder if I ever knew what I was about. Did I question, as I slaved to get a competent knowledge of the subjects, to what purpose I would later apply the expertise gained? Why did I decide to study for a degree in commerce or an arts B.A? The answer is simple: I did so because most women students at that time chose to do so and I followed the herd.

I was conscious in my time in university of a degree of social snobbery, perhaps engendered in upper class schools and in the better off homes. Urban students had the edge on those from rural areas.

I left college with B.A., B.Comm, and H.Dip. in Education, and with skills in shorthand and typing acquired in a secretarial college when time allowed. With this baggage I set out to test the market. There was no great rush to seek my services; the lean thirties had extended into the Forties. I worked variously for a time in Cork and Tipperary as secretary and bookkeeper, and taught for a couple of years in a secondary school. As there was no security of tenure there, when an opportunity arose I moved to the technical school in Dundrum, County Dublin with the prospect of permanency. Within a year I had fallen in love and in due course got married. I lost my job, the ultimate irony. My long struggle for permanency in the public sector came to an end when it was within my grasp. The ban on married women in employment was not revoked until 1973. There must be a lesson there somewhere. Employment in the private domestic sector proved stable — for me. Sometimes you win.

Cliodhna O'Neill

Caitlin Uí Neill (Ní Chaoimh)
Trailblazing

My grandmother, Caitlin Ní Chaoimh, was from Dublin but was educated at the St Louis convent in Monaghan. As she wanted to attend university and had been unable to study Latin formally at school, she studied it alone and mastered it sufficiently to matriculate, starting her B.A. at UCD in 1933.

Her nickname in college was Citi na gCumann, or Society Kate, because of her prodigious involvement in various student activities. This carefully guarded secret was recently discovered due to a reference in a letter my father found, written in the 1950s by Cearbhall Ó Dálaigh (later President of Ireland) to her husband, my grandfather. Citi was indeed, by her admission to me, heavily involved with student activity and spoke mainly of the people she had met in the English Literary Society. On hearing of my own involvement in the Students' Union, and of my friends in the L&H, she remarked that she had always thought the L&H 'a load of old nonsense'. It transpired that she had in fact often sneaked in to a debate or two, and had appreciated the wit of the hecklers, to whom she referred as 'the gang at the door'.

Academically, she spoke of the horrors that First Year Latin held for her, and of the patience of the professor who shuffled herself and a similar group of non-starters through their First Arts exam. In like manner she opted out of the mathematics exam, choosing instead logic — which she claimed was anything but. Her memories of those who taught her in history were particularly fond.

Some of the memories that our discussions about UCD evoked were obviously painful to recall. One member of her peer group, a friend of Spanish parentage, was recalled to Spain to fight for the government. Another, a member of the Blueshirts, volunteered to fight with Franco. They were killed within a month of each other. Like herself, many of her friends in UCD at the time were the children of those who had been politically involved in the War of Independence and the Treaty negotiations, many of whom had spent long periods in jail for their activities. She remembers that as de Valera's party had just re-entered the Dáil, many academics who had previously held seats in the Dáil returned to the University to resume their positions.

She clearly remembered Miss Norah Greene, and to my amusement recounted that this formidable lady would fine her for wearing trousers, attend the College balls as Chaperone, and generally ensure a high level of decorum amongst students. My grandmother remembers a young man being intercepted by Miss Greene, who enquired as to whether he had been formally introduced to the young lady whose attention he was seeking. The young man replied, 'Why yes, but I'm afraid since I have not yet been introduced to you, Miss Greene, I cannot stay and talk.'

When my grandmother spoke of UCD she spoke not just of her own time there, but referred to a variety of developments which she had observed throughout her lifetime. While attending the National Concert Hall in Earlsfort Terrace a number of years ago she was outraged at the destruction of the grand staircase, but showed great interest in the renovation of Newman House. She retained a close link with UCD, having many friends in various departments, and eventually attended the graduations there of all four of her children. As her first grandchild to attend the University, my father tells me that I have followed the trail she blazed. I hope so.

May O'Meara (Carroll)

A Trip in Time

Time, I know, is only a dimension of the universe, but a few years ago as I watched on television the opening of the new Government Buildings it became for me much more than that, a kind of magic carpet taking me back to my lost youth. As the pictures unfolded I realized that the new Government Buildings were a reincarnation of the College of Science, my old Alma Mater.

In the Dáil Chamber itself, I saw the embodiment of what must have been our old chemistry and zoology lecture theatres, and there where Mary Harney was sitting, there surely was where I had sat that day when Professor Bailey Butler hypnotized the alligator during a zoology lecture. And a little higher up near Proinsias de Rossa, that's where the boy sat who had whistled loudly in the hushed room and woken up the hen that the professor had done as an encore when the alligator was such a huge success. Near the front beside John Bruton was where the German boy was sitting listening attentively and unsmilingly as the professor enlivened a lecture on the life cycle of the body louse by a description of the delousing machine he had invented when he was a medical officer to the Allied Forces during World War I looking after the health of the men coming back from the trenches. I wondered if Hans was thinking of a father who had perhaps fought in the opposing trenches, who had perhaps even died there. I never knew.

Life was very pleasant in college in those days. There were lots of hops and céilís, but if you lived in a Hall of Residence you did not get late leave to go to those desirable functions. You did, however, get leave to go a play. Going to a céilí on a late pass for *The Old Lady Says No*, some of us got into hot water because we didn't know the first thing about it the next day when Mother Rose wanted to hear details. This was 1936 and that week at the Gate Theatre was the first performance of Denis Johnston's wonderful play. We were very careful about our late passes after that. In spite of our eagerness to go dancing there were very few romances. There were lots of society meetings. These meetings were held in the afternoons and were very well attended. There was always tea and plenty of lovely cakes. Some boys claimed that they got a delicious free tea every day of the week by a judicious choice of society.

This idyllic existence could have another side, like the time that myself and four other girls lived under the threat of expulsion. It happened so simply, and we almost got away with it. It was all my fault. I persuaded the others to ignore the edict issued by the Head of Science that First Years were not to avail of the invitation extended by Trinity College to the entire Science Faculty of UCD to a prestigious occasion in the world of science. In short, a team of scientists had succeeded in splitting some of the neutrons away from the nucleus of the atom. One member of the team was Irish and happened to be a graduate of Trinity College, which was why Trinity was chosen as the venue for the team's first lecture on their really wonderful achievement. It was a truly memorable event attended by most of the crowned scientific heads of Europe.

The Trinity lecture theatre was hushed and waiting when we five arrived late and breathless and were directed to seats at the very top. We knew we were intruders in this august assembly. Was it guilt that made me stumble on the unfamiliar steps in the half dark? Was it conscience that cursed me with one of my unfortunate fits of laughter? I'll never know. All I know is that we spent some days of sheer horror. But we were not sent down. True, we had to endure some caustic comments, made more in sorrow than in anger, from our professors. Relations between TCD and UCD in the 1930s were delicate to say the least, and we knew that we had let the side down. Why did I do it? — Professor Walton, the Irish member of the team came from Cloughjordan near my home town.

The boy who had whistled and woken up the hen had also escaped expulsion. But everyone knew that the boy who owned up was not the guilty party.

As the picture faded on the screen I came back through my time tunnel. On telling my family about my exciting discovery I was scathingly informed that the Dáil I had been watching was the old one beautifully restored. My old lecture theatres were now the Taoiseach's and Tánaiste's offices.

Really, families have no finer feelings.

Máire Redmond

Lightening the Mood

My years in college coincided with the War Years, or Emergency Years — late Thirties, early Forties. I was a science student in the former College of Science, Upper Merrion Street, where one attended a 9 a.m. lecture, the audience consisting of First Medical, Agriculture, Engineering, and Science students. At mid-morning we walked or cycled to Earlsfort Terrace for maths and oral Irish. In the afternoon we returned to Merrion Street for practical work in the laboratories, whether for chemistry, botany or zoology. At around 4 p.m. we 'treated' ourselves to tea — in beakers, if cups were scarce — and delicious cream buns from the DBC situated near the Shelbourne Hotel. Sometimes we held a Society meeting after tea.

At that time, Belfield was a large country house surrounded by playing fields and situated along the Stillorgan Road. What must we owe to the founding fathers for their foresight in acquiring that property?

In those days the students held a 'Rag Day' to amass funds for charities — probably St Vincent de Paul — and, as traffic at that time could go down Grafton Street, one enjoyed the thrill of a ride on a float in carnival clothes with painted face. Another fund-raiser was a midnight matinée in the old Theatre Royal (now demolished) in Hawkins Street, at which I was a programme seller on one occasion.

Yes, I think I must say that I enjoyed my years in college, cramped though that large lecture theatre in Merrion Street may have been at 9 a.m. each day with so many First Year students, and in spite of the fact that the 'black-out' situation made it a dark and dreary time in Ireland generally.

The 1940s

Following the 'Emergency' (as World War II was known), conditions in Ireland were actually worse for a couple of years than they had been during the war, and then very gradually the 1940s improved.

Everything was in short supply, including money. Some food and all clothes were rationed. Fuel was scarce and unsatisfactory: no coal except anthracite, which was not suitable for ordinary open fireplaces; wet turf and not enough of it, which was not satisfactory in kitchen ranges. In cities and where there was a gas system the supply came on only for limited periods each day and was policed by the 'glimmerman' who could cut off supply to any household found using the small amount of gas that remained in the pipes.

Paraffin oil was rationed, and one's quota of electricity was based on one's consumption in a given period. This was probably a fair enough system, but some households had a very poor ration because they had been on holidays for part of the period on which the ration was based.

Jobs were scarce and changing conditions meant that traditional ways of earning a living disappeared. Merchants who imported from England or the Continent found that they were getting only very reduced supplies from England and none at all from mainland Europe. Some fruits disappeared from the shops and a whole generation of children did not see a banana until they were seven or eight.

Accommodation at all levels was difficult to come by. No houses were built during the Emergency and there was a very limited supply of materials to repair existing buildings. Paint was practically non-existent so that all buildings became shabby.

A family's standard of living depended on the skill of the housewife to 'make do' and improvise, and also on what could be obtained on the Black Market or by barter. Parcels of tea from relatives in America or India were like manna from heaven, and smuggling from Britain or the North was a recognized way of life.

During the war years Ireland was insulated from actual combat, but threats of invasion and the bombing of Belfast and of the North Strand in Dublin gave us some idea of how bad it could be. We knew we were better off than our neighbours in Britain, but until World War II ended no one knew what conditions were like on the Continent because of strict censorship of all mail leaving or entering the country.

Everything improved after the terrible winter of 1946–47. Food became more plentiful and varied; fruit came from abroad; a huge cargo of chocolate came from Holland to Dungarvan but we found it very bitter. Clothes rationing ended and exotic materials like corduroy and organdie appeared in the shops. Nylon stockings became commonplace and skirts voluminous.

In the first half of the 1940s Ireland must have been a very insular place, but we did not know how insular we were and we did not care.

Nellie O'Cleirigh

1940   German invasions in Europe.

John Charles McQuaid consecrated Archbishop of Dublin.

1941   German bombs in Belfast and Dublin. Japan bombs Pearl Harbour.

US enters the War.

1942   Ration books in the Free State.

1944   Children's Allowances Act provides for an allowance of 2s 6d (12.5p) a week for a third and any further children under 16.

D-day. Liberation of Paris.

1945   Suicide of Hitler. Surrender of Germany.

Sean T. O'Kelly elected as President of Ireland.

Surrender of Japan. End of World War II.

1947   Archbishop McQuaid allows people to ignore fasting laws because of undernourishment.

First coal ration in Dublin since 1941.

1948   Rationing of gas, bread, flour and other commodities ends.

First coalition government since the establishment of the Free State.

1949   Ireland leaves the Commonwealth.

Irish delegates attend the first meeting of the Council of Europe in Strasbourg.

Breda Ryan (O'Brien)

Parking? No Problem!

Commerce was my faculty at UCD and Professor Barney Shields was Dean of the Faculty. There were five of us who were friends and we were known generally as 'The Four Blondes and the Ink Spot' (the latter had dark hair). We went everywhere together. Needless to say, during the Emergency we cycled everywhere, or sometimes, depending on pocket money, we travelled by tram. Distance was no object and I remember cycling with a group of commerce and other students to a commerce outing in Howth. Some of us rowed over to Ireland's Eye and then back to the usual brown loaf sandwiches — there was no white bread available during the Emergency — and tea. This was followed by a hop and then probably in the early hours we cycled home — what energy in those days! There were no muggings then and your only worry was of being stopped by a policeman for having no light on your bike. However, we had the excuse of the Emergency and the difficulty of getting batteries. I cannot remember hearing of any bike stolen from the college bike shed. Professors, lecturers and office staff, as well as students, cycled or travelled by tram, and maybe there were a few buses on special routes. Sometimes after dances you lent your bike to a fellow student who had walked to the venue, and you took a crossbar from another, all cooperating.

We were a small crowd in the 1940s, and as well as knowing most in our own faculty we knew many from other faculties, and the Main Hall was the meeting place for all. I think we spent a good deal of time chatting under the various notice-boards, arranging dates for the pictures, dances, matches, and discussing the doings of the SRC, etc. When we went to dress dances we rolled up our evening dresses and put them in the baskets of our bikes and parked the bikes, usually in the O'Connell Street Bike Park, for 6d (2.5p). After the dance we would change in the dressing room back into jumpers and skirts (no trousers in our day!) for the cycle home. Sometimes if an escort was 'in funds' one might travel home in luxury in a horse-drawn cab.

I can remember collecting the Ashbourne Camogie Cup (I was the goalie on the team) the night before we travelled to play UCG in the final in Galway. I got a phone call from the captain around 9 p.m. to say that we had forgotten to collect the cup from the previous year's captain and could I collect it as I was in Rathgar and the cup was in Rathdown Park. I got on my bike and collected it and with another teammate brought it to Westland Row station by tram. We met the rest of the team and our chaperone there and headed for a great weekend in Galway. Unfortunately, Galway won, so we returned minus the cup.

We really had a very happy time during our student days and had not the same pressures as nowadays, so we were lucky in many ways.

Marie O'Neill

Doing Two Things at Once

I spent the years from 1944 to 1947 as an arts student at the old UCD, situated in Earlsfort Terrace. Having been born and reared in Dublin (except for two years in London) I was familiar with the city and did not have the problems of country students who had to find their way around for the first time. I lived with my parents in Ballsbridge and came in to college by bus or bicycle, depending on the weather.

The college itself was in many ways a bewildering place. There were no Freshers' courses, and information about various options was not easy to find. For First Arts you needed five subjects. Most of us chose the subjects we had liked and/or been good at in school. My choice was to study English, French, Latin, history, and logic. The latter subject was the only alternative to mathematics and was regarded in general as a softer option. The next task was to work out the timetable for lectures. In my case, as I was also a solicitor's apprentice, I had to juggle my time between UCD and the Law Society lectures in the Four Courts building on the quays, a distance of about a mile which required two bus trips if you were not going by bicycle. I was supposed to give some time to office work with my 'Master' who had undertaken to train me in practical day-to-day work. This system of doing the two courses at once was a bad one and has long since been abolished. Nowadays you have to obtain a degree before starting the professional law course.

When I had settled into the routine of college lectures, I enjoyed most of them. In the English department Dr Roger McHugh was lively and stimulating. We admired him but his personality kept most of us in some fear of betraying our ignorance. I remember one unfortunate student who ventured to disagree with something he had said. Dr McHugh coolly asked him for his source and on being told it was the *Reader's Digest*, he reminded the student with a touch of sarcasm that that periodical was not a prestigious publication nor one to which any credence should be given. In history we had lectures from Professor John Marcus O'Sullivan and Professor Robert Dudley Edwards. The latter, universally known as 'Dudley', had been promoted to his Chair at an unusually early age. I got to know him better in my second and third years when I was concentrating on history for my degree. He was extremely kind to his students, taking a personal interest in all of them. I remember how quickly he memorized our names and never mixed us up, which was quite an achievement in the early months. Professor O'Sullivan, then in his later years, gave wonderful lectures. He had been Minister for Education in the early years after the Treaty settlement and was a prestigious figure in the college.

In the evenings there were numerous clubs and societies for students. The L&H was the foremost debating society, where the skills of speakers were put to the acid test. Constant interruption and heckling was the norm. At times the debates became rowdy but they were in general very good-humoured. In those days the Society was considered too rough for girls. Few of us dared to speak there. Among the exceptions were Maeve O'Higgins, a law student who later became a Carmelite nun, and Máirín Maye, a brilliant classmate of mine who died tragically young from tuberculosis. The Law Society and the History Students' Society were more sedate groups. There were numerous sporting clubs too.

Informal dances known as 'hops' were held regularly at Newman House, and during the summer months, at Belfield. Female students tended to go in much larger numbers than male students, so it was a great relief when someone asked you to dance! In those days the girls did not do the asking unless it was a 'Ladies'

Choice'. The Lady Dean of Residence, Miss Norah Greene, who looked after the welfare of the girl students, attended these hops as a kind of chaperone. I have often thought since how boring it must have been for her. She was a charming person and I often met and talked with her long after my student days had passed.

Apart from the educational benefits one of the great advantages of UCD was the wide circle of students you got to know. The various backgrounds from which they came provided a new perspective on life, particularly for Dublin girls like me who had little knowledge of rural Ireland. In those years most of us formed close friendships that lasted for life.

All too soon my three years in college came to an end. Serious revision and reading had to be covered before the degree exams in the autumn of 1947. The spring months that year were marked by very cold weather. Ice and snow persisted for some time but the summer weather was warm and sunny. We tried to vary hours of study with breaks for sport, in my case swimming and tennis. By the time my class graduated I felt a certain regret at leaving UCD. At the same time, however, I was anxious to finish my law course and begin the serious business of earning a living.

Nellie Beary O'Cleirigh

Looking Back

This article first appeared in *Alma Mater* 1995–96 and is reprinted here by kind permission of the author.

A first sight of the Belfield campus today cannot be any more daunting than a first sight of the large black and white squares of the Main Hall in Earlsfort Terrace in 1944. If you were the eldest in your family and no one from your year in school came to UCD, it was a very large and lonely world. Seventeen and straight from boarding school, being a student in Dublin during the 'Emergency' was another life entirely.

The geography of the city was a complete mystery and it never seemed to occur to us to spend precious pocket money on a map. Coming in to the city from digs in Ballsbridge was a major worry as you had to ensure that you got off the bus at the right stop in Nassau Street. After a few weeks a bicycle was the obvious mode of transport but it was an expensive commodity and spare tyres and tubes were often smuggled in from Northern Ireland and Britain.

Finding out about lectures and clubs and societies was another problem. There was no Freshers' Week, but after a few months one discovered that the person to ask was 'Professor' Paddy Keogh in the Porter's Office in the Main Hall. He knew everybody and everything.

Meals were in the basement of 86, with the smell of mashed potatoes and boiled cabbage wafting towards you halfway across Iveagh Gardens. Nell Whiteside and her mother ran the restaurant, which provided cheap but basic fare. Facing in on your own to collect your tray was an ordeal in the beginning but was probably very good training for all types of social situations in later life. You were glad to meet the few students who came from your home town. Contacts made at Irish College in Ring, Co Waterford, were particularly useful as these covered both sexes and varied faculties.

War time was a great leveller. No one had lavish wardrobes, although a few Dublin girls were better dressed than most of us, who were glad to have warm, sensible clothes and a few changes. The 'in thing' at one period was a 'Highland Twinset', or its poorer cousin, a 'Paula Set'. If you were lucky, a kind aunt might give you a present of the correct accessory — a single string of pearls — or you might get one for your 21st birthday. The male architects were very distinctive, being the only students sporting corduroy jackets, dickie bows and beards. I still wonder where they managed to acquire their ensembles, as all fabrics were strictly rationed at that time.

The student population in 1944 was regarded as enormous — 3,000 full-time students — but as all teaching was conducted within Earlsfort Terrace and the College of Science in Merrion Street, it was not difficult to get to know 'characters' from other faculties.

During 1944 and 1945 there were a few German Prisoners of War on parole from the Curragh. One or two came to the history lectures and anyone who attended the First Arts maths class may remember the Luftwaffe pilot who, at the end of the lecture, marched down the steps of the theatre to give the Nazi Salute to the lecturer!

The L&H offered great free entertainment on a Saturday night. A number of today's politicians began their careers there. I was in college at the same time as three students who went on to head political parties: Charles Haughey, Garret Fitzgerald, and Tomás MacGiolla. I recall that Charles Haughey, in particular, was a regular performer at the L&H. Probably the most entertaining character was Ulick O'Connor. He had a disappearing birdcage and was a good conjurer. At one stage he was banned from the L&H but he got around this by appearing as a woman, having arranged for Jackie McGowran of the Abbey Theatre to take care of make-up.

Apart from the L&H, which attracted all-comers, Irish societies such as the Cumann Gaedhealach, Cumann Seanacais, and the Cumann Litheardha had large memberships. The Dramsoc also captivated a variety of characters from all disciplines.

There were a few particularly memorable members of the teaching staff. Professor Robert Dudley Edwards of the History Department loomed largest in my circle. He knew each of his students by name and had a shock of white hair which stood out all round his head. We regarded him as an old man, but he can only have been in his thirties. He had just replaced Mary Hayden as Professor of Modern Irish History and was considered a very young appointee. As many of us were neither familiar with the public libraries in Dublin nor had access to the Royal Dublin Society Library, we were blessed by the great concession of tickets to the National Library, which 'Dudley' had obtained for us. Decades later, I stopped to offer him a lift on Highfield Road, Rathgar and was thrilled that he remembered me, especially as I had not been one of his more brilliant students.

Another staff character was George O'Brien, whose head preceded his body as he came through the door of the lecture theatre. He used to start speaking the minute he entered, so one needed to be ready to take notes. Professor Bailey Butler's botany lectures attracted many students who never even studied science. They were considered good entertainment, and perhaps he might hypnotize a hen!

When it came to examination time we sat in the enormous cavern that is now the National Concert Hall, a large, cold place, with drops of rain or condensation coming in from the roof. A Supervisor who clanked up and down in heavy shoes on the concrete floor was no help at all.

Most of us managed to 'get through' this gruelling ordeal, some with distinction. Apart from those who went into politics, the 1940s produced a number of public figures and academics: Fr F.X. Martin, Michael MacCormac, Louis Smith and Con O'Cleirigh are some who come to mind. Postgraduate students such as Tom O'Neill, Oliver McDonagh and Donal Kerr became history professors. Others such as Ciarán Mac Mathúna, Denis Meehan and Maeve Conway went into radio. Seán MacRéamonn and Benedict Kiely are also remembered. Later, television lured talent like Donal O'Móráin and Brian Farrell.

Today's students would find it hard to believe that Belfield was merely a place where you went to play tennis on poor courts or to attend the occasional hop in Belfield House. And in those days it was considered a long way when you had to cycle home.

Marie Fennell

The Age of Innocence

To use Oxbridge phraseology, I was 'up' at UCD between the years 1945 and 1948 and I read science there. In those days before the points system UCD accepted students with a good Leaving Certificate or Matriculation or both. I bought my Matric from my Leaving Certificate and also sat a Latin paper to matriculate. Academically gifted students could win scholarships from their Leaving Certs or from some county councils; generally, however, students' fees were paid by hard-working and ambitious parents.

For a 'country girl' there was the added cost of accommodation in Dublin. Our choice was Dominican Hall on St Stephen's Green. The gentle penumbral atmosphere of that splendid Georgian house I now recollect in tranquillity. The wonderful architecture of Earlsfort Terrace, St Stephen's Green, University Church, and the College of Science buildings must have formed my early standards in city architecture.

The student body was an interesting mix at that time. The 'Emergency' was in force. Young German airmen, blond and handsome, created quite a flutter among the girls. Cohorts of black-suited clerical students would swoop down on their bicycles from Clonliffe College seminary. Young and pretty nuns wore their traditional habits and always sat in the front row of the lecture theatres. Future politicians Garrett Fitzgerald and Charles Haughey occupied chairs in the Library in Earlsfort Terrace.

Our social life was a reflection of 'the age of innocence'. The weekly hop in the Aula Maxima at 86, or out at Belfield during the summer term, were favourite meeting places. We knew nothing of the Pill or condoms then. The free and easy sexual habits of the

Sixties were light years away; the Ten Commandments and the word 'No' were the only contraceptives known to us.

The slow-growing sense of our own worth as young women contributed to our greater expectation of status and fair play. Some notable women staff members such as Dr Carmel Humphries, Professor of Zoology, and Dr Helen Doyle, were obvious role models. It became both admirable and praiseworthy to have academic success and a 'good job' as well as marriage and children. If it sounds like *la vie en rose* we were not totally ignorant of poverty and deprivation, and many young people entered religious orders to comfort the poor and sick. The idealism of youth will always produce excellence. *Plus ça change, plus c'est la même chose!*

Carmel Duggan

Seats for Sale!

My four years at UCD in Earlsfort Terrace in the second half of the 1940s now seem part of another world. A First Year student staying at the Dominican Hall, St Stephen's Green at that time could not be out later than 7.30 p.m., until 10 with permission, and there was an 11 p.m. special concession for the Friday night hop in 86. I recall getting in free to the Friday hops and to the Wednesday afternoon céilí by playing the piano with another student as a duo during the band's interval.

The term began with a Retreat in University Church, St Stephen's Green, and at coffee at Hall's Corner after the first night of the Retreat, a Second Year medical student 'sold' me and friend two seats in the Library — a well-worn practice, as we discovered too late.

I studied Irish, Latin, music, history, and logic. In Second Year, I proceeded to a two-year honours degree course in Irish. Irish history in First Year with Professor Dudley Edwards was never dull. The class roll included names like Róisín Dubh, John Bull, Caitlin Ní hUallachain, and Grainne Mhaol, and these he read out on the first day with mock solemnity, and responses were given with equal seriousness. There was in the history class a genuine 'Claudia Hapsburg' who lived at Áras an Uachtaráin with President and Mrs O'Kelly. When this girl answered the roll call on the first day, Professor Dudley Edwards looked up and asked, 'Do I see a crown?' Claudia answered politely, 'No, Professor, I do not wear a crown.' The professor did not make that mistake again.

John Marcus O'Sullivan's European history lectures were a great experience. He opened my mind to vistas I had not previously imagined and I am indebted to him for reinforcing my lifelong interest in history.

I recall the civilizing effects over three years of the classics, and the weekly discipline of translating modern literature into Latin prose. The encyclopaedic minds of Professor Semple and Professor O'Meara made the politics, the culture and the literature of the Roman Empire seem alive and relevant to our age, to represent, as it were, a microcosm of contemporary world affairs.

I was privileged to enjoy Tomás de Bhaldraithe's scholarly learning, Cormac Ó Cadhla's *Gnas na Gaelige* and *An Fhiannaíocht*, Fr Francis Shaw's clarity of exposition in Old and Middle Irish, the analysis of the sonata form under Dr Larchet, Mairéad Piogoid's exposé of the history of Irish music, and the happy experience of the Musical Society and its repertoire, which included productions of Gilbert and Sullivan's *Gondoliers* and *Patience*, and Coleridge Taylor's choral work *Hiawatha's Wedding*.

The cut and thrust of the L&H in the Physics Theatre was always a Saturday night highlight, and the fortnightly symphony concerts at the Capitol Theatre and queuing for seats in the gods for the operas at the Gaiety never failed to entertain. *O tempora, O mores!*

Teddy Burke

The Coldest Winter

I came to college in 1946, planning to do arts and subsequently a librarianship course. I went to Dominican Hall, where I was fortunate enough to be put in a room with six other girls. I had been horribly spoiled by my parents, so it was the best thing that could have happened to me. For a week I hated it and wanted to move out. By the time my mother next came to Dublin and asked about moving, I was perfectly happy and had made friends with the others. We learned later that we had been put together because we were from different Ursuline convent schools in Waterford, Thurles, and Sligo. Two from Dominican Convent, Taylor's Hill, were there to maintain the balance, and we had plenty of late night chats about our respective schools.

To me college seemed enormous; at that time it consisted of Earlsfort Terrace for lectures, and 86 for coffee (which was called 'mud' by the more discriminating, but our twopences did not go much farther, and, in any case, coffee was mostly an excuse for long discussions about how we would run the world if we had the chance). We enjoyed the Language Society meetings but we also had friends among science students. With one of these I used to go to study in the Science Library in Merrion Square, as it was much warmer in winter than the Arts Library, which was cold and draughty.

In 1947 came the coldest winter I had ever experienced. Some of my brother's friends had a little car called 'Lulu', of which they were inordinately proud considering its size and vintage. One of them, I presume the owner, thought he would try Lulu on the snowy slopes of the Wicklow Mountains. But she refused the test and died on the spot. I hope they gave her a decent burial when the snow melted.

One professor who remains forever ingrained in my mind was nicknamed 'Fish' in reference to the first word he taught us to decline in the Old English part of our course. As he must have gone to his hard-won heavenly reward by now, I hope he won't mind my using this name because I don't recall his real name. I don't know whether, in fact, we ever knew it. He was overflowing with enthusiasm for his subject and enjoyed every moment of his class. I was rather less than enthusiastic and attended only because one had to make the attendance list. I have regretted it since, having become much more interested in the formation of, and historical change in language.

I remember coming down the stairs in Earlsfort Terrace with a friend who was also an Old English student. 'Fish' had been lecturing us for an hour and we needed coffee. Suddenly he appeared between us. 'That was an interesting lesson, wasn't it?' he said with a beatific smile. It was said as a child would say it, without the least pride or conceit. He just wanted to share his joy in Old English with us. My friend had been reading a newspaper under the desk and I had been copying poetry into my book. However, we both hastily assured him that it had, indeed, been most interesting. Looking back I think it probably had been, and I sometimes wonder whether he was as unaware of our lack of appreciation as he seemed.

College was a great place to expand the mind because you encountered so many different points of view, both from lecturers and students. When I hear the Forties and Fifties described as repressive, intolerant and illiberal, I wonder whether these people are talking about the same era through which I lived. In the family in which I grew up we were free to come and go as we pleased, but we more often pleased to be with our families and friends. And in college everyone seemed to me to express themselves as they wished. In those days it was not as competitive as it is for students now, and there was time, therefore, for those extra-disciplinary exchanges in debates and meetings that broaden understanding for others' interests and awaken one's own. We did not, either, have that growing anxiety about securing work when our college careers ended that weighs so heavily on young people today. We were lucky and, better still, we partly knew it; one never fully knows how lucky one has been until afterwards, I suppose.

On the subject of debates, I remember that Sean MacBride, as leader of Clann na Poblachta, came to chair an L&H Society meeting in 1948. The Physics Theatre was packed to the doors and the speakers — students in law, medicine, science, arts or whatever — could find no proper room to stand to make their speeches. One speaker stood on the demonstration table to speak — perhaps they all did. The topic, as far as I can remember, had to do with cooperation among all sections of the community: for and against. Whether Sean MacBride was for or against, I don't remember. What I do remember is that he started to say the 'Our Father'. He said it all the way through. I still remember how I froze in my seat, praying that they wouldn't interrupt him or jeer him, as was typical L&H at that time when the non-participants got bored or annoyed. They didn't. My relief was not so much because I had wanted them to respect him; rather, I had wanted them to respect God.

All that is more than fifty years ago now. I do not think we were repressed or unable to express what we wanted to do, or to do it. Many of the people I knew then I have never met since, but I remember them very plainly as they were. Some of them I have met in later life and it has always given us great pleasure to look back on those far-off days when we were so sure that we knew what we were going to do with our lives and where we would spend our years. For most people, however, whether college students or not, I think life brings many surprises. It certainly did to me.

Sister Kathleen Sullivan

Observing the Silence

Happy years, delighting in new experiences, broader vision, and above all, the people. Without the people, much would have been lost.

In those days, silence reigned between clerics and female religious. But silence is a powerful language; it can often reveal much more than the spoken word. Years later some of the gaps in communication were filled on discovery of the fact that the clerics used to bet on the cleric–religious results. No doubt using buttons as coinage.

Dr Lorna Reynolds for English was both challenging and supportive. My first essay, 'Impressions of UCD', was pedestrian, getting more than it deserved with its conventional shackles; a further effort, however, written at the request of a harassed student on condition that I could 'let go' by giving my impressions as Thomas Mann, was the initial stimulus for future writing.

I was intrigued by Professor Dudley Edwards and his elite History Group VIII. As a classics student I was curious to 'get inside', being ignorant on the subject of modern history. I thought I would have an enjoyable session doing nothing but exploring. The professor, however, was the one who had fun — at my expense. A history student, renowned for the illegibility of his handwriting, was absent; I was commandeered to read the scrawl. My ignorance of history, combined with my tendency to see all in Latin terms, resulted in my proclaiming nervously and loudly as 'mal-e tal-e' what the well-informed class recognized as a simple historical term: 'male tail'. The ensuing laughter ensured a welcome if I cared to return.

I read a paper at the Classical Society. As the first religious woman to do so, I was scared stiff. I agreed on the condition that I would not answer questions. The reason was quite simple — anything I knew was in the paper I was presenting. Professor Semple, the perfect gentleman, handled it beautifully and I got away safely. Some time later Des Fennell told me how disappointed he had been, as he had come expressly to riddle me. It would have been a simple matter indeed and quite unworthy of his skills to have done so, I told him.

Professor John O'Meara influenced me more than anyone, an influence that lasts to this day. He elicited one's best effort and was generous in his recognition of that effort, but he never accepted poor work. His humanity and kindness were and are remarkable.

My sweetest memory is of stolen breaks in Iveagh Gardens. My eye there was always open for Paddy the Porter's little son, whose innocence and frankness were a delight. Through the child, I earned a place in Paddy's heart. My final examination results, coming earlier than I had dared hope for thanks to Paddy's unexpected wire, were all the more welcome because of the human relationship that prompted the kind deed.

Máire Gibbons

Standing Room Only

My Dublin will always be Rathfarnham, and the old buildings at Earlsfort Terrace that now house the National Concert Hall. A recent visit evoked many pleasant memories of my years spent in that part of town. The entrance hall in the Terrace was known as the Main Hall of UCD. It inspired awe in most First Year students and I was no exception.

I went there in October 1947 when the chill of winter was in the air. I felt that chill within as I looked around shyly and made straight for the nearest notice-board, more to hide from the gaze of onlookers than to read what was written there. It was my first taste of city life. Rathfarnham, where I lived, was then a quiet suburb on the outskirts. The crows resting in the tall trees behind the walls of Rathfarnham Castle were seldom disturbed. Traffic was light on Grange Road. This was probably why W.B. Yeats could come down that road in his wheelchair. I vividly remember him when I was a child. He smiled at me as he passed by the church on his way up to the village. Such was the quiet peace we enjoyed.

During my college years I stayed in Dominican Hall on St Stephen's Green with ninety others. Though the accommodation was not luxurious, Sister Columban and Sister Perpetua were unsparing in their attention. The hub of college life centered on this part of town and there were students everywhere. A walk in the Green was a favourite pastime. On one occasion I was there with a friend, when we spotted a newly appointed professor strolling along with his wife. As he was renowned in his field, we assumed that his conversation would be in keeping with his erudition. As we passed them, however, he proclaimed in a loud voice, 'I'd rather have rashers!' He fell from his pedestal immediately, just another mortal as far as we were concerned.

We got a new Professor of Logic in those years, Professor O'Doherty. He was famed for being able to handle twenty philosophical enquiries at the same time. No lecture room was big enough to accommodate everyone; you had to be there well ahead of time if you wanted a seat. On one occasion Ulick O'Connor entertained us to a magnificent parody on one of Shakespeare's speeches while we waited. We kept moving from one lecture hall to another. Overcrowding kept getting worse. Finally one day the professor asked, 'Is there anyone here who should be at another lecture?' We could see plenty who should, but there wasn't even a whisper. All he could do was laugh.

The Singing Kettle, a café on Leeson Street, was a favourite haunt. Discussions and conclusions on philosophic topics were hammered out in the billowing cigarette smoke. The coffee was oh-so-bad!

Though every day has something new and exciting to offer, those days in UCD were unique in that they opened up a whole world of culture to be explored in the future.

Maedbh Ní Concubhair

A Scoop

In the late 1940s I was one of twenty students of social science in UCD. We were one of the first such groups and often shared lectures with students from TCD. My sister Nessa was also a student at UCD, studying Celtic Studies and Archaeology under the famous archaeologist, Professor O'Riordan. This was the era before television, and college life revolved around the various college societies, which provided a continuous source of recreation and amusement. This ranged from the L&H on Saturday nights to various dress dances. Coming from an Irish-speaking family we were heavily involved in the Cumann Gaedhealach in addition to the other societies. The Cumann Gaedhealach published a monthly literary magazine called *Comhar*, which still exists today.

Comhar contained articles and poems by students and graduates, and both my sister and I were on the committee. One day we were given the formidable task of seeing if we could entice the famous actor Michael MacLiammóir to contribute an article in Irish. We made an appointment to see him and at the agreed time we arrived at the apartment he shared with Hilton Edwards in Harcourt Terrace.

We were received most graciously, and without hesitation Michael agreed to contribute to *Comhar*. He and Hilton were about to leave for London and they offered us a lift in their car back to the city centre. We set off in grand style with our most attentive hosts and were driving down Grafton Street when there was a dramatic exclamation from Michael — they had forgotten their tickets. There was a frantic dash back to Harcourt Terrace where fortunately the two tickets were quickly found, then a speedy drive once more to Grafton Street where we took leave of our hosts.

The editorial committee of *Comhar* decided that Nessa and I should feature on the cover of subsequent issues of the magazine. We made many enduring friendships in UCD, and were fortunate to know and enjoy it when it was still small and everybody knew everybody else, before the pressure of today's points system.

The 1950s

The Fifties in Ireland could be criticized for being a very narrow and introspective time. Thinking for oneself was rather difficult in a country where books were subject to heavy-handed censorship; Alan Simpson was imprisoned for producing Tennessee Williams' *The Rose Tattoo* because of the appearance of a condom on stage. Added to all of this there was a boom in almost all capitalist countries while Ireland suffered chronic unemployment and emigration throughout the decade. The European Economic Community came into existence in 1958 but Ireland did not apply for membership until 1961. There was no evidence in the Fifties of any likelihood of the changes that started to take place in the Sixties.

Lest we think, however, that Ireland was alone in fearing the consequences of freedom of expression, it is worth remembering that it was in this decade in America that McCarthyism flourished. American Senator, Joseph McCarthy, helped to engender a frenzied fear of Communists in the American people, and 'Reds under the Bed' became the catchphrase of the day.

On the lighter side of life, this was the era of rock and roll; 'teddy boy' fashions for the young and not-so-young males, waspie belts and billowing skirts for the females as they rock 'n' rolled to Bill Haley and Elvis Presley.

Life for the students, and particularly the women students, of University College Dublin mirrored the larger society. There was control of College societies by the authorities, with a list of banned guest speakers; women were not allowed to wear trousers; the charming Lady Dean, Norah Greene, kept a wary eye on behaviour between the sexes in the precincts of the College and attended the College hops and dress dances as a sort of general chaperone.

Despite these negative aspects of life, college for the students in the Fifties was free from a lot of the academic and competitive pressures imposed on students of today. Career choice was influenced by the fact that one had a Matriculation Certificate and £30+ for fees — and often by what queue one stood in for Registration. It was not unheard of for students to change their minds while queuing for one faculty and move to another.

Although the total number of students would only have been around three thousand, those arriving on their first day in college still found it a daunting experience; they were not surrounded, as often happens today, by friends, all moving from school to third level together.

Belfield in the Fifties only provided the sports facilities for the College and was the venue for Sports' Day, when refreshments were provided afterwards in the big house beside the athletics track. The building of the new university did not start until the Sixties.

Although exams were relatively stress free (with students repeating and moving faculty when a number of repeats failed), there were pressures afterwards since jobs were not necessarily available even when one had obtained a degree.

Despite the current perception of this decade as one that was marked by repression and little economic prosperity, it had, nonetheless, unacknowledged freedoms associated with a pace of life that is cherished and much sought after today.

Eithne White

1950   Minister for Health, Dr Noel Browne, proposes 'Mother and Child Scheme' whereby all mothers and babies get free postnatal treatment; Catholic bishops condemn the scheme, saying it infringes on the rights of the family.

1952   Death of Stalin. Queen Elizabeth II crowned.

1955   Protests against Sean O'Casey's play, *The Bishop's Bonfire.*

       First regular TV service in Ireland.

       Archbishop McQuaid unsuccessfully calls for the cancellation of a soccer match between Ireland and Yugoslavia because of Tito's imprisonment of a Croatian prelate.

       Ireland joins United Nations.

1956   Ronnie Delaney wins gold in Melbourne Olympics.

1958   European Economic Community comes into existence.

1959   De Valera elected President of Ireland.

Joan Trodden Keefe

Course Work Optional

Sister Paul, headmistress of my convent school, was responsible for my getting a university education. She insisted that I get enough tuition in Latin in my last few years of school to qualify for the university entrance requirements. She also whisked me through the final two years of school at a pace that got me, somewhat breathless, into college at the far too immature age of sixteen. Her strategies were dictated by a practicality; if I hadn't gone then, I would never have gone.

In First Year Arts I registered for English, French, Irish, Latin and maths. It seems a tall order now. However, notions of serious learning or study soon evaporated in the heady climate of the extra-curricular activities into which I irresponsibly plunged. For the three years it took to graduate with a B.A., course work was not high on my list of interests. Otherwise the daily life of a student was pure heaven.

The first and lasting impression of the College on students of those generations was the checkerboard marble-tiled Main Hall, a place a-swirl in smoke, bustle and din, misty and expectant as a railway station. Each well-defined group had its stakeout: EngLit, Dramsoc, Cumann Gaedhealach. At intervals some would drift off to a lecture, others amble down the stairs at the left to the Annexe, an underground den lit like an interrogation cell, where 'coffee' (God knows what it was made of) and cream buns were consumed.

In English Literature, Jerry Hogan — truly one of Flann O'Brien's professors 'distant in the web of his fine thought', a man with a cadaverous face and a kind of hollow booming voice — intoned scenes from Shakespeare with gusto:

And thou, O wall, O sweet, O lovely wall,

That stand'st between her father's ground and mine!
Thou wall, O wall, O sweet and lovely wall,
Show me thy chink, to blink through with mine eyne!

What were we to make of it?

Senator Michael Hayes, Professor of Irish, delivered his lectures (in English) with a swaggering bonhomie, generously larding his speech with peasant stage-Irishisms. A bellowed, 'By Gor, Sor, 'tis terrible late ye are!' would crush some tardy jackeen creeping into class.

These two polar opposites characterized an uneasy schism in Irish education. Those who took English seriously were considered to be sophisticated, to have their eyes fixed across the water. The *gaeilgeoirs* were seen as frumpish, given to sporting *criosanna* and *fáinní*, and to crying up the charms of the Blaskets. Some of us, jostled by odd loyalties to our parents and grandparents, tried to belong to both groups. Joyce catches these strains in the edgy sparring of Molly Ivors and Gabriel in *The Dead*.

The first book I read after becoming a student was *Ulysses*, lent to me by a new friend. It was a revelation, and heavily though unconsciously under Joyce's spell, I wrote a tiny piece called 'Poor Mangan' and timorously pushed it under the door of the office of *The National Student*, the student literary magazine. It was accepted and published and I thought I was made for life.

There were brilliant people around, some already moving into the real world of politics and the arts. More than anyone, Anthony Cronin has given us in his writings vivid descriptions of the wilder shores of bohemian excess. P.J. Connolly was auditor of the L&H where Ulick O'Connor was already tweaking the nose of outraged respectability. Poor John Jordan still glowed with the promise of great things. *As Gaeilge*, Desmond Fennell whipped into shape aspiring playboys of the western world. Of course, the rest of us applauded delightedly the antics and achievements of the great.

My initial small success in *The National Student* made me a devoted disciple of the magazine, but lack of serious purpose enfeebled my subsequent contributions. Even so, I was appointed editor for the Spring 1951 issue. I was fortunate to have the unflappable Sean J. White as sub-editor and we produced a worthy but perhaps not inspired edition. Still, my gadfly editorial roused the *Evening Mail*'s 'Man About Town' to devote a column to it. Fame indeed. Almost as an afterthought, I graduated in 1951.

Writing about Brian O'Nolan (Flann O'Brien) in the *New York Review of Books*, John Banville remarked: 'It is possible that Brian O'Nolan's happiest, or his least unhappy, years were those he spent as a student at University College Dublin.' I think the same, without the qualification, could be said of some of the rest of us also.

Anne Kernan

A Bygone Era

I entered UCD in autumn 1949 at the age of sixteen. I took my B.Sc. and Ph.D. in physics at UCD and continued there as College Lecturer before moving to the United States in 1962.

We science undergraduates were very busy, our days filled with lectures and labs. We dashed back and forth between Earlsfort Terrace and the College of Science in Merrion Street. But long afternoons in the labs gave us time to become acquainted.

I have very good memories of the UCD faculty. One person who had a special impact was Carmel Humphries, lecturer in zoology and later, professor. She was a handsome, hearty woman. During our first class she quickly concluded that our group needed sex education and gave us a lecture on human reproduction. In the Ireland of 1949 this was an electrifying experience; it was the first time for most of us to hear from a responsible adult that sex was a healthy, natural human activity. On meeting years later, members of the group would recall this lecture as a milestone in our personal development.

Others I remember are Professor Wheeler, the charismatic Professor of Chemistry, Mr O'Grady, College of Science Librarian, who allowed me access to the shelves, and Professor Gormley, reputed to be a genius because his mathematics lectures were near incomprehensible and he seemed barely aware of the students. Professor Nevin in Physics was always kind and encouraging. He was intensely loyal to UCD. When I decided to go to the United States he asked, 'Why? They're doing nothing in America that we're not doing here.'

I was the only woman continuing in physics after First Year, but I was readily accepted by fellow students, faculty and staff in the Physics Department. In 1953, during my fourth year, Professor Nevin sent the following handwritten letter to my father:

> *Dear Mr Kernan,*
>
> *Each year it is the practice for the College to send students who are doing a special Honours Degree in Physics on a visit to Physics departments of some English universities. This year they are visiting Manchester, London, and Cambridge. It is very unusual for us to have a young lady doing this particular degree so that she will be the only girl on this tour. The tour is an official one and is in the charge of two members of the Department staff, Mr D. Keefe and Mr F. Ó Foghludha. You may regard this as a purely formal letter informing you of the circumstances.*
>
> *Yours sincerely,*
> *T.E. Nevin*
> *Professor of Experimental Physics*

This letter seems to me now a charming souvenir of a bygone era.

In retrospect I feel that it was quite remarkable that women science students in UCD in the early 1950s had so many female role models. In addition to Carmel Humphries in zoology, women occupied senior faculty positions in chemistry, botany, and mathematical physics. All of these women went on to become professors and heads of their departments at UCD. By comparison, women were extremely rare in the science faculties of major universities in the United States and northern Europe before the 1970s.

Mary Fahey Mc Keogh

One Hundred and Seventy-Two Women Grads

Some years ago I went to an exhibition in Newman House about women graduates over the years — I've forgotten the exact title. Two things remain with me about it. First, I had seen a letter in the *Irish Times* some months earlier asking women graduates for photos, mementoes, etc. pertaining to their days at college. My immediate reaction was to get out my picture of the hockey team that had won the Peat Cup, and my engraved silver badge, but then I thought, 'We were only the Second XI, and they'll have lots of stuff.' But they didn't really have all that many exhibits when I got there, although what was on view was fascinating.

What made a huge impression on me that day, however, and keeps coming back to my mind quite frequently, is the fact that one hundred and seventy-two women graduated from UCD in 1952. A year chosen at random, but my year. Yes, one hundred and seventy-two, not from the Arts Faculty, not from arts and commerce together, not even from medicine, dentistry and science combined, but *in total* from UCD. Sure there were often one hundred and seventy-two women trying to push in to the mirror in the Ladies' Reading Room. Or so it seemed to me, coming from the quiet and remote suburb of Howth, and the Leaving Cert class of six in Santa Sabina, Sutton.

I spent three years in UCD studying French and Spanish. A whole new and wider world was opened up to me, a world of ideas and travel and other cultures and independence. People started treating me as an adult, and being encouraged to think for oneself and work out one's own ideas was quite different from the school ethos I had operated in over the previous twelve years. Our Professor of French let us know very early on that we were to read everything, and that, in that era of censorship in Ireland, there was nothing we could not obtain if we ordered it in French.

Societies opened up this adult world to us. We mixed with professors and lecturers, as well as students of other subjects and faculties, through common interests in theatre, dancing, music and sports. I attended German lectures in my second year — I was interested in finding out about other languages, but in addition, a young German-national lecturer who read Goethe's romantic poems aloud was attracting extra students. The German Society meetings added to my knowledge and enjoyment as that year their secretary had a family link to a Dublin bakery and their teas were superb!

I don't ever remember feeling in UCD that as a woman I was in any way inferior, but that may have been because there was a high percentage of women in Modern Languages. I always felt eligible, entitled — but then I never tried to join the Rugby Club. I played hockey in Belfield and changed into my saffron gymslip and long black stockings in the old house and had tea there afterwards. I played table tennis somewhere up near the attic of 86, and also sang in the Choral Society somewhere there too. I studied in summer in the Iveagh Gardens. I sat with about two hundred clerical students from Clonliffe College in a large lecture theatre for Latin classes in First Arts. Just recently when a friend invited me to lunch in The Commons Restaurant, it was impossible not to think back to all the economical meals we had had in 86 when, even then, it was considered a more upmarket canteen than Earlsfort Terrace.

M. A. F. Carley

The Idea of a University

When I visit the National Concert Hall and see Count John McCormack's portrait hanging from what was the wall of the old Aula Maxima of Earlsfort Terrace where our fate was sealed at exams, cherished memories of my three years at UCD flood back.

My first recollection of being in UCD is of a golden October day when I stood in a queue all day waiting to pay my fees and to register. I felt like 'Ruth amid the alien corn'. I had just qualified in a Manchester Teachers' Training College where my class numbered only eighty-five; there were hundreds of students in UCD First Arts.

As my five compulsory First Year subjects I chose Irish, English, Latin, history, and maths. Several excellent teachers remain in my memory. I shall begin with Professor Timoney, who waltzed up and down the lecture room at full speed teaching calculus and other branches of abstract maths, my weakest subject. I attribute my success in First Arts maths to Mr Timoney. Tomás de Bhaldraithe and Bean McEntee opened for us the windows of wonder in Celtic culture. Professor Dudley Edwards in history entertained us daily with his witty sayings. He informed us that Irish policy was always: 'The auld stock versus the rest.' Moonan and Hayden's *A Short History of the Irish People* was our handbook.

In Latin, Professor O'Meara and Mr Harrison stand out like monuments to that prestigious department. Mr Harrison was a born teacher whose teaching techniques were outstanding. I remember his method of conveying the Latin *either/or* construction: '*Either* Cosgrave *or* de Valera is *aut.*' I took honours Latin for B.A. and wasn't it a wide course! We had to wade through twenty-seven books, including twelve books of Virgil and four books of Horace's *Odes*. Professor O'Meara believed in expanding our horizons by extramural courses, during which he treated us to the *Confessions* of St Augustine, and accounts of his own annual wanderings in Greece and Rome.

My real love was, and still is, English literature. Professor Hogan and Dr Lorna Reynolds, neither of whom I shall ever forget, were my mentors. In their hands Shakespeare came alive and poetry became the music of my life.

UCD has meant so much to me — its teachers, its students, the friendships I have forged. John Henry Newman's essay, 'The Idea of a University' is as valid today as it was one hundred and fifty years ago. If we have seen further, we must acknowledge with Isaac Newton that it is because 'we have stood on the shoulders of giants'.

Susan McKenna Lawlor

The Road to Damascus through Merrion Square

It is a sobering thing to realize that time has moved so far on since I was a student at UCD, that use of the Merrion Square building which then housed the Chemistry Department, and of the Earlsfort Terrace building which housed the Experimental Physics Department, has long since passed to politics and music respectively.

In those days there were two ways to enter university. One could either 'matriculate' at an appropriate level in one year, or take a more leisurely two-year route via the Leaving Certificate. In my case, I matriculated, and on a fateful day cycled to Earlsfort Terrace to pick up the entrance regulations. It was expected by my family that I would follow a career in music (I had studied both piano and cello while at school), and indeed I duly asked for the regulations covering that option. To this distant day, however, I can never attend a conference or exhibition without picking up every brochure in sight and so it was that in my saddle bag going home was a goodly collection of brochures covering a diverse range of subjects. I can still see in my mind's eye those austere white booklets bearing the UCD crest.

To read these brochures was a sobering experience. Although at my school we covered many subjects relevant to the arts, science had never been mentioned. I thus realized with a dreadful clarity that, as hard as I had worked on some nine subjects, if art and science were deemed to be the twin pillars of civilization then I was leaving school with a very unbalanced education. With the enthusiasm of the very young, I decided that I would spend the year I had 'gained' by matriculating early in trying to balance my education by studying science.

This decided, it turned out that according to the Regulations, I was, by several months, too young to enter university at all. My mother was not in the least put off by such a difficulty and on another fateful day she and I went to Merrion Square to meet the then Dean of Science (Professor Wheeler) to ask if I might be accepted. I remember our standing outside the Office of the Dean, which, to my eye, was equipped with traffic lights; red meant 'Stay without,' green indicated 'Come in,' and yellow signalled: 'You may enquire of my Secretary what to do.' For many years thereafter it seemed to me that the ultimate expression of importance must be to have such lights on one's door. The Dean was very kind. He offered no substantial opposition to this very inexperienced and relatively youthful person entering the Science Faculty, and I duly registered to read experimental physics, chemistry, mathematics, and botany.

At my first lecture I saw how things were structured. In the front row sat the nuns, and in the next row a rather small number of girls. Behind the girls were the boys, the most rakish and daring of whom occupied the back row. Lecturers received a level of attention that depended on the awe they might strike into those in the back row, and among the most awesome was Professor Johnny Nolan. I was reliably informed that when, in another class, the daring and the rakish released a ping-pong ball that descended with a plop, plop, plop down the steps while this professor was writing on the blackboard, so much hilarity was engendered that the trick was tried again. This time, however, the professor swung about, pointed to the guilty party and ordered him out. How could he know? Had he eyes in the back of his head? Then it dawned on the onlookers what had happened. He had simply counted the 'plops' and looked up to the row concerned, where the body language of the guilty party was easy to spot. Before such a formidable intelligence the rakish and the daring were silent.

For me, things were initially very difficult. Everyone in the class it seemed had school honours in every conceivable scientific subject, and the boys, in particular, were very blasé and told me that they did not need to study as they 'knew everything already'. The sight of dangerous acids bubbling in the chemistry laboratory, and of electronic equipment with mysterious dials in the Department of Physics, filled me with dismay. It all seemed very alien and in the first week I went home and wept. My father was extremely kind and reassuring. 'Why bother with all that?' he asked, 'You have your music — why not simply go back to that? It's what you know and like.' One does not always change with time, and I remain dogged to this day. 'I will not be put off by the first difficulty,' I told him; 'this is a challenge.' And, with a profound sense of suffering, I went on.

It was not very long before another fateful day arrived. I was sitting on my bed surrounded by open books when, like a bolt from the blue, came my personal 'Road to Damascus'. In some blinding flash I recognized that what I was reading was profoundly beautiful, and it seemed that, could I but summon up the capability to understand and absorb this material, my life would be filled with wonder. It was indeed a special insight, because that sense of wonder, awakened many years ago, has remained to illuminate every day that has since passed.

I can provide another snapshot from UCD. Now a little further up the student ladder, I was working on a Master's thesis in a room at the end of the long 'Physics Corridor' (which had been created by the simple expedient of blocking off the area concerned and adding a door). In this inner sanctum I was busy looking through a microscope when the door burst open and the Head of the Physics Department, Professor Nevin, appeared at my side.

'I have just recommended you', he announced, 'for a scholarship to study astronomy at the Dublin Institute for Advanced Studies. Will you take it?'

I could not have been more surprised if he had said that I was to be assigned to study Ancient Greek on Mount Parnassus, and I had, besides, a panicky feeling that the whole future course of my life was being decided at that moment. 'But, Professor,' I said weakly, 'I know absolutely nothing about astronomy.'

'I am aware of that,' he said briskly. 'Will you take it — people are waiting?'

I looked at him wildly and stammered, 'Professor, do you think that it's a good idea?'

He looked at me with considerable impatience and exasperation. 'Of course I think it's a good idea,' he said. 'I suggested it!'

With the profound faith people had in those days in their professors, I made a decision. 'If you think it's a good idea,' I told him, 'I accept.'

With that, he turned on his heel and disappeared through the door. It had all happened so rapidly that it was almost as if he had never been there. Looking back over the years I realize now what a gift he offered to me, one that ultimately led to undreamed-of possibilities within the space agencies of the world. In trusting his judgment I was, indeed, leaning upon a rock.

These are but vignettes, yet in recalling them I see with great clarity what it was that UCD gave to me: namely, a life of intellectual beauty and the scientific education and opportunity to pursue a challenging, deeply fulfilling career at an international level. It is what universities in every country strive to provide for their students, and these treasures UCD gave to me in full measure. It is a pleasure to be asked to provide memories of my time there, to take the opportunity to publicly say, 'Thank you'.

Eda Sagarra

Jobs for the Girls

The analogy often invoked by late twentieth-century authors of local reminiscences between their own work and Proust's *madeleines* in *A la recherche du temps perdu* has been rather overplayed. But the fact remains that taste and smell are usually the first responses when one attempts to recapture times long past. In my own case, my instinctive response on being asked to recall my own days as a First Arts student of history and German in 1951 was to feel the disagreeable smell of carbolic soap mixed with drains pricking my nostrils, as if I were once again descending into the women's cloakroom in the basement of Earlsfort Terrace. I expect the continued potency of the mixture derives from the fact that this was the place to which most First Years gravitated, to comb their hair and peer into the grubby mirrors over the washbasins in the hope of finding solace in what they saw reflected back. Few did.

By contrast, the women students' Common Room on the ground floor of Earlsfort Terrace just inside the right-hand entrance, with its scuffed parquet, untidy tables and broken chairs, was warm and welcoming. Its notice-board held tantalizing offers of holidays in distant places — a week in the Balearic Islands cost ten shillings plus fare, which, of course, nobody had, or at least nobody one knew.

The notice-board was full of *dos* and *don'ts*, more of the latter than the former. The *don'ts* were liberally supplied at a higher level also. 'Don't say you "wouldn't know" when you mean you "don't know",' enjoined Ronald Knox at the students' retreat preached in University Church. 'It is insincere, and bad English.' I don't recall what else he said. Our first public lecture, on the other hand, I remember very well, or at least one part of it. It was given by the Professor of Ethics, Monsignor Horan. Coming from the liberal tradition of an Anglo-French convent run by an ancient great-aunt, where I had spent the last four years of school, I was taken aback to be advised that, at least *sub specie aeternitatis*, it would not matter if we left college after three years without learning anything, provided we avoided mortal sin.

One of the methods evidently devised to help us all to retain our innocence was the unwritten disposition of the lecture halls: nuns in the front, clerical students to the right, girls to the left, boys at the back. The clerical students, who constituted at least one quarter of the student body at history and logic lectures (German was almost exclusively female), were not allowed to speak to the women students unless actually addressed by them. In our VIIIB history class of eleven where there were five clerics, we soon put a stop to such nonsense. But all relished the day when Miriam O'Connell, with her bobbing ponytail and neat waist emphasized by the then fashion for elasticated belts with metal clasps, pranced up the steps in Hugh Kearney's lecture and sat down in the centre of a row of blushing clerical students, whose novice masters had evidently not prepared them for the boldness of Jezebel. A French girl who came into college in slacks on an icy January day in 1953 was given much shorter shrift: she was sent home by the Dean of Women Students for causing a scandal, and told not to come back except in a skirt.

We must have been extraordinarily passive to have taken this sort of thing without a murmur. Or rather, to have put up with the quality of teaching we got from some departments and the flagrant disregard for our basic rights as students by some staff. One professor failed over and over again to turn up to lectures, or cancelled them at the last minute without apology. True, one of his colleagues, Desmond Williams, also frequently kept us waiting or failed to appear, but *he* knew human nature well enough to feel that our acceptance — or even connivance — would be guaranteed by his self-deprecating excuses and the squintly witty glance he levelled at every individual following each lapse.

Latin, taught by the learned Professor Bieler, was a slog, but history and German lived up to all expectations, the latter not on account of the course, but rather because of the attractions of the language and the (lifelong) friends I made in the class. The contrast between the German and History departments could hardly have been greater. The German Department in UCD in the 1950s was like most others in Britain in the 1930s, consisting of a professor, a tutorial assistant and a language tutor. Student numbers were similar: six or seven per year. I had only done German for a little over a year at school and failed some First Year exam, but was allowed to proceed because I represented a significant percentage of the cohort. Lectures and classes were without any intellectual stimulation; literature consisted of reading plays aloud and translating every word, the one (Polish) male student taking all the male parts. (German classical drama has relatively few female roles and the rest of us took turns to read those few.) Most of what we learned was from writing essays, though the Librarian made it extraordinarily difficult for us to extract books from the locked cupboard and only allowed us to do so under duress. Medieval classical literature, with the excellent annotated editions that we bought, was a revelation in the second year, and the whole degree course would, we later agreed, have been worth it just for the sheer marvels of Goethe's *Faust*.

Professor Cunningham, small, red-haired and hot-tempered, with her torn gown covered in chalk, had been appointed to the Chair in 1950 from Bangor, having done her doctorate in Bonn. She never ceased to lament to us her decision to return home, hinting at dark conspiracies by her male colleagues to do down German. She was utterly single-minded in her devotion to her students, securing scholarships in Tübingen for the entire class in the summer term of their second year — though the History Department would not let me go. But she had already got me a summer scholarship the previous year to repair some of the deficiencies in my command of the language. I owed more to her personality than her teaching, for though she was a learned women, she published virtually nothing after her German doctorate on Schiller and Racine.

A critical event in my academic path in UCD was the day in First Year when Professor Cunningham and I were called to the Dean's office to find a solution to my problems with the regulations. It was not possible in those days to combine German and history to do an arts degree. I was set on doing history whatever else I did; she was determined not to lose one of her First Years. The Dean, Aubrey Gwynne, S.J., was tall and unyielding. Miss Cunningham protested that history took no account of the needs of her students. She wept tears of rage, I tears of disappointment when it seemed clear that nothing could be done about it and it was going to be French and history after all. Fr Gwynne, towering at least a foot above his colleague and clad in an inordinately long gown, kept his eyes closed throughout the interview. Now, dismissing us, he opened his eyes, raised them to heaven and murmured, 'Oh God, I thank Thee for clerical celibacy.' That afternoon I had a tutorial with Desmond Williams. I told him my sad tale, to which he had an instant solution: why not do VIIIB, the single honours history degree, and do a half degree in German? I hesitated at the thought, to which he responded, 'Yes, I don't suppose you could manage the workload. Of course, I did degrees in history, law, economics, and German all at the same time and got a First in all. But then I am a man.'

Desmond can have been only 31 or 32 at that time, and had held the Chair for two years. Already he had succeeded in internationalizing the department by the appointment of able and interesting scholars from across the water: Hugh Kearney, John

Morrall, and Jack Watt, who with Maureen Wall imitated Desmond's mastery of the Socratic method in our tutorials. These required the submission of fortnightly essays with massive bibliographies for each. On top of all one's other work, they were immensely demanding, but the tutorials were so stimulating that everyone looked forward to them. Our group was rather international for those days, including a Belgian, two Poles, and a brilliant Italo-French nun, Sr Philip Anthony. We discussed endlessly with each other. On one occasion, thanks to Dudley Edwards' 'experiment', discussion lasted until nightfall.

The experiment took place in the early summer of 1954 and was billed as a preparation for one of our Finals papers in Irish history, which consisted of a single essay title. A group of about fifteen students was assembled in one of the classrooms at 9 a.m. and given three hours to write our essays. The next day we returned at the same time to read out our papers, to listen and respond to criticism from the rest of the group. Everyone had to make a contribution on each paper and the author had to respond to each. We were still there at 9.15 p.m., despite the flutterings of the nuns who had to be home 'in Hall' by 6 — apart from the worldly-wise Sr Philip Anthony who, it seemed, had her own Rule. Dudley dismissed the nuns' worries airily: 'I will deal with Reverend Mother.' When the porter called him to take 'an urgent telephone call' at 9.10, he returned looking a little sheepish and we were sent home.

It was only when I went to Freiburg that I recognized Dudley's 'experiment' as an eccentric variation of the pedagogically effective seminar format. Another particular merit of the UCD History Department in the 1950s was the access given to Second and Third Year students to some of the leading historians of the day. The most exciting intellectually were Sir Herbert Butterfield and Denis Brogan.

One of the most original initiatives of the combined History and German Societies in the winter of our third year was the staging of a historical fancy-dress ball with the Trinity students, in Trinity, a place with which we had normally no contacts apart from the occasional lecture by one of their staff. I was one of the main organizers. Plans were complete and costumes finished. Two days before the ball, I received a letter summoning me to the President's office.

Michael Tierney was a neighbour of ours in Shankill, a friend of my father; I had played with his children and learned a great deal from his beloved eldest daughter, Una, my Latin teacher, who was to die in her early twenties. Professor Tierney looked across his desk at me in a friendly way. The Archbishop, I was told, would not like to hear of what we were planning. He was very sorry indeed to have to have to say it, but in the interests of my degree result, it would be imperative to give up the idea. It was typical of those days that neither I nor any of the organizing committee considered defying the absurd demand. Madeleine Margey's father, who was manager of the Metropolitan Cinema in O'Connell Street, offered us an alternative venue and the ball, a great success, went ahead.

UCD Arts Faculty was a firm believer in examinations in those days. Examinations were invariably sat under umbrellas in what is now the Concert Hall, because roof leaks were alleged to be insoluble. The only moment of pleasure I can associate with it was when the daughter of an ambassador — a dainty, pretty girl — let *Gray's Anatomy* fall with a resounding crash onto the floor. Papa pleaded diplomatic immunity successfully, it was said.

Finals consisted for me of ten three-hour papers in history, and five in German, all in less than three weeks, followed by a German oral and — the worst experience of my undergraduate years — an hour-long viva in history. Desmond Williams affected to read *The Times* throughout the proceedings, but whenever one was stuck for an answer, shifted the paper slightly and fixed one of his eyes (was it the one with the squint?) on the unfortunate candidate. 'Not one of your best performances, Eda,' he remarked afterwards.

I continued, like most of his ex-students, to keep in touch after I graduated. When I went to Zurich and later Vienna on the NUI Travelling Studentship, I consulted him about my planned doctoral thesis. It was to be on the mid nineteenth-century Austrian railway system, a fascinating subject, I thought. He agreed and I rose to go, but just before I reached the door, he said, 'Do you suppose that will get you a job in Ireland?' I looked at him in horror. Such mundane matters had never entered my head. 'In any case,' he went on, 'if there is a man up for the job, he'll get it no matter what you say or do. By the way, there'll be no men looking for jobs in German.'

Nothing for me underlines more clearly the ideological chasm separating UCD of the 1950s from the decades that followed than my response to that piece of, I have to say, good advice.

Sarah H. J. Poyntz

Who Am I and What Am I Doing Here?

I came to UCD from New Ross, Co. Wexford when I was twenty-six years of age. Professor Lorna Reynolds set us our first essay in English: 'Who I am, what I am, and what I am doing here'. I was down for a pass degree but after reading my essay Professor Reynolds sent for me and asked why I was not taking honours. To this day — and I am seventy-two years of age — I remember the sheer exhilarating pleasure I got from such encouragement, the very first in the scholastic sense.

Then there was the fuss of changing and *begging* permission from Professor Jeremiah Hogan to be allowed to do a combined honours English and Modern History degree. A sister from the Dominican Order and myself were the only two students allowed to proceed in 1952 with such a degree — I think we made history in that sense. The English Department, except for Professor Reynolds, were very much against it, stating that the reading would be too much. It was not for Sister Veronica and myself — we loved it and we both got honours degrees.

I certainly remember my first history lecture. We were all waiting for Professor Dudley Edwards to arrive when the door opened and in walked a man with a great domed forehead with, at either side, a bunch of fuzzy grey hair. He wore a black jacket, black striped trousers, a white shirt and a long, flowing black tie. I thought, 'I'm in the wrong lecture room — he's an art teacher.' It was, of course, Professor Edwards. I got to know him. I think he liked me because he often called me for chats in the State Paper stacks. He seemed to treat me as a kind of racehorse on which he'd placed heavy bets! He and Dr Hugh Kearney, together with Professor Reynolds, were wonderfully encouraging. They had that spark that fires students, the prerogative of good teachers. I owe them a great deal. Throughout my life, especially my life as an exile teaching in the United Kingdom, I always knew that if ever I needed someone, I could call on Professor Reynolds. For me she combined the highest intellectual gifts with a deep humanity, a delightful sense of humour, and a marvellous forthrightness.

Then there was the lecturer in Old English always called 'Fish' from the first noun he made us all learn to decline: *fisc*. I recall that he was detailing the French origin of some words in English when there was a fierce racket from the back of the room caused by a French-speaking Belgian student. 'The word *vivacity* is also of French origin!' said Fish immediately.

From my Ed. Year I remember with gratitude Tommy O'Neill who was my supervisor during my teaching practice in Loreto, Stephen's Green.

My undergraduate years at UCD were wonder years for me, full of intellectual vigour and inspiration. This was mainly because of the people I have mentioned, and because of being able to read, read, and read again.

Katie Kahn-Carl

Out of Africa

Because I was at school with the Irish order of Loreto nuns in Kenya, it seemed somehow natural to come to Ireland to study after I won a scholarship from the East African Government in 1952. UCD was suggested and the nuns looked after the application for me. Naturally I was booked into Loreto Hall, one of the two girls' hostels on St Stephen's Green.

I was enrolled in the autumn of 1952 but 'twas no ordinary registration; waiting for me in Loreto Hall was a message to go to the President's Office. There I was welcomed by Miss O'Doherty, President Tierney's secretary. Apparently the President was related, or connected in some way, to one of the nuns in Nairobi, who had asked that I be 'seen to'!

It transpired that the Kenyan nun had written saying that I should do an honours arts degree in the languages of my forebears, i.e. French and German. My father was a Jew, who had been killed by the Nazis; his family was from Alsace. My mother was from Frankfurt am Main. My mother and I had gone to East Africa in May 1939 as refugees, just before World War II broke out in September of that year.

I started in the First Year French class with the much-feared Professor Louis Roche, and Messieurs Congnon and Gagnepain, and in German with Professor Kathleen Cunningham. As we had to take four subjects and Latin was obligatory for my degree course, I chose logic for my fourth subject under Reverend Professor O'Doherty.

While my background was a Franco-German one, English was my mother tongue. I only had the same school French as everyone else and even less German. Several times I was banished from the

Gentlemen,

1. We desire for all women in Ireland the full advantages of University education & that the same teaching, privileges, prizes, honours & degrees shall be open to them as to men-students.

2. In Ireland, at present, while Trin: Coll: & the three Queen's Colleges have thrown open these advantages to women, those women who cannot attend the above Colleges are almost wholly shut out from University teaching in Arts. This includes the large class of Catholic women-students who are debarred from attending Trin. Coll: & the Queen's Colleges, also all women-students of the Royal University who do not reside within reach of one of the Queen's Colleges. Both these classes of women-students have entered the University in large numbers & taken Honours & Prizes, in proportion to their numbers, as numerous as those won by men-students.

3. In University College, Dublin, fifteen Fellows in Arts of the Royal University lecture, but, except to certain public lectures given each session, women-students are excluded from their teaching. About 120 lectures in Arts are weekly given to the men-students. From these women students are excluded; yet they have to compete against men-students so taught by the Fellows (who are also Examiners) for Honours & Prizes.*

They also lose the greatest benefit of University Education — teaching by scholars & experts in the various subjects, & contact with men of academic learning & ability.

4. We submit a correspondence with the authorities of Univ: Coll: showing our failure to induce them to alter this unjust treatment & extend to this class of

---

* The Medical School has been for some time open to students with satisfactory results; also students who make special application are sometimes allowed special teaching in Arts.

1. (This page and following): Statement from Agnes O'Farrelly to the Robertson Commission requesting full advantages of university education for women.

benefits open to all others. We also give a memorial on the subject addressed to the Chief Sec: for Ireland in 1904.

We now desire to reiterate the prayer of that Memorial.

We earnestly beg that in laying down any scheme for Irish Univ: Education as a whole, your Commission will recommend that no charter or endowment be given to any University or College which will not give to women the same teaching, privileges, degrees, honours & prizes as those open to men-students.

We desire to point out that these Irishwomen are the only class of women in the United Kingdom thus shut out from University teaching in Arts, every College in England, Scotland, Wales, & also Trinity College Dublin, having, with the best results, thrown open their advantages to women. Yet nowhere is such education more needed than in Ireland. Every day women have a larger influence in the education of their children & in home & social life: they are increasingly in Ireland sharing in public & philanthropic work, & it is now the rule & not the exception, that the Irish girls of the middle classes have to adopt some means of livelihood.

We look to your Commission to be the means of putting an end to a great injustice which is a drawback to the well-being of the whole community.

Statement continued.

SPECTACLED "BLUE STOCKINGS" SUPERSEDED BY PRETTY GIRL GRADUATES.

Miss M. Hogan, B.A.

Miss Boyle, B.A.

Miss Coghlan, B.Sc.

Miss E. Stainer, M.A

Miss J. Kelly, M.A.

Miss Hogan, B.A.

Not many years ago people were laughing at collared women, and calling them "goggle-eyed blue stockings" and many such insulting things as that. But the above series of photographs of girl graduates, on whom the beauté of the National University of Ireland conferred degrees at Dublin last week, will show that it is no longer necessary for a woman to be plain in order to be clever. All the girls photographs—and they are chosen at random—show that the originals are typically charming Irish ladies whose looks are not exceeded by their brains.

Lafayette, Dublin.

2. From the Daily Sketch, *November 1913. The caption states that 'the above series of photographs ... will show that it is no longer necessary for a woman to be plain in order to be clever'.*

To the President and Members of the Executive Council

MEMORANDUM ON THE STATUS OF WOMEN

Gentlemen,

We are directed by the National University Women Graduates' Association to lay before you a statement of their views on the Status of Women under the proposed new Constitution. We are Members of a University in which perfect equality of rights and opportunities has been enjoyed by women both in theory and practice since its foundation in 1908.

While our anxieties with regard to Articles 9 and 16 have been met by the assurances of the President given to our deputation, we still view with alarm the Articles in the Constitution which appear to us to menace the citizen's right to work in whatever legitimate sphere he or she may deem suitable. We regret to find clauses in the Constitution which might be a directive to future Governments to pass legislation worsening the economic and social status of women.

In the following Article 40:

1. All citizens shall, as human persons, be held equal before the law. This shall not be held to mean that the State shall not in its enactments have due regard to differences of capacity, physical and moral, and of social function.

We object to this clause because it leaves it open to the legislature and the Courts to restrict the legitimate liberties of any citizen or group or class of citizens. We ask either for the deletion of this clause or for the insertion of a safeguard such as; provided there is no discrimination merely on the grounds of class, sex, or religion.

3. This page and opposite: Memorandum of May 1937 outlining NUWGA opposition to the Draft Constitution.

While the Women Graduates welcome the proposal that mothers be not forced to engage in labour to the neglect of their duties in the home, they regard with the strongest misgivings the provisions of Article 41. Clause 2, Section 2:

> The State shall, therefore, endeavour to ensure that mothers shall not be obliged by economic necessity to engage in labour to the neglect of their duties in the home.

which suggest interference on the part of the State with the affairs of the family. We consider that the husband and wife, knowing best what is necessary for the support and happiness of the family, should decide what work is necessary to these ends.

The same objections apply to Article 45, Clause 4, Section 2:

> The **State shall endeavour** to ensure that the inadequate strength of women and the tender age of children shall not be abused, and that women or children shall not be forced by economic necessity to enter avocations unsuited to their sex, age or strength.

in so far as it refers to women. If the Constitution is aiming through these clauses at remedying the unemployment of men and the exploitation of women, we suggest that the application of the fundamental principle of social justice, equal pay for equal work, would go far to maintain a satisfactory balance.

As we regard a Constitution as a Charter of the rights of the citizen which in normal circumstances is inviolable, we appeal to you to give our proposals your favourable consideration.

Mary T. Hayden

President National University Women
Graduates' Association.
University College Dublin.
23rd May 1937.

The Irish Press

FRIDAY, DECEMBER 17, 1937.

Of the day.

WOMEN GRADUATES AGAIN

IT would seem that the body of women styling themselves the Emergency Committee of the National Women Graduates Association are still determined to carry on their campaign against *Bunreacht na hEireann*, that they are not ashamed to rely on the most unblushing perversion and misrepresentation of its provisions with regard to the status and rights of women, in order to mislead the public with respect to its true purport, and that they are resolved to pay no heed to the most complete confutation of their arguments, no matter how often made, but to go on audaciously repeating statements which are demonstrably false and without any foundation in fact. We recognise that these are serious allegations to make, but we shall prove them up to the hilt.

But the first thing which we must do is to prove that this group of University women are in actual revolt against the authority and teaching on the questions at issue of Pope Pius XI. When they are attacking the terms of the Constitution in this respect they are in reality assailing the weighty and deeply pondered words of the Sovereign Pontiff. They are deliberately placing themselves in opposition to the advice, the solemn exhortation, the paternal admonition given by the venerated Head of the Catholic Church to all who would listen to his voice as to the position, the sphere, the duties of woman in the world in which we live to-day.

This is a matter which can best be demonstrated by placing side by side Article 45, which is supposed to have filched from women rights to which they were entitled, and the relevant passage from the Encyclical *Quadragesimo Anno*:—

ARTICLE 45
" The state shall endeavour to ensure that the inadequate strength of women and the tender age of children shall not be abused, or that women and children shall not be forced by economic necessity to enter into a vocation unsuited to their sex, age or strength."

ENCYCLICAL
" But it is wrong to abuse the tender years of children or the weakness of women. Mothers will, above all, devote their work to the home and the things connected with it. Intolerable and to be opposed with all our strength, is the abuse whereby mothers of families, because of the insufficiency of the father's salary, are forced to engage in gainful occupations outside the domestic walls, to the neglect of their own proper cares and duties, particularly, the education of their children."

We beg our readers to examine carefully the words of the Holy Father and then to compare them with the language used in Article 45. Can there be any doubt that they both express the same idea, that the object they have in view is identical, and that what *Bunreacht na hEireann* has done is to translate into language appropriate to a legal document the vigorous and emphatic pronouncement of the Pope? It will be observed that His Holiness does not mince his words on the matter. The abuse which it is sought to safeguard against in the Constitution, the Sovereign Pontiff describes as " intolerable and to be opposed with all our strength." For most people that will end the matter.

Now let us test the allegations made by Professor Mary Hayden as to the menace, the danger, the hostile intentions to women involved in the Article which we have quoted. She asserts that it contains " a threat to women's economic freedom, and that it possibly foreshadows a project to make some outside authority the judge whether an individual woman shall or shall not work outside her home." Where is this threat to woman's economic freedom to be found in the Article? Can one syllable of its terms be adduced in support of such a contention? Of course not. It is a mere figment of the imagination. It is the result of attempting to read into plain, unambiguous phraseology a meaning which it is incapable of bearing and which never entered into the minds of those who framed the Article.

Again, where is the foundation to be discovered for the statement that the section would authorise the setting up of some " outside State authority to judge whether an individual woman should or should not work outside her home?" Surely, when a specific assertion of this kind is made, the language should be cited which was held to justify it. No attempt was made to do so and for a very good reason. There is no such language. The whole thing is pure invention. But it must be borne in mind that if the charge brought against the Constitution be well-founded, then it must also be levelled with far greater force against the Pope's Encyclical. The truth is, the whole thing is no better than a mare's nest.

Professor Mary Hayden also quotes Article 40 to prove that it would be quite possible under it " to forbid the employment of women in any particular industry or their entrance into any particular profession." Here are the terms of the Article in question:

" All citizens shall, as human persons, be held equal before the law. This shall not be held to mean that the State shall not in its enactments have due r e g a r d to differences of capacity, physical and moral, and of social function."

Where can be found the power or the intention in these words "to forbid the employment of women in any industry or their entrance into any profession?" There is not a shadow of such intention or authority. It is a pure myth. What the Article aims at is to give the State the right to intervene in certain cases to prevent abuses and protect women and children from dangers to their health and morals which are too obvious to dwell upon. That is a power which is now exercised by the Governments of every civilised State, and it is rightly regarded as one of the most e s s e n t i a l and indispensable functions of any Government. But in Professor Mary Hayden's eyes it is all mere " blarney " and she would evidently wish that the Government of Eire should deprive themselves of it and leave women and children to fend for themselves. That learned lady must have, indeed, a peculiar conception of " blarney."

We think it will be admitted that this is a case where the women of the country may well pray to be saved from the advocacy of the academic group who have constituted themselves their champions, who have set themselves in opposition to and conflict with the principles laid down by the Pope for the guidance of the nations, and who can bring themselves to describe the finest charter of woman's rights extant as mere " blarney."

Graduation, then and now ...
Above: The Great Hall, Earlsfort Terrace
Below: O'Reilly Hall, Belfield

honours classes, but I was determined; I took grinds, managed to pass the House Exam at Christmas, and was allowed to stay on.

I remember it snowed quite early in 1952 and, as I had only ever seen snow on top of Mount Kilimanjaro, I went a little berserk and walked around nearly every bit of untrodden, virgin snow in St Stephen's Green. My friends nearly died laughing as this rather oversized 'toddler' did her thing.

Early in First Year I received a letter, which I opened while sitting next to Des Keogh during a German lecture. Out of the envelope dropped a photograph of a nun and Des said, 'What on earth are you doing with a picture of my aunt?' It was 'my' Reverend Mother, who had just celebrated her Silver Jubilee in Nairobi.

Another classmate in German was Dorothea Brummer, the foster child of John and Gertrude Hunt (of the Hunt Museum in Limerick). She sometimes asked me to her home, a flat in Merrion Square, to study. I remember, on the odd occasion when I was invited to tea, thinking how strange it was that none of their china matched. Little did I know then that they were all priceless pieces that would end up in the Limerick museum.

Despite the fact that Louis Roche was generally feared by First Year students, I struck up a good student/professor relationship with him, mainly due to the fact that he sent me down to the pass degree course on a regular basis, as he did with many others, but I refused and kept coming back. So when I got a chance, through my Scholarship Award Authority, to do an extra year in France and Germany to perfect my knowledge of the languages, he organized it all, getting me into the Université de Grenoble for two terms and, with the help of Professor Kathleen Cunningham, into the Goethe Universität in Frankfurt for a further term. I was eternally grateful to him for his help, as in those days it was most unusual to go to other universities during one's degree course.

In my last year I became 'Lady Vice-President' of the Student's

Council and had a great time, though there were some rough spots, and I often had to take tea with President Tierney, charm him and iron out whatever row was going on between the students and the administration — I was sent on the basis that a 'girl' would do it better than a 'fella'.

One of the big problems for students staying at Loreto Hall was that you had to be in every night by 11 p.m., so if you were invited to a dress dance, you had to stay out either with friends or in a hotel. I remember after a particular dress dance that some of us Loreto girls stayed in a reasonably priced Harcourt Street hotel. In those days you left your shoes out to be polished by the porters; we exchanged and moved all the shoes outside the rooms from the second floor to the first and then slept blissfully, unconcerned about whatever mayhem we had caused.

Lelia Doolan

Dramsoc

Dimly visible above an immense radiator at the back of the Main Hall, near the stairs down to the Annexe, that's where the Dramsoc notice-board was. That's where the worthies leaned — ostensibly to warm their bottoms in that draughty acreage, really to see if the director of some forthcoming epic had had the brilliance to include them in the cast list. I did a bit of lurking there myself, between intense sessions over slabs of gur cake and milky coffee downstairs, and the less demanding schedule of lectures overhead.

The Musical Society, with the inimitable John F. and the absolutely redoubtable Mrs Larchet, also beckoned. Through some fluke (hardly of birth), I managed to land the part of Ruth in *The Pirates of Penzance*. Basically, I suspect, it was because I had a sizeable presence (the gur cakes), a deep voice, and I appeared fearless to the unknowing. The Larchets were wonderful taskmasters, Hilda White O'Brien directed with great panache, and the singable music and mad Victorian plots made everything delightful and frightening at the same time.

Some talent scout may have spotted my attractions, for before you could say 'Goneril and Regan', I was frenziedly mixing paint in Iveagh Gardens in all weathers, boiling up buckets of size, slapping it onto naked hessian, and carrying furniture, lumps of timber and stageweights from A to B and back again, boring all comers about gels and dimmers, and telling my mother lies about where I'd been all night.

Then Eddie Golden of the Abbey Theatre was engaged to direct Christopher Fry's *The Lady's Not for Burning*. Sheila Brennan played The Lady with red-haired haughtiness, and

Dramsoc's Director, Val Joyce, was her smooth-voiced lover. Brian Price and Brian Farrell played the twins; I, a mere raw rookie, was Margaret, their mother. The diminutive Neil Porter was there as well. Was he my husband? Or was it Tony Portley? No idea. Jimmy McGoris was a rascal of some sort. The only line of Margaret's that I remember is: 'One day I shall burst my bud of calm and blossom into hysteria.' Lovely Gay McCarron did the sets. The costumes came from Gings and weighed a ton, but by this time, five and nine had me firmly in their grip. *The Lady's Not for Burning* had a mysterious, lyrical air about it; a whiff of cordite was never far absent.

Many midnight work parties, many vats of size, many auditions and readings and disasters and romances and Ag. hops and broken hearts and tragedies later (my beloved father died at the end of my second year), shows in the Little Theatre, shows in the Royal Irish Academy of Music in Westland Row, and shows in the Aula Max where the stage was higher than the launch tower at Cape Canaveral, it came around to my time to be (the first female) Dramsoc Director. I'm sure that many of the dates have been telescoped, but I definitely remember undertaking to direct Goethe's *Faust* — the kind of project that would make any sensible human think twice — and any student with notions plough straight on.

I had a great cast — Mick O'Shaughnessy as Faust, Eilish MacCurtain as Marguerite, Henry Comerford as Mephistopheles — and a spirited band of witches and warlocks who included several Ferguses, Cecily Kelly, Barbara Becker, and Paddy McEntee. My German Professor, Kathleen Cunningham, sent me a friendly note of congratulation, while Roger McHugh's tore into the shortcomings of the production with vigour and some justification. Later in the year, we took it to Newry to the UDA Festival, where a tiny Gerda Redlich adjudicated with kindness. We made good friends, and Cecily Kelly (director), Kate Binchy, and the ubiquitous Henry Comerford walked off with the one-act award for Edna St Vincent Millay's *Aria Da Capo.*

Later on, we encouraged student writers to present new work in The Little Theatre (way up in the eyrie of 86 St Stephen's Green, where George and Dick minded the house and many a student too, and covered for us in times of closure, lockout, inebriation and plague). Letty Barron and I played two Russian women in a play of (then) Joe McArdle — now J. Ardle McArdle — called *The Escalator,* which Liam Redmond came to see. Carrol O'Connor's wife, Nancy, staged an in-the-round production of *Anastasia* in which Mairín O'Farrell played the eponymous heroine. The highlight of that year was a first: a revue entitled *Idle Chatter,* consisting of sketches and satires and songs and a bit of political shafting with new and old singing and acting stars. Ann O'Dwyer made her debut. Dermot Kinlen directed, and he and Finbarr Callanan wrote most of the material. Paddy Murray did the music. We gave it our all and achieved a minor smash hit. The President, Michael Tierney, objected to the programme cover, which showed a lady on a barstool, wearing the bare necessities and lifting a glass of (possibly) champagne to her pouting lips — pretty harmless stuff. I think we got around it by putting a pink banner across her middle.

Galway's Dramsoc swept the boards at the next Universities' Festival, which we hosted in the Aula. Michael Garvey did an electrifying production of Arthur Miller's *The Crucible* from an acting, setting and lighting point of view. Through a piece of Garvey enterprise, it was also the world premiere of the play. UCD did a serviceable *Murder in the Cathedral* in which we all wore very scratchy frocks (from hessian left over from the sets, I'm sure) as the women of Canterbury, and Thomas was a very convincing Noel Deisniu: 'The last temptation is the greatest treason / To do the right deed for the wrong reason.'

That festival and the meeting of our two societies probably

sealed many of our fates: Kate Binchy, Henry Comerford, Michael Garvey, Celia Salkeld, myself and others founded Guild Players and combined to run a season of plays in Kilkee over the summer of 1955. In spite of blazing sun, we presented World Theatre — a dozen plays or so in repertoire, changing the play every night and encouraging our next door neighbour to take part (a very small part, of course), in our festivities. His name was Richard Harris.

Passionate involvement; sleepless nights; great 'new' ideas; lasting friendships; re-inventing theatre over and over out of thin air   these our revels hopefully go on and on in today's Dramsoc — and will never stop.

Clare Mc Donough (Connolly)

No Trousers Please, We're Ladies

I scrambled through a B.Sc. in 1954 after a false start in architecture, where the atmosphere was bohemian and relaxed. When I cut my losses and restarted in science, a simple remark addressed to one of the boys (and I do mean boys) caused him to shy away and practically bless himself. Obviously, I was all that Father Misogynist at school had warned him about.

At lectures in science we had set places in the lecture theatres, most usually nuns in front, then girls, then clerical students and boys at the back. There was a great gulf in place between the girls and the clerical students. I was allocated one as partner in the Physics Laboratory, but I always called him 'Mr'. We did not speak to them outside, or expect them to acknowledge us, for fear of getting them into trouble. When my first cousin, a clerical student at Clonliffe College, came to UCD to do his B.A. his mother warned me not to speak to him if we met, or he would be up before his superiors.

Girls were at a disadvantage in science because of the abysmal teaching of maths in (Catholic) girls' schools. There was very little science either, except for botany. It was an article of faith in the educational system that girls were no good at maths and there was even, shamefully, a special paper called 'Elementary Maths For Girls Only' at the Intermediate level, which meant that to get from that low level to the Leaving Certificate pass standard was very difficult. The result in the Science Faculty was that after the compulsory maths of First Science, most girls opted for low status 'soft' subjects such as botany, zoology, biochemistry, and chemistry, which led only to teaching and were beneath the dignity of boys.

I chose to stick with Physics and got a lot of harassment from one of the Physics professors, who hated women and usually succeeded in laughing them out of his classes. The toady boys, of course, laughed at his sexist jokes. A really brilliant woman student could compel respect, but the average student had a hard time and usually retreated. My father, himself a UCD graduate, warned me not to do engineering as the professor there hated women and would give me a hard time, although he could not technically refuse to admit me.

At the beginning of the academic year there was always an extremely High Mass to invoke the blessing of the Holy Spirit on the year, or something to that effect. All the staff and students processed from Newman House into University Church, the staff in gowns, hoods and mortarboards (or squashy hats). Women were represented by the Dean of Women Students, at that time Miss Norah Greene B.Sc. There was a second woman Dean whose name I forget. We felt that Miss Greene pointed up the absence of women in this overwhelmingly male display of power.

Miss Greene used to accompany us when we went away on hockey trips, usually to Belfast, Cork or Galway, and with her opposite numbers saw that we didn't get out of our depth on formal occasions. I think it would have been up to her to deal with any unacceptable behaviour on the part of women students and hush up any scandal, in which she was one hundred per cent successful as far as I ever knew. Miss Greene and one of the two chaplains sometimes put in an appearance at the College hops. Obviously we thought she was staid, but that was acceptable in grown-ups, and we respected and liked her. I believe one of her successors was even more staid.

There were female professors and lecturers then, even in science: Sheila Power (maths/physics), Helen Ryan (zoology), Mabel Kane (zoology), Phyllis Clinch (botany), and Eva Philbin (chemistry).

What I think present day students will think most peculiar is that women students were not allowed to wear trousers on College premises, so that if, for instance, one were out on a field trip, one could not go back to the College without going home and changing.

Co-existing with my women friends who played hockey and went ballroom dancing was another set who played camogie and went to céilís where Irish was spoken. There was also a large number of non-Dubliners who started by staying in the women's Halls of Residence on St Stephen's Green. To hear them tell it, these were a cross between a boarding school and a jail, though they were very convenient and provided study facilities. I am sure that many girls whose parents would not have allowed them to be at large in the big city were allowed to come to UCD on condition of staying in Hall.

It is impossible to isolate the College from its time in the history of the State — isolationism, unemployment, emigration, the Irish-language revival, etc., — or from the city, over which, like the shadow of Sauron, brooded the baleful influence of Archbishop John Charles McQuaid. It was he who saw to it that there were no dances during Lent. It was he who re-introduced the full Lenten Fast after the relaxation of the Emergency years. For those over twenty-one, this meant only one full meal and two 'collations' on all weekdays in Lent. Some categories were exempt, and one could ask for a dispensation in confession. The first year it came in, the College Chaplain issued a blanket dispensation to all students.

Every year Dr McQuaid issued a Lenten Pastoral setting forth the Lenten restrictions and reiterating that it was a 'reserved sin' (one which could not be absolved by a priest, but was reserved to the bishop), for parents to send their children to Trinity College, as it was a grave risk to their faith and morals. This increased the proportion of Catholics in UCD above the national average, and meant that we knew hardly any non-Catholics, except in subjects that Trinity did not offer.

Rosaleen Linehan

First Good Revue

'In the days that were early the music came easy,' wrote the poet Louis MacNeice, and I suppose I must take on the accusation of misplaced affection and nostalgia for an era that is now often portrayed as drab and nasty. We had no money, no foreign travel and no expensive clothes, yet I wouldn't change one petal of the plastic flower I dashingly pinned on my grey pinafore then for all the designer trainers and mobile phones in the world.

They say you should start as you intend to continue, but my first entrance through the doors of Earlsfort Terrace on a sunny October day in 1954 was coloured by the fact that the aspirin that was holding my suspender to my right stocking started crumbling on my third step. So began four years of disorganized laughter. Well, to be honest, not completely disorganized, because I've always loved studying and to this day have an undiminished hunger for self-improvement. Mind you, I did have a certain problem with my English style, which our Professor of Politics, Conor Martin, told me was difficult to describe. 'It's like a curious mixture of *Dublin Opinion* and the Old Testament,' he said.

Of course the first month in college was completely coloured by the arrival in one's life of Men! Having spent fourteen years in Loreto on the Green, it was amazing to find that this cornucopia had existed all the time almost across the road. You collected invitations to dress dances like scalps. The Hall Dance, the Colours Ball, the Clongowes Union Dance, even some hunt ball the name of which I can't remember. It didn't matter who asked you to be their partner as long as you were asked, and to them all I wore the same apple green dress I had worn as a bridesmaid to my sister the previous August.

And then there was Dramsoc. I still remember the time I first saw the notice-board with the magic word 'Auditions' on it. The 'Green' kept all its energies for music, so I had never acted at school. By myself I used to clown and write little songs, so without knowing it I was preparing myself for something of which I'd never even heard: revue. It was sheer luck that I arrived with a bunch of people who had a similar interest. They included the late Jim Harrington, a medical student who wrote words and music, Aideen Kinlen in the Law Faculty and another young law student called Des Keogh.

There was also Fergus Linehan. I met him at a History Society hop in a long-vanished venue called the Swiss Chalet and he uttered the magic words, 'dress dance'. He had to leave early to catch the last bus to Dalkey, and when he rang a week later to say where he'd pick me up for the dance, I'd totally forgotten what he looked like. We won a spot prize — I think it was a Christmas cake — for being the first couple up to the bandleader pretending to be engaged. We sat up on the balcony of the Gresham Hotel, the long table marked with jugs of orange for the girls and Guinness for the boys.

I remember that first winter in college was cold a lot of the time. I remember freezing when I'd get up in the morning, freezing at bus stops, and being petrified while pancake make-up was applied to my back when I was wearing low cut dresses. One of the few places you could keep warm was beside the fire in the Ladies' Reading Room in Earlsfort Terrace, but the armchairs there always seemed to be taken by the Glam Set. These were girls from another planet, beautiful shining, groomed creatures with magnificent clothes. (Most of them seemed to have been at school at Sacred Heart convents). They paraded the Main Hall and the corridor outside the History Library like supermodels, with callow youths (and indeed callow lecturers) gaping in their wake.

Of course not everything was roses. I suppose if I'd been more radical I would have been angry at the despotism of a College President who wouldn't allow female students to wear trousers in freezing weather and who told our societies who could and who could not speak to us. But I came from a time and a family where rules were strict, and if I considered them stupid I would try to skirt around them, and if I couldn't, I would try to have as good a time as possible. Some of our lectures too were ill-prepared and delivered with a cynical indifference. But, in a strange way, even that prepared you for later in life when, inevitably, you came up against the same thing in people with whom you worked.

Economics was my main degree subject and I really hated it, though I loved politics and the other minor subjects I studied. I suppose it would have been better for me to have done English — at least I wouldn't look blank so often now when people talk about such and such a play. But I really had no choice. My father said economics, so economics it was. Maybe nowadays I'd have dropped out. But dropouts were thin on the ground back then. We felt lucky to be in college at all (there were only two of us there from my class at school) and we knew it was hard for our parents to afford the fees.

I suppose those college years all that time ago gave me an extra slice of youth. I still had my long, happy holidays in Donegal for four months every year. I never had a job and never really had pocket money. Fergus had an account in the canteen in 86, so we had free coffee and buns, and he got ten shillings every Friday, which looked after Saturday night (usually the pictures). He also visited the pawnshop in Cuffe Street from time to time. For years his mother lamented over the 'theft' of a beautiful overcoat she had bought him. Once we Second Year economics students were told that there would be summer jobs for us in Guinness's and I applied. The Personnel Officer, a very elegant lady called Miss Coulson, told me not to take it, as it was going to be a lovely summer and I should get up to Donegal.

Back in Dramsoc I took to borrowing my sister's clothes and wearing them back to front, she having a figure like Marilyn Monroe, while I could be described as having two backs. We also made costumes out of curtains, like Scarlett O'Hara in *Gone with the Wind*. There seemed to be endless hours of happiness in the Little Theatre at the top of 86, where George the Porter was our father figure and philosopher. In the main office over in Earlsfort Terrace Hilda White O'Brien, who had a mordant wit, presided over all the stormy romances that seemed to be going on all the time. Of course, she had seen it all over and over again. Young people lucky enough to be given a few extra years in which to grow up, to learn, to laugh, and to love.

Teresita Durkan

From Goldenbridge: A View from Valparaiso
(Dublin: Veritas, 1997)

I had always suspected that I wasn't cut out to be a teacher of small children. Now I was certain. So it was a relief of sorts when the beginning of the new school year came around and I was assigned to teach Standard Five in the classroom with the sinking foundations. It wasn't a bad year, but it wasn't a great one either. I had to face the final inspection for my teacher's diploma. I had growing doubts about my vocation to be a primary teacher. I was nervous and edgy and cross. Pity the poor youngsters who had to put up with me that year.

The good news — it came during the summer holidays, I think — was that the central council of the congregation in Carysfort had decided a group of us should enrol as night students at the university. We were odd fish in the university too, even though religious black — along with a ubiquitous chalky grey and an ingrained, colourless scholarly grime — was a pervasive feature of the decor of Earlsfort Terrace during those years.

We travelled to and from the College in the beginning by taxi — you couldn't have black novices walking the streets of Dublin at night, Archbishop McQuaid had said. So our Blue Cab was only a shade less conspicuous than the long black chauffeur-driven limousine that dropped and collected the Loreto Sisters from Rathfarnham Abbey during the day.

Goldenbridge was the last stop on our taximan's three-convent run. This meant that we rarely got home before 11.30 p.m. With a bundle of school copies on the table waiting to be corrected, a cookery class to be prepared, and sometimes an essay to start or finish before you turned in — and look sharp again at 5.30 a.m.

for community prayers — the life of a junior in Goldenbridge in those days was no bed of petunias.

University College Dublin in the 1950s was nobody's dream of the groves of academe either. But it had its moments, and I think it saved me. From what? Well, from being made over into the likeness of the PO or the Town Planner, for one thing. It also moved me further and further away from the likelihood of ever having to work in an orphanage or even in a primary school, for the rest of my life.

I wouldn't have thought of it that way or put it into those words for myself, back then. Much less would I have confessed it to anybody else even if I had been conscious of it. But looking back now I know that it was an unspoken and comforting truth somewhere in my subconscious during those early and decisive years in Goldenbridge.

Eithne Bennett

Ellen Power

When I arrived at UCD in the Fifties little did I think that it would become a vital part of my life for nearly the next forty years, and that the Library was to be the central point. My decision to go to college came about because two of my brothers were there and seemed to be having a hectic social life. Their advice to me was that I should become a poultry instructress, as the only single female with a car of her own in our town was pursuing this career, and they thought I would have the opportunity of meeting with a wealthy farmer!

My knowledge of UCD Library began outside what students termed the History Library — I subsequently discovered that it was in fact called the Council Chamber. Outside were red benches where a group of us would congregate on many an afternoon. (Note — *outside* the Library, not inside.) At some stage (I suspect it was in the degree year), I moved to the then Arts Library, situated at the back of the main building at Earlsfort Terrace. My move was prompted by the fact that I had discovered that the American Embassy had made a large donation of contemporary American fiction to UCD Library and I was wallowing in it.

But reality hit one day and I realized that I had to start thinking about what to do when I left college. I can still recall the moment clearly when I looked up, saw a person sitting behind the library counter reading, and thought, 'What a lovely idea — sitting reading all day and just looking decorative'. On enquiring as to how one got such a delightful job, I heard for the first time the name 'Miss Power'. Not only was this Miss Power the Librarian in UCD but she also ran something known as the Library School.

And so it was that I entered the School and learned all about bibliographies, abstracts, citation indexes, cataloguing, classification, how to evaluate one encyclopedia against another, and even a little bit about architecture. On completion of the Diploma in Library Training I was offered a position in the Library at UCD, and it was then that I really got to know Miss Power, as she was always called.

It was then too that I discovered that the other side of the library counter was a different story to what I had imagined. Today everything is computerized and technology has taken over, but in the Sixties and Seventies, Library staff at UCD were more visible and dealt directly with students at all levels.

This state of affairs led to an interesting situation during the time of the Gentle Revolution, as it was called. I was neither fish, flesh, nor good red herring, and was caught between the students and Miss Power. The students were very sympathetic to my plight and often gave me ample warning as to when they were going to demonstrate against Library policy. On the other hand, Miss Power thought that as a staff member I was fit to sit in on arbitration meetings. I find it very interesting today when I see these 'revolutionary' figures featuring as business executives, politicians and pillars of society.

It was at this time that I matured into a fully-fledged member of the Library staff and came to respect and admire Miss Power, who was running what was, in effect, the largest department in the College, with many out-lying libraries, all of which inter-related with almost every other College department. By this time, in the mid Sixties, the old arts and history libraries had moved to the Dr Coffey and O'Curry Halls in Earlsfort Terrace, but the space problem was critical. The increasing pressure caused by the growth in numbers of students and staff made it evident that not only was there an accommodation problem for the Library at Earlsfort Terrace, but for the College as a whole, and UCD was actively considering the move to what is now the campus at Belfield. Naturally it fell to Miss Power to oversee the planning of a new library. This she did with foresight and vision, making sure that what was known as 'Phase One' of the Library building could operate on a day-to-day basis, catering for the immediate needs of staff and students, while at the same time making provision for expansion which would eventually incorporate all elements of a modern library.

Not only did the Library move from closed to open access at this time, but technology was taking over. While Miss Power was not particularly interested in the technological side of information control and retrieval, and although she was not personally involved in the implementation of computerized cataloguing, she saw to it that her staff were in on the ground floor of its development and were prepared for its installation at UCD.

At the same time Miss Power was running the Library School at UCD, which was supplying trained librarians to academic and public libraries, and in many cases supplying graduates to establish specialist libraries in private institutions and help in the development of libraries in many state-sponsored bodies. Today the former Library School is the Department of Library and Information Studies and is separate from the Library with its own teaching staff.

Miss Power had been faced with a daunting task when she became Librarian at UCD in 1951, but by the time of her retirement in 1974 she had laid the foundation of a modern library for the College. To me she was a woman before her time, a woman of vision who brought personal traits of intellectual integrity to her chosen career. A whole generation of librarians in Ireland owes her a debt of gratitude.

Some time after she retired I visited Miss Power. She was reading a book about Vienna. With a faraway look, she told me that when she was studying for a M.A. degree in German there in the 1920s, a young man had taken her punting on the Danube. As I left I wondered what both our lives would have been if I had become a poultry instructress and she had stayed in Vienna.

Ellen Power died in 1992.

Helen Burke (Binchy)

Not Just Ivory Towers

In the 1950s you did not need hundreds of points to get into UCD; all you needed was a matriculation certificate or its equivalent. The annual fee for a degree in the Faculty of Arts was then £50. If you were a student from the country, as I was, you also had to have enough money for digs, entertainment, and the odd book. The educational reforms that opened up second and third level education to children of ability, irrespective of their financial situation, still lay in the future then. There were no HEA grants, and scholarships were few and hard to come by. So really UCD in the 1950s was a small, privileged place, reserved for those whose parents could afford to send their children to college. I think few of us who were students in the 1950s were aware of this at the time, but what most of us did know was that UCD was an exciting and fun place to be.

There was a buzz about the Main Hall in Earlsfort Terrace, the like of which I never experienced anywhere else. Groups of undergraduates, mostly male but including a scattering of madly glamorous women, seemed to hang around there all day, smoking, laughing, plotting and appearing ever so sophisticated. To cross that Main Hall without a supportive gang around one while a green First Year seemed an impossible task.

There was the L&H on Saturday nights, the best free spectator sport in town, sharpened by the hope that someone might ask you to a party afterwards. There were the endless cups of lukewarm coffee in the Annexe, where gossip was garnered and swapped and plans for parties were made. There were the hops in 86 and in the Four Courts, sometimes great, at other times heartbreaking. There were the tennis, ping-pong and badminton matches, with the

UCD teams greatly enhanced by skilled Malayan students and stars such as Mary O'Sullivan. There were the hilarious inter-varsity trips to Cork and Belfast (including the unlikely diversion to do penance in Lough Derg en route), Des Keogh building team spirit with his rendition of 'Do join the Tennis Club, do!' There were friendships made that lasted a lifetime, and the agony and ecstasy of falling in love for the first time. We were hugely innocent then.

The gaiety and fun of those 'salad days' was in marked contrast to the seriousness of the subjects I was studying for my social science degree and B.A. in economics and politics. (In that more casual era many degree combinations were possible). Mrs Agnes McGuire in those days ran the Social Science Department singlehandedly from her office under the rafters of Newman House. She was a brave and wise woman who for thirty years introduced her students to social work and to the social problems of our country: poverty, unemployment, emigration, illegitimacy, mental illness, bad housing — the list could go on and on. She not only opened our eyes to the injustices of the world we were living in, but inspired many of us to try and do something about it. Agnes McGuire had a great sense of humour and was marvellously outspoken. She did not hesitate to tell her students what she thought of them: 'You are quite unsuitable for social work; why not try Aer Lingus!' For those she deemed suitable, she went to endless trouble to help them get on postgraduate courses abroad, for there was no professional training for social work in Ireland then.

Like many of those who graduated from UCD in the 1950s, I joined the thousands that emigrated from Ireland every year of that decade; however, I was one of the lucky ones going on a fellowship to take a Master's degree in Social Welfare at Florida State University. During my last term there, I applied for a Junior Lectureship in Social Work and Social Administration in Queen's

University, Belfast. I got the job, moved to Belfast and learnt an awful lot about the island of Ireland that year. In 1961 I moved back to UCD as assistant to Agnes McGuire. My salary was £500 per annum and my office a converted cello cupboard — space has always been in short supply in the ever-expanding UCD.

Father Conor Ward, with his doctorate in Sociology from Liverpool University, had joined the department a year before. Although we were rather isolated in Newman House, I thoroughly enjoyed my job. We worked very hard with far fewer students than nowadays and got to know them well. Both Conor and Agnes instilled in me that as social scientists, the city and country around us was our laboratory, and that we must work in that laboratory as well as in our ivory tower. Agnes sent me off to do voluntary social work one day a week, and I also learnt about the basics of social research through assisting Conor Ward with research tutorials and projects. Then one grim November morning in 1963 Agnes did not arrive. We later learnt that she had died in her sleep the night before. Agnes McGuire was the great pioneer of social work education in Ireland. She was never sufficiently recognized by the university for which she had worked so hard. Although revered by many outside UCD, she was never promoted; she herself had to pay for occasional secretarial assistance out of her meagre salary. Was this because her department was then outside the mainstream of college life, or was it because she was a woman?

Not long after Agnes McGuire's death, Father James Kavanagh became Head of Social Science and subsequently UCD's first Professor of Social Science. Under his leadership the department expanded greatly, with new courses and new staff, ending up, after a sojourn in the basement of Earlsfort Terrace, in the spanking new Arts Block in Belfield. When the 'Gentle Revolution' hit UCD in 1968, Jim Kavanagh showed what a brave leader he was by encouraging his staff to join the students in the heady and sometimes threatening dialogue of those days, rather than try to ignore it all, as many other professors advocated.

I remember one of those meetings particularly. I was conspicuously pregnant and sitting up at the back of a lecture theatre in the Terrace, while a very angry student was telling us everything he could think of that was wrong with UCD. I wasn't particularly comfortable myself and I remember thinking, not too constructively, 'Wouldn't I give that fellow a right fright if I had my baby right here in front of him!' Fortunately I didn't. UCD learnt a lot from the Gentle Revolution: proper tutorials, better staff–student contact and improved administration were some of the reforms that followed it.

Both Professor Jim Kavanagh and his successor, Professor Conor Ward, carried on Agnes McGuire's philosophy of commitment to work outside as well as inside the university; thus, when staff were asked to serve on different advisory bodies, they encouraged us to do so. I think I learnt more about Irish social policy that I was able to pass on to students from the five years I spent chairing the Social Policy Committee of the National Economic and Social Council, than twenty books would have taught me. Likewise serving on the board of the Combat Poverty Agency and the National Planning Board, were terrific learning experiences. In my view UCD has always been very open to encouraging its staff to undertake these forms of community service and has benefited greatly from fostering these links between town and gown.

The women's movement hit Ireland with great excitement in the 1970s, but it took a while before it gained a foothold within the patriarchal university system. Early in the 1980s a group of women, mostly academics, Library staff and postgraduate students, started meeting informally to explore the newly emerging field of Women's Studies and to discuss how the position of women in UCD could be improved. I had got elected to the Governing Body on the graduates' panel in 1984 and shortly afterwards was invited to join the group, which I gladly did. This group became the Women's Studies Forum, an open forum that anyone interested could attend. There were interesting research papers, poetry readings, and fascinating discussions about the lives of women. It was both enjoyable and effective and out of it grew two important new structures in UCD: the Women's Education Research and Resource Centre (WERRC) and, after the publication of Ailbhe Smyth's report, *Breaking the Circle*, which clearly identified the lowly position of women academics in Irish universities, the Equal Opportunities Committee of UCD's Governing Body. But that was just the beginning of the struggle to give equal opportunities and equal rewards to women and men in UCD; it is, alas, a battle that has still to be won.

Sister Eveline Loreto McLoughlin

Seasons in the Sun

Figuratively speaking, I rode on the merry-go-round for my first term in UCD. It was my season in the sun; I felt joy-filled, excited and carefree. There were so many of us there, 'nuns' as we were called, young and eager for life. We resided in Muckross Park with the Dominican Sisters. We had our own hostel and lots of freedom. Generally we walked to the college in Earlsfort Terrace, coifed, gimped, and wearing long black habits. Other people just took us for granted, including our co-students in the college. I found the college building dull, dark and overheated — very different from the beautiful Concert Hall which now replaces it. The 'nuns' room' was good for the studious, but in those early days I preferred the corridors of the great outdoors. I loved the Iveagh Gardens; time stood still as I soaked in the sun or gathered with other Sisters there for chats and camaraderie. On one occasion we stayed so long that we were locked in, only to be rescued by the college porter, who seemed to have a certain penchant for the nuns.

Despite good intentions all around we were somewhat cut off from our colleagues, by our dress, our culture, and our constant occupation of the front seats in the lecture halls. This, however, did not weigh too heavily on anyone; we had our identity and, unlike Alice in Wonderland, we knew who we were and where we were going. There was no rat race, no force-feeding, no points system. It took me until Christmas to realize that I was responsible for my own study and development. During my second semester I grew more accustomed to the 'nuns' room' and the dull, drab darkness faded from the building. I started to study.

Lecturers and professors made a big impact on us. The staff

was mainly male but I remember one woman clearly. She was *Bean* McEntee. She had a melodious voice, a lovely *blas* and a very serene disposition. The Ags joined with us arts students for our weekly reading session by *Bean*. The text was *Peig — a Scéal Féin*. Emotional outbursts greeted all Peig's tribulations and triumphs with ooh-ing and aah-ing from every backbencher. *Bean* furrowed ahead serenely, seemingly oblivious of the outbursts. So in my first year in UCD Peig's life story rolled on and on each week — time out only for a roll call that was met with a magnificent response. Who can tell if the hundred per cent clear *'Anseo'* was fact or fiction? One way or the other we were all accounted for and marked present.

Our weekly *explication de texte* was another story. The idea originated with M. Cognon, the French lecturer. He seemed to delight in calling forth the timid and bashful to sit on his high chair and explain, in French, to the whole class, some obscure passage. It was an ordeal. I can still remember some of the quake and tremor that silently filled the room before M. Cognon selected his victim. However, once your day was done, you could sit back and relax. Lightning rarely strikes twice in the same spot, and M. Cognon observed this dictum. M. Louis Roche was the professor. He had his moments. He seemed to me to harbour some small dislike of Sisters in general, or perhaps in particular, some small dislike of our over-diligence in note taking. Regularly he interspersed his lectures with shouts of, 'That's right, Sister, write it down'. It didn't sound as comic as Hal Roche's, 'Write it down, it's a good one', but I saw some fun in it.

As the weeks sped by I began to realize that if I hoped to attain the expected standards in French, I would do well to spend some time among the natives. In July 1956 a few of us set sail for L'Insitut Catholique in Paris. We had joy, we had fun. We went to the top of the Eiffel Tower and under the bridges of the Seine. We visited the Louvre and Lisieux. We attended High Mass in Notre

Dame, and the Greek Orthodox in Julien le Pauvre. On our return M. Roche and M. Cognon accepted us with open arms, metaphorically speaking of course, into the honours French class. I could now major in French and Irish, the subjects I liked most. Those subjects fascinated me, though not to the same degree as they fascinated our Professor of Old Irish, Fr Shaw S.J. He could cover the board in chalk as he showed us, 'in point of fact, eh,' how the Irish definite article '*an*' was derived from the Sanscrit '*sinda*'. An Doctúir T. de Bhaldraithe, with his *Gaeilge Cois Fhairraige* was as keen on correct pronunciation as any 'rolling rrrr' Frenchman in L'Institut Catholique.

Those were the days before Vatican II, and the days before participative education. The jug/mug method was in vogue. The professor/lecturer was the jug who poured out his knowledge into the mug, namely the student. We were passive receptacles. Tomás de Bhaldraithe made tentative efforts to break the mold. At the end of each lecture he would raise his eyes and ask, '*Ceist ar bith?*' [Any questions?] After seconds of profound silence he would say, '*Ceist ar bith eile?*' [Any more questions?] and with a wry smile leave us.

It seemed to me that strong demarcation lines separated professors, clerics, lay students, and Sisters. We used to hear that Dr Garret Fitzgerald frequently invited his students in the commerce classes to coffee, but my own experience and perception was that this sort of thing was beyond the ken of the Arts Faculty. All four groups ran in parallel lines towards the same goal.

As I look back now I am amazed at the lack of interaction. I am amazed too and a bit sad that as Sisters we did not get involved in college life, more especially in the social/pastoral organizations. Was there a Vincent de Paul Society in the College? Was there an awareness of Third World famine? Were there homeless and destitute on the streets of Dublin? We did not know. We were sent by our congregations to the university to get our degrees and, after a slow start, we were, by and large, single-minded in our endeavours. I was part of the parade and acknowledge that I did not see the whole picture, but as I perceived it UCD was a great place to be in the Fifties. There was a relaxed and easy-going atmosphere. I have always been grateful for my time there. I imbibed from staff and from some students a life-long love of learning. I formed long-lasting friendships with Sisters from other congregations as well as our own. For those gifts I thank God. I ask his blessings on my co-students and on all my erudite, if aloof, mentors. *In iothlainn Dé go gcastar sinn.*

Paula Loughlin (Doyle)

Girls Do Honours Now

It was fashionable to sneer at the B.A. — maybe it still is — but I felt privileged to be there. There were only sixteen in our Leaving Cert class at school (many girls had left after the Inter) and only two of us were given the opportunity to try for college.

It wasn't the usual thing for girls to go to university back then. In our school we weren't expected to be able for the rigours of honours level papers, so the talk was of 'baby' maths and 'baby' Latin. (A book I read later entitled *Girls Don't Do Honours* throws light on this custom.) But to give them credit, two Loreto nuns in Beaufort, Rathfarnham decided to offer extra tuition in these subjects and Irish so that at least we could sit the Matric. Thank you, Mothers Consuelo and Redempta.

The next hurdle was the fees. My parents had many doubts about spending that much money on a girl who spent her spare time going to the tennis club and dreaming about romance. Other parents decided to send only their sons to college as university education would be wasted on girls who, most likely, would get married. (Most families, I am aware, were excluded by second level fees in the days before they were abolished.)

I do remember the excitement and fear of those early days in Earlsfort Terrace. There were huge numbers doing English and it was easy to feel lost. It seemed odd that our English lectures took place in a hall called the Physics Theatre. The professor read to us from *Paradise Lost* and if you paid attention you would notice that he smoothly skipped over the lines describing the passionate coming together of Adam and Eve.

In the French Department, Professor Louis Roche was determined to raise the standards and had a poor opinion of convent-school French. By the end of First Year he had weeded out the weakest. I turned to Spanish and found support and encouragement from the lecturer we knew formally as 'Miss Crowe'. What was initially a huge disappointment became a consolation prize as the doors opened to a fascinating exploration of Spanish literature, music, drama and dance.

In other ways too First Year was a humbling experience. English essays that would have got an honours mark at school were failed by Denis Donoghue. He used to startle First Years by asking them to write an essay on any piece of literature *not* on the syllabus. This was a lived experience of learning for its own sake, a concept we studied in the writings of 'silver-tongued Newman'.

The social life was hectic. A day could include lectures, lunch in the Annexe, tutorials, Library, milling around in the Main Hall, and going for coffee. This last ritual was performed in places with exotic names like 'Inca' or 'Kilimanjaro'. Coffee as a drink seemed quite sophisticated to the children of tea-drinking families. It never crossed our minds to go to a pub. The evenings were devoted to the student clubs: Dramsoc or the Music Society, or the Legion of Mary, which was flourishing in those years. Then there would often be a hop in 86 or a party that 'really needed girls'. (We were vastly outnumbered so constantly in demand.) One highlight was the commerce picnic when we all went by boat to Dalkey Island on a perfect summer's day. We swam, we sang, we danced the *Siege of Ennis* on the pier to the music of a mouth organ. We thought we would always be young.

The highlight of my first year was putting on the Gilbert and Sullivan opera, *Patience, or Bunthorne's Bride* under the long-suffering direction of Professor Tony Hughes. I still have the programme. It cost 6d. I was thrilled to be chosen for the eponymous heroine and abandoned study for rehearsals. We learned all the choruses ('twenty love-sick maidens we') and fell in love briefly and serially with the romantic lead and the members of the men's chorus. The show ran for four nights in February 1959 in the Aula Maxima in 86. The audiences were enthusiastic, the newspapers not so kind; they criticized the principal ladies who 'looked the part but had hardly the vocal resources'.

The greatest and most prestigious society was, of course, the L&H. For a sheltered schoolgirl who had only dabbled in polite debates this was a revelation. A note I wrote at the time conveys the dream-like quality of the first evening, describing as it does 'the long-haired chairman looking for all the world like Beau Brummel or Darcy'. I sat amazed at the earnest, angry, or witty speakers, and the perfect 'Palace of Variety' guest chairman, Alec Newman of the *Irish Times*. It was enough to sit and admire; few girls dared to speak.

I suppose we had no role models. All the professors and the vast majority of the senior lecturers were men. The exceptions I remember were Miss Crowe from the Spanish Department and Lorna Reynolds in English. The most powerful woman I knew in UCD seemed to be my aunt Rita who guarded the Registrar's office like a dragon. We came largely from a culture of quietness; girls were supposed to be ladylike, studious and amiable. We wore straight tweed skirts from Clerys, and dark stockings, never trousers. For parties I remember frills and stoles and stiff under-skirts, high heels and pointed toes that my feet now regret.

I have revisited UCD a few times since my graduation, once to do a belated H.Dip where I learned about the mistakes I had been making as a teacher. It was a novel and challenging experience then to be a married mother-of-two juggling lectures and babysitters, study and home duties (as the census used to call them). Now further education for older women (and men) is widely accepted, if greatly under-funded.

The most recent course I did as a mature student was Women's Studies. It was the Belfield campus again and far in time and distance from the haunts of St Stephen's Green and Baggot Street.

There were wide-open spaces, lovely shrubs and birdsong. The architecture seemed modern and functional with heavy double doors to restrain possible riots. There was a student bar. The Library was brighter; even the way we studied was changed by technology. In Earlsfort Terrace we used to sit for hours copying key sentences from precious books; now the photocopy machine makes it almost unnecessary to take notes. The Internet has revolutionized the way students do research. And girls do honours now.

Maeve Binchy

Another Circle of Friends

This article was first published in *UCD Connections* and is reprinted here by kind permission of the author.

I was very young and silly and overexcited when I first went to UCD in October 1956. It was a cold sunny day and I was wearing (much to my rage) a good quality green coat which my mother had said joyfully to my doom-stricken face was a coat that would last for years and years. This was deeply depressing because what I yearned for was a duffle coat, a navy thing, with a hood and sort of toggles to keep it fastened. I thought I would look a dish in that, and vaguely Left Bank and experienced as well.

I walked up from what was then Westland Row station, which is now Pearse station, to what was then UCD in Earlsfort Terrace, which is now the National Concert Hall. I walked with a new friend, Mary, whom I had met on the train and we joined up with my schoolfriend Philippa so that we would be three and that this would somehow take the bare look off us as we walked nervously up the stairs. Thank God some things don't change. University premises and railway stations have changed utterly but Mary and Philippa are still close friends.

I remember that first day as if it were yesterday. We hung around the Main Hall eyeing people, laughing loudly at things to show we were having a great time. A lot of girls seemed to be wearing much more make-up than we were so we discovered the Ladies' Reading Room (a place where I never read a book during my four years at UCD), in order to put on more paint. And there I met Catherine and Rose Mary and Geraldine and others who also became friends for life.

Then my cousin Helen, who was two years older and therefore knew everything came and took us all on a tour. Helen Binchy — later Helen Burke — already had all the kindly firm feelings towards students that led her on to the academic life of UCD, and she insisted on showing us the libraries and the lecture halls as well as the Annexe.

In fact, she delivered us to our first lecture which was a First Arts English with about four hundred students. It was given by a man in a clerical collar whom we all called Father Dunning, because in those days that was about the highest compliment and form of address for any man, be he professor or doctor or whatever. When he went to rub out what he had written on the blackboard with a duster, eight girls sitting near the front and myself got to our feet automatically. Nice convent girls would never let a teacher struggle to erase a board. Nearly four hundred people laughed at us and we never did it again.

We had our first lunch in a place called The Singing Kettle on the corner of Leeson Street. The first of hundreds of lunches there. They all seemed so confident, these young women of seventeen and eighteen. I was younger, bigger and louder than all of them. Suddenly school seemed safe in retrospect.

Then fellows came to the café, shuffling and smoking and wondering where they'd sit. My companions looked up with interest. By the greatest fluke I knew one of the guys who had come in. I, who knew no fellows in my life, actually knew this great hunk in a duffle coat. From Ballybunion days. And what's more he acknowledged me with the appearance of being pleased to see me.

There were introductions and I think that at that moment my college life began. I got the feeling that the future might not be just one more beauty contest where the race went to the tiny and the svelte. Fellows might be people you could talk to. A blinding insight to someone just out of convent school in 1956.

And so began four years of talking, and ambling around Stephen's Green, and coffees in Grafton Street, and afternoon films in the Green Cinema, and the L&H on Saturday nights. There was a bit of work too, not a huge amount to be honest. I wish I could tell you how I sat in the Library lost for hours in what I was reading but that literally would not be true. I was full of observation, though. The difference in those days between people who came from the country and the Dubs; the way the clerical students (who were totally out of bounds to us) were much cleaner than the other students and actually washed their necks.

Then there were the nuns, always sitting in the front rows so as not to miss anything, grateful to their religious orders for the education. We might have worried about letting our parents down by failing exams but the poor young nuns were totally terrified in case they would let their Sisters down and you felt that the occasional vision of a disapproving Reverend Mother was there too — so they worked like little demons, to use an inappropriate simile.

The holidays from UCD seemed dull at first, but they were filled up with long stays in France being pinched black and blue by the Monsieur who must have got some vague pleasure from it all but it certainly gave none.

Then we all went to get summer jobs in London where we shared flats with people who were later to become judges, MEPs and captains of industry. 'Shared' was an interesting word. The women had day jobs and the men worked at night; nine of us lived in an apartment for four. Quite amicable but interspersed with huge arguments about changing sheets and people's feet smelling.

And then it came to graduation day. I just scraped the honours B.A. and I did the Higher Diploma in Education. I hated leaving UCD, hated it with a passion. Well, wouldn't anyone? Hundreds of friends on tap, a social life at the ready, the belief that we would change the world. Total disbelief that College would ever move out to what we thought of as the sports fields at Belfield. How could we leave the centre of town for the suburbs?

I couldn't get a job teaching in Dublin, which was a major tragedy at the time but in retrospect was probably just as well. I think if I had stayed in the capital city I would have spent all my time hanging around Earlsfort Terrace looking for the ghosts of those who had passed through and got on with their own lives.

Instead, I went to Cork where I knew nobody at all and nobody knew me and where I spent months licking my wounds and telling everyone it was a desperate place instead of getting on with things and realizing that you make your own life wherever you are.

It was, as it turned out, the best thing that could happen to anyone, to leave Dublin at the same time as leaving UCD. By the time I got back again I felt I was too old to go back and look for a life in the Annexe or in 86 Stephen's Green. And soon it was part of the past and I didn't need it anymore.

Need no, but remember yes. It was the luckiest, most privileged and happiest thing to have been able to spend four happy years there, to learn something — not early enough, but that was my fault. To have fallen in love — which didn't last — to have made marvellous friends who did.

When I wrote the novel, *Circle of Friends*, it wasn't my own story that I was talking about, but it was my own time. Our innocence and silliness compared to the students of today, the way we took a university education as a sort of right if our parents were middle class or saved enough to pay for it. The way we all talked non-stop about sex but (as far as I know) very few of us had any.

I thought the book was set in a time capsule, the last period of innocence or idiocy before the Sixties, depending on how you look at it. Oddly enough, when the book was published and when the picture came out later people everywhere and of all ages said that it reminded them of their own student days. Art students who had been in Paris in the Eighties, engineers who had qualified in Scotland after the last World War — it all seemed familiar.

So maybe though Fifties UCD seems special to those of us who lived through it, it's just not all that different and dinosaur-like as we thought. Perhaps young, hopeful, eager people lucky enough to have the time to think are roughly the same in different lands and different generations.

Gemma Hussey

Was it a University?

It is difficult to stand outside early experience and to be dispassionate about its effects. For this writer, arriving in UCD at Earlsfort Terrace in the autumn of 1957 was exciting. The train from Bray (the Harcourt Street line — soon to be resuscitated) dropped me just around the corner. These were the days of the ban on Trinity (it never occurred to any of us to go anywhere other than UCD) and it was before the points system. If you had £33 and some kind of a 'Matric' you were in.

We were immediately caught up in the whirl of the social life of UCD, simple though it was (and it was simple!). It came as heady stuff to a 17-year-old who had just spent several years in one of Ireland's most strictly enclosed convent boarding schools. For many of us, the social life centred around the hops in the Aula Max, and the dress dances of the various College societies, when we could afford it and parents allowed us to go. We wore the same dress all the time, varied with a rose or a sash, and thought we were at the hub of the smart universe.

Lectures? The huge numbers in all the lecture rooms and theatres (they seemed huge after the tiny classes at school), along with the poor punctuality and lack of communication skills of most of the lecturers combined to make any learning experience boring to say the least. Boys, sports occasions, dances, and cream buns in Fullers and the DBC were what turned us on, not to mention lighting up the sophisticated cigarette in the Annexe amid the murk and smoke and cooking smells of that underground attraction. Rampant hormones and newfound freedom were a powerful combination. By Easter of that first year I had still not bothered — or been encouraged — to discover where the Library was. As a result I spent my second year at UCD in a pass B.A. class, even more bored academically. It was desperation that drove me to find out that I could repeat Second Year, switching to honours economics and politics.

Most of us leaving school in the 1950s were simply not ready for higher education. We were thrown into a situation where there was no one-to-one encouragement, tutorials, general guidance. Silly rules like 'no trousers for girls' took the place of real efforts to encourage learning. Student societies were rigidly controlled. The results of that unreadiness and out-of-date attitude were seen all around in people achieving less than their potential, girls in particular. Women played hardly any role in the major College societies, where young men jousted verbally on their way to becoming future leaders of Ireland.

Trinity College, just down the road and across Stephen's Green, might have been on Mars for all we knew of it, except for a vague notion that they were all Protestant and/or English, and that the girls were 'fast'. The Bishop's ban worked efficiently in that respect.

I can hardly believe my memories. Girls pretended to be less intelligent then they were for fear of being thought too clever, too serious. My reaction on discovering a relatively good examination result was to wonder how I would tell the boyfriends. Would I be despised as being too clever for my own good? Would I be accused of cramming on the quiet? And, despite a casual remark by the late lamented John Kelly (T.D. and university lecturer) that I might consider going on to take a higher degree or study law, I opted out of it all and got a job in advertising, not out of economic necessity, but because of a lack of any clear picture of where I might go, and an unfocused attitude towards any career structure.

It wasn't easy to get advice. I remember an occasion when I tried to have a talk with one distinguished professor, George O'Brien, about possible future directions of study. He was obviously acutely unwilling to communicate at all, looked everywhere but at me, and escaped down the corridor as soon as he could, gown flying, without suggesting any follow up. I don't blame him; he was an agonizingly shy man, and a clever one, but he was not backed up by any system of student counselling or support. That experience made sure I didn't try again. With the honourable exception of Patrick Lynch, who lectured to us on political economy, there did not appear to be much interest.

I left UCD with a good honours degree in economics and politics without having set foot in Leinster House or having any idea of how Irish politics worked. There was no attempt to introduce us, the honours group, to our own country's systems or political players. Ten years later, when I had a growing business and a growing family, it was the Women's Movement that steered me towards a political career. The first time I set foot in Leinster House was the day after I was elected to Seanad Éireann, representing the graduates of UCD and all the other NUI colleges. By that time I was 37 and had begun to grow up — I think.

Do not misunderstand. I was very happy in UCD. I met a huge number of people, made many good and lasting friends, grew up a little, had some fun, and discovered that I could do well at examinations. But I can't say that those four undergraduate years at UCD all that time ago enriched my knowledge in many fields, or helped in a critical understanding of the larger world and its challenges, or greatly developed my mind. That kind of development came much later, and it was only then that I realized how narrow the education at university had been.

UCD was an institution very much of its time. Perhaps it could not have been any different; perhaps all the other colleges were about the same for young women like me. In Ireland it was a time of intellectual stagnation and gloomy introspection, along with economic depression. The first decade of change, the 1960s, had yet to come.

The 1960s

The UCD move from Earlsfort Terrace to Belfield coincided with the beginning of change in Irish society. Perhaps this is not unconnected with the opening of the national television station in the earlier part of the decade, and a growing awareness of the world outside our small island. What was happening in other countries and our own was brought home to us more forcibly through the new medium. The Civil Rights movement, the anti-Vietnam war protests in the USA; the Cuban Missile crisis; the debate provoked by the Second Vatican Council; CND, and later the anti-Vietnam war movement in the UK; 1968 in France; the stirrings of a Civil Rights movement in Northern Ireland; all had an effect on students in Ireland. Public protest, which was rare at the beginning of the decade, was commonplace at its end.

Criticism of lecturers in UCD mirrors this trend. It was muted, if voiced at all, in the earlier part of the decade, but was heard more frequently as the years went on and students became less accepting of the status quo. The rows between the L&H and President Michael Tierney in 1960 were recounted with relish throughout the decade, and in the telling the Society does not back down, so that clashes with authority were glorified by the end of the Sixties. Memories of Michael Tierney striding through the Hall of Earlsfort Terrace in his bicycle clips gave way to a less authoritarian and old-fashioned image — though as a member of a delegation to the new President, Jeremiah Hogan, said, 'He's nicer, but it's still the same answer: "No!"' Donogh O'Malley's plan to merge TCD and UCD seems to reflect the idealism of those years.

Who would now suggest such a scheme, and why was it considered necessary at all? Our differences are now cherished, and the new universities with their own individual strengths have shown that in modern Ireland there is room for many different institutions.

Earlsfort Terrace is remembered by many of our earlier writers as an idyllic spot, but students in the last years in the Terrace were coping with overcrowding, and the mid-Sixties protests about the Library had swelled into a major complaint that eventually gave rise to the occupation of the Great Hall and the student revolt. This led in turn to a more democratic UCD with student participation in the administration regarded as the norm.

Reflection on the music of the Sixties brings to mind not only the Beatles and their visit to Dublin, but also the rebirth of folk music in Ireland, with The Dubliners and the regular sessions in O'Donoghue's epitomizing the decade. Fashion also changed enormously as we started out dressed like young ladies in tweeds and sensible shoes but ended up in boots and mini-skirts, hoping we would look like Julie Christie. With the advent of the French *nouvelle vague* and Italian directors like Fellini, cinema became a subject of intellectual excitement, and was discussed endlessly over cups of coffee in the New Amsterdam or the Coffee Inn as well as in the Annexe. The issues of the day also exercised us; we were very idealistic and thought we would be different from our parents' generation. We were going to change things.

Looking back, things certainly changed in Ireland — but did we do it, and was it for the better?

Sally Corcoran

1960	Seannad Éireann approves a move to Belfield for UCD.
	John F. Kennedy elected President of the United States.
1961	Yuri Gagarin first man in space.
	First TV broadcast by RTÉ.
1962	First *Late Late Show*.
	Meeting of Second Vatican Council.
1963	Beatles play Adelphi Cinema, Dublin.
	Assassination of John F. Kennedy.
1965	Rolling Stones play Adelphi Cinema, Dublin.
1968	Pope Paul VI issues *Humanae Vitae*, an encyclical condemning artificial birth control.
1969	Riots in Northern Ireland.
	Neil Armstrong first man on the moon.

Eleonore Tuohy (Johnson)

No Registration Necessary

The first thing that amazed me in 1960 heading for UCD was that, unlike nowadays, no registration was necessary beforehand. A phone call from me elicited the information that I should just turn up on a given date in October. I was surprised that no one in UCD administration would be aware of my impending arrival, and that no one was awaiting me, eagerly or otherwise. I had come from a boarding school that had a very strict regime, which was quite the norm in the Ireland of the time. It was rather a culture shock, almost like being released from prison, into the big bad world.

From the age of twelve or thirteen I had wanted to study for a science degree, unlike some of my contemporaries, who entered university without having the faintest idea what faculty they wished to enter, let alone what subjects they wished to study. My confidence in knowing what I wanted to study was short-lived, however. A week or so after I had started, various faculties held their advisory sessions for First Year students. I attended the sessions for science students, having decided on taking chemistry, physics, botany, and zoology. My advisor told me that if I wished to continue with chemistry in Second Year I would have to take maths in First Year, a fact I had failed to notice in the College calendar. Maths was my best and favourite subject, but in most girls' schools in those days, honours Leaving Certificate maths was not an option; I was therefore afraid that I might not be able for the maths course. However, without checking on my ability in the subject or asking how I had fared in Leaving Cert maths, this 'advisor' told me that I had no business studying science. I felt deflated, inadequate, put down, and left the room in tears, while my advisor calmly and matter-of-factly called on the next person in the queue to come forward. What was I to do? How could I return home and tell my parents that I would not be accepted into science? The advisor had not actually said as much, but that was my interpretation. I spent the evening contemplating my position and eventually decided to give it a go. After all, in my five years at secondary school I had sat fifteen exams, and on fourteen of those occasions had finished in first place in my class. My self-esteem restored, I registered for science, and, as they say, the rest is history. Ironically maths was to be one of the subjects I took to degree level.

I feel that studying subjects with a practical content greatly contributed to getting to know my classmates. With practicals lasting three hours there was ample time to get to know the other people in the laboratory, and practicals all through my time in college were almost social events.

Because of my choice of subjects my memory is of forever to-ing and fro-ing between Earlsfort Terrace and Merrion Street: 9 a.m. in Earlsfort Terrace, 10.15 in Merrion Street, 11.15 in Earlsfort Terrace, was a regular morning's timetable. Although I used a bicycle to get to college it was mostly faster to walk between the two lecture venues because one's bicycle had often to be retrieved from behind about twenty others and that took too much time. Saturday morning lectures were the norm during my time in UCD and for every one of my years in college I had a 9 a.m. lecture every single day. That must be a record!

I very much enjoyed the L&H debates on Saturday nights and though I was too shy to speak, I hung on the words of Emer O'Kelly, Louis Courtney, Tony Clare, Ruth Dudley Edwards, Patrick Cosgrave, Ricky Johnson et al. So interesting were the debates that I frequently missed the last bus. However, Dublin was a much safer place then, and I often walked back to my flat alone and unhindered except for a hiss or a namecall from a prostitute or two around Hatch Street who thought I was taking up their beat.

During a break from studying in the Library one night I was introduced to Gordon Colleary, a classmate who was very involved with the SRC. Gordon took a shine to my friend and invited us for a coffee in the Singing Kettle after study. While waiting to be served I got a kick under the table and a whispered request for the loan of a half-crown from Gordon, who was obviously 'skint'. When later he became a millionaire I was tempted to look for my money back — with interest.

A sad occurrence that comes to mind was the sudden death at a relatively young age of T.E. Wheeler, Professor of Chemistry, one lunchtime on the steps of the College of Science.

Taking a conducted tour about five years ago of the beautifully restored Newman House, I was reminded of the many plates of egg and chips (costing 4s 6d) that we consumed at tea-time, before facing the rigours of a few hours of study in the Library. No smell of chips lingers in this present showpiece.

In these days of seeking gender equality it is interesting to note that in my time in UCD the Professors of Chemistry, Botany, and Zoology were all women. (Eva Philbin became professor following the death of Professor Wheeler.)

The late Fr Joe Dunne was chaplain during part of my time at UCD and it was plain to see even then that he was a very outspoken man and quite charismatic.

In my final year myself, a classmate, and a First Year student shared a flat in Kenilworth Square. The landlady, from Lismore, lived on the ground floor, a very kind, friendly, and motherly lady who brought us soup on cold days. It was here that I first heard of Dervla Murphy, a friend of our landlady. Dervla was then cycling in India and had yet to write her first book. However, she gave graphic descriptions of her trip in letters to our landlady, who passed the letters on to us to read. When I finished my studies at the end of the academic year, the three of us went our separate ways. Imagine my surprise on discovering some years later when the landlady died that the good lady had willed her house to one of my flatmates! Where did I go wrong?

My degree was not my only acquisition from UCD, for during my second year there I met a Final Year Engineering student who shared my own passion for hurling, and we have been happily married since 1965.

Barbara Prendergast

On Your Bike!

I began a B.Sc. degree at UCD in September 1964. We were one of the first classes to use the new Belfield campus; however, our first year was a continuous round of travelling. I remember I had a Physics lecture at 9 a.m. in the old Physics Theatre in Earlsfort Terrace, which lasted for a full hour. We then had either a chemistry or a maths lecture in Merrion Street at 10 a.m. None of the timetable organizers seemed to have realized that it took a good ten minutes to walk from Earlsfort Terrace to Merrion Street and we would frequently have our names taken for being late. I can never remember anyone complaining. I can't see that happening today. We had lectures in Merrion Street some days until 1 p.m. and then had to get ourselves out to Belfield for practicals at 2 p.m. This didn't allow any time for lunch. I also remember that the only ladies' toilets in Merrion Street were on the fourth floor along a huge long corridor towards the back of the building. It was very inconvenient.

In my first year I used buses and spent an inordinate amount of time on them. In Second Year I started cycling to Belfield every day from my grandparents' home in Marino, the only place I could afford to live. By this time at least we had all our lectures and practicals on one campus and we did feel rather special, even though we were virtually living on a building site. I can still remember the monstrous great earth-remover trucks trundling up and down outside the geology/botany/zoology block. The facilities were marvelous: a good canteen, comfortable lecture theatres, clean and well-appointed cloakrooms, and a good library. The seating in the Geology Department was not the best. The stools were too high and you had to sit sideways on to the desk and bend down to write notes, a very uncomfortable position.

Because I cycled across the city in hail, rain or snow every day to college I wore appropriate clothing, usually warm jeans or slacks and a pullover. In my third year I got myself a motorbike to cut down on travelling time and used to wear black leathers. There were no concessions at all for the female students in regard to what we wore at college; we were expected to wear dresses or skirts to attend lectures. Once we arrived in college we had to go to our locker rooms and change. I would not have minded changing on really wet mornings, but it was quite unnecessary on dry days and the male students could wear what they liked. There was a big protest towards the end of my time at UCD and this very sexist rule was eventually changed.

The teaching during my time in college ranged from excellent to abysmally bad. On the whole my geology lecturers were a good bunch, and with one or two notable exceptions the chemistry lecturers got their information across. Without exception though the mathematics lecturers were hopeless. I am not saying that they were bad mathematicians — in fact they were probably all brilliant mathematicians — but their failure to instruct was unbelievable and their teaching capabilities non-existent. Having failed maths twice in Second Year, I had to repeat a year doing maths only, and I failed again in the summer exam. It was only then that I became aware of a geology lecturer called Kevin O'Kelly who gave grinds in maths in his home. I would never have got my degree without his help. From then on I only attended maths lectures for attendance purposes, still failing to understand anything that was being 'explained', and it was only during Kevin's evening classes that the penny would drop. I was not the only student who owed a very great debt of gratitude to this wonderful teacher.

I think it was in my second year, at a Science dance, that I was voted Miss Belfield. The other girl in the running at this beauty contest was a very beautiful Siamese girl called Ploumirudi Devahastin. How I managed to beat her I really do not know. I won a white satin sash embroidered with the words 'Miss Belfield', which I still have, and a photograph of me wearing the sash appeared in the student newspaper.

The principal event in my university career was meeting my wonderful husband, Sean Prendergast. During my repeat year, I worked for Mrs Monaghan in the canteen in Belfield at lunchtime, and occasionally during evening receptions. I used to collect and clean the trays, cutlery and dirty dishes. It was during lunchtime that Sean, a Ph.D. student who used to sit in what we called 'Pets' Corner' (an area of the canteen reserved for staff and postgraduate students), noticed my potential as a good housekeeper. He apparently used to leave notes for me on the trays but I worked so fast that they disappeared without trace into the bins. He eventually made contact through one of my friends in the Judo Club. We met at a Christmas social in 1967, married in December 1968, and are still very happy.

Nicola Jennings

Starting Out

Everyone standing around waiting as I walked into Earlsfort
Terrace in October 1964 — that was my first impression. We
glanced suspiciously at each other, crossing the black and white
tiles to the far side of the hall and waiting there. Fooling ourselves
and no one else that we knew what we were doing. Of course we
knew. We all knew, but we were all just a little bit bewildered.
Reading out-of-date notices and shifting the body weight from one
foot to the other. Right foot, left foot, over to the chaplain's
notice-board, stop for seventy-five seconds, back to the telephone
kiosks. Sitting on dusty red velvet benches. 'So this is university
life,' everyone was thinking in unison. The thought so strong it
was almost audible. A thousand and twenty representatives of Irish
youth, Freshers all, the majority baptized, processed, and
matriculated. A few from overseas. A large number of black-clad
clerical students and nuns. Here we were, the largest unemployed
population per square mile of any area in Ireland. The dregs of
humanity or the cream? It depended on your point of view.
Suddenly a look of relief would spread over a vacant face. Two lost
souls approached each other. Contact at last.

The Freshers' Exhibition added to the confusion. Societies and
clubs proliferated. Who to join? What to do? There were so many.
The English Literary Society, the Spanish Society, the History
Society, the L&H, to name but a few. Dramsoc touted for talent.
The Boat Club took men only — the first hint of inequality.
Women row too. Didn't they know that? The College Dublin
Society explored the city and its surroundings, with an emphasis
on Georgian architecture. *St Stephen's* published would-be writers.
Awake published gossip. There was even an AgSoc, which ran

dances. The choice was endless but resources were low. The pubs on Lesson Street — O'Dwyer's, Kirwan's, and Hartigan's — provided a refuge when things got just too much.

Another place of refuge was the Ladies' Reading Room, a spacious room furnished with large and very worn-out armchairs and sofas. Miss Greene, the Women's Dean of Residence, looked after the needs of women students. Miss Ellen Power looked after the Library. A strict dress code was in operation and a clear demarcation of roles. Women were not allowed to wear trousers, not a great hardship at the time as lacy white tights and pointy shoes were the height of fashion, but later it became a major issue.

These were shifting adolescent days when sunshine and a cheerful greeting were enough to make us delirious with happiness, crazily, deliciously lost in that joy-of-living feeling. These were the first days of discoveries, acquaintances, experiences, and a rich, innocent, platonic style of loving. These were unrepeatable days.

The invitation to the first dress dance was nerve-racking, but who would admit it? It was first time evening out, wine-drunk, dance-tired, and it all went wild until three o'clock in the morning. Dance followed dance. The Law Society and Commerce and Economics Inaugurals. The SRC Jubilee Ball. The Shelbourne Hotel. The Gresham. Living it up. *La Dolce Vita. Amarcord. Elvira Madigan.*

The morning after the night before, and there were many. The head was full of music: *A Hard Day's Night; Sergeant Pepper's Lonely Hearts Club Band; Puppet on a String.* Time to get up. Hard not to sink back into oblivion, to forget about studying. The cherry blossom was out. The first lecture had begun. The libraries were busy. Paddy Keogh, Head Porter, marshalled us in the right direction. We sat up high on a hard bench in the Physics Theatre, or hurried to find the soft seat at the back of general history. The hall was full of people talking. Would it be like this in eternity? Would we be forever talking? The Annexe drew us like a magnet.

Coffee, buns and cigarettes. Beans and chips. Milk in glass bottles. Clerical students were required to lunch elsewhere. We strolled across Iveagh Gardens to 86, where Alice cleared away the saucers while we still held the cups in our hands. Others crossed Stephen's Green to the Grafton Cinema, forgot exams, and smiled.

Graduation Day came all too soon. Gowned and topped with mortarboards, we sat in the Great Hall, received our scrolls and said our goodbyes. How differently we all turned out. Some successful; others not so. Some of the best and brightest lost to us forever. Only the memories remain and strong enduring friendships. Was this what it was all about?

Ita Daly

Skies Always Blue

I have been in Belfield a dozen times and each time I leave I think how lucky I am to have escaped spending my university years in such a bleak, windswept place. I think of it as a ghastly, south Dublin Gulag where the sun never shines, but where grey, concrete buildings are mirrored in permanently grey skies.

In my UCD on the other hand, the skies are always blue and the walk down Grafton Street to drink coffee in Robert Roberts was through the leafy, fragrant delight of Stephen's Green, which to us always seemed part of the campus. There is something very civilized about having a university in the heart of the city, for it encourages the students to expand into the city instead of remaining corralled within college grounds. The streets around Earlsfort Terrace were our playground; the pubs, the coffee houses, the bookshops were every bit as important as the lecture theatres — at least to those of us who were being properly educated in the liberal arts.

I remember the Main Hall, where one lingered to meet friends or to strike an attitude or to flirt, while Paddy looked on benignly from his Porter's Office, philosophical about the antics of the young. I remember the Ladies' Reading Room where one went for respite from the fray, to gossip, to weep, to re-do one's make-up before returning to the rigours of unisexdom. (Remember, most young women students had only just been released from long years of hand rearing by the nuns.) And speaking of nuns, I remember the Loreto sisters arriving in college by car, a sort of clerical stretch limo, chauffeur driven and disgorging what seemed like dozens of black-clothed Sisters, all wearing gloves. Other nuns came on the bus like the rest of us.

My UCD was a very relaxed place where most First Years were in no hurry to discover the delights of the Library. It was well into the month of December before I made my entrance, and then I was so terrified of Miss Power that it was months again before I plucked up the courage to return. Besides, there was not much time for libraries. There were so many calls on our time; there was coffee to be drunk, friends to be made, boys to be snared, societies to be engaged with. In other words, there was Life demanding to be lived. And if we did get worried about exams there was always the shining example of the 'chronics' — students, mainly medical, who had spent years repeating their exams and who appeared to us to have benefited from this lengthy exposure to university life.

And yet, one of the great pleasures of those years was the intellectual excitement I experienced. I found that learning could be thrilling and that attending lectures could actually be enjoyable. I imagine that good teaching at third level is rare enough and I do remember being bored on occasion. More often though my imagination was caught and held by such memorable teachers as Denis Donoghue, Alan Bliss, Isabel Foley, Sean Page. I think all of those people must have liked the undergraduates they taught and they were all good performers, very necessary when you are competing with hangovers and raging hormones. I also remember being very impressed by the way all the staff treated us as adults and addressed us as Mr or Miss. Everybody smoked in those days and drank vast quantities of beer. Drugs were only entering the scene when I was leaving college, and wine was something you drank when the beer ran out. There were also far more student parties than there are nowadays when young people go on to clubs after the pubs close. At half eleven most nights of the week you used to see groups of students wandering around Leeson Street and Harcourt Street, brown bags full of beer bottles under their arms asking one another, 'Where's the party?'

Aside from these parties there were regular dances in Newman House, 'hops' as they were known. And there were dress dances, what students nowadays call 'balls' but more formal, as most of life was then.

Most people who left school in the early 1960s went into jobs and only a minority went on to third level, which then meant university. University students were more of an elite than they are today. What I remember though was how modestly we all lived. We cycled or took the bus. Many students did not have telephones at home, never mind mobiles in their briefcases. Dining out was something that was reserved for big occasions, like graduation. I remember how much we envied English students who were over here on grants and lived like pashas in splendid flats with their own bathrooms. Irish students for the most part when they had to rent rooms, lived in bedsits and queued for the one bathroom on draughty landings.

There is one moment of supreme magic that I often recall. I must have had a nine o'clock lecture and walked in to college though a snowstorm. After the lecture I needed to go to Newman House for some reason and I walked out into Iveagh Gardens to find them transformed by a blanket of pure, untouched snow. Nobody had yet walked across it, and trees and statues were enshrouded and strange. I stopped and stared, and then, as I was wondering if I dared put a footprint on all that pristine beauty, a snowball came flying through the air and hit me on the ear. It hurt, and shattered the mood of tranquillity. And I knew that it was one of the Engineers probably, behaving with their usual crassness.

Life was always difficult for the aesthete, even in my UCD.

Sally Corcoran

Three Ages of College

When I think of my undergraduate days in Earlsfort Terrace the first place that comes to mind is the Ladies' Reading Room with its warm fire in winter and capacious armchairs. In fact I don't think I spent that much time there, but it was a private place for women students where you could arrange to meet or spend a few minutes checking your appearance before making your entrance into a lecture. It was also a place you overheard the troubles of others, as frequently there were tearful scenes with friends rallying around to cheer up the afflicted. One couple comes to mind. The wife-to-be bawled her head off then; now they are happily married for thirty-something years. Another woman talking loudly about her boyfriend was in fact being two-timed according to my inside knowledge; she was subsequently very subdued. I felt that she had had a lucky escape but could not say so as I did not know her very well and the other woman was a friend of mine.

Lectures in history were stimulating or extremely dull depending on the lecturer and the time of day. Dudley Edwards after lunch could be either brilliant or incomprehensible. Desmond Williams was always stimulating and missing a lecture was unthinkable. English was another matter. Denis Donoghue went on about appearance and reality and the philosopher Kenneth Burke. It had to do with his next book, and we were allowed to listen to his thoughts on this theme as it applied to Shakespeare. It was all very interesting and disposed us to read the plays and stay awake, which was more than other lecturers managed, though I do recall reading the Jacobean tragedians with enthusiasm as a result of lectures from Tom Kilroy. By far the greatest enthusiasm that has remained with me came as a result of public lectures given by Tom Dunning during which he talked about the medieval world, the topics ranging from philosophy and religion to history, poetry, art and music. The first time I heard medieval music, which has remained a lifelong interest, was in his study with a group of us listening to his records and singing along!

The Sixties were a time of idealism and I remember taking part in various protests and the first demonstration in the Library, which was about lack of space. In the late 1990s the Students' Union organized another demo in the Library about lack of space — *plus ça change*! The first intimation of the Troubles in the North came in a tutorial where a student from Omagh burst into an impassioned statement about life in the North as a Catholic, which left the rest of us dumbfounded. After a debate in the L&H we were convinced that the world would be a better place when we got our hands on it — the illusions of youth once again.

When I came back to UCD in the 1980s it was to a different place and time. It was Belfield now and the bleak and unattractive place of my memory had matured. It wasn't the buildings that took my attention, but the plants and trees that had grown as their designer had intended. Now I have some favourite times of the year where I make a point of going to see the cherry trees in bloom or the sorbus coming into leaf on the way out to the Clonskeagh gate.

Library Studies in middle age was more demanding than I had anticipated and I nearly went round the bend in the first term staggering from one deadline to another. Staff assured us that we would survive and that managing deadlines was all part of the package. I graduated and went on to work in UCD managing a small library called the Development Studies Library, which concentrates on developing countries. This has shown me another side of UCD. I admire the academic staff who work hard to take good care of their students. There is a downside, however, as nine years (to date) on a contract with no pension rights is also part of the package. But I love my job and again and again encounter the idealism of students, which is still focused on injustices both at home and abroad, as well as the hard work involved in getting a degree. They give me hope for the future.

Sister Vera Mc Grath

Infinite Possibilities

The Sixties for me, living a strict religious life of stern routine and thrown suddenly into the mental, psychological, spiritual, and literary liberty of UCD, Earlsfort Terrace, were enough to produce schizophrenia! But as time went on, I found my 'at home-ness' in the circulation of open philosophical ideas, pondering the imponderable, and discussing infinite possibilities of many forms of world political and social change. Brian Farrell in politics knew all the historical facts but went much further, to speculate on change, freedom, and a new life in Ireland. Gus Martin in English was a fund of reverence for literature, old or new, and he evoked in us the same great reverence and respect for the written word. An hour with Nuala O'Faolain on Anglo-Irish poetry flew by. There was never enough time to listen to the richness of her ideas and language.

I did maths too, and calculus re-introduced me to infinity. I remember my excitement just trying to conceive of the idea.

Beatles-rhythmic breezes were sweeping through the checked corridors. Garret Fitzgerald, although he had a big heavy-doored room on the ground floor, was continuously arguing the toss about anything from autocracy to democracy with a bunch of students on the corridor. Mary Finan swept through the foyer in her enormous black hat, and all heads turned at her elegance and freshness. We voted on everything from the President of the College to the length of an essay. The nuns' room was dank, dark, inadequate and stuffy — though the discussions and arguments were anything but. The Library was a haven of order, peace, and bound information to be researched. We did our exams under the sweltering glass roof in the huge RDS.

The college door may have closed behind us, but the door of the mind has been ajar ever since.

Deirdre Carroll

Changing Times

Increasing participation by women in third-level education is a hallmark of the Sixties. In my school class in the Dominican College, Eccles Street, up to one third of my peers entered third-level institutions, a sizeable increase on even the previous year's class. We were the product of the post-war baby boom, of, typically, middle-class urban and rural parents who wanted their daughters to 'do well' — not necessarily (yet) to have life-long careers, but to become educated and upwardly mobile and, ideally, to marry similarly mobile young men from the same educated elite.

That is indeed what many of that generation did, and in the process we surprised both ourselves and our parents by becoming the early flag-bearers of the soon-to-flourish feminist revolution, which would in the decades ahead see changes in occupational structures in areas such as journalism, medicine, law, and the Civil Service.

I say we surprised ourselves, because for many of us in the mid- to late-Sixties the cultural expectations for females were to a great extent unchanged from those of our own mothers. Perhaps it is easiest to illustrate this in my own personal recollections of that time. The 'rewind button' for me is most easily stopped when I recall Earlsfort Terrace — its Reading Room, corridors, Main Hall and Library — and also Newman House and the Iveagh Gardens. Within that geographical space I recall virtually the entire spectrum of my UCD experience: the feminine discourse in the Ladies' Reading Room; the frenzied back-combing of hair; the putting-on of the obligatory pale pink lipstick and black eye liner (the facial uniform of the

Sixties). One listened in to myriad conversations on who was going out with whom, when the next 'big' dress dance was taking place and where, who was 'in' at the L&H, when the next auditions for Dramsoc were taking place, whose name was appearing in the gossip column of the university magazine, and so on. By the second term of the first year, it was quite usual to be 'going steady', and indeed many of these relationships endured through college and beyond. The advent of the mini-skirt and jeans threw Miss P, one of the librarians, into a flap, and one would be upbraided by her for simply lounging against a heater in such attire! This state of affairs was, however, undergoing rapid change, and by 1967–68 a cultural revolution altered previously held values and attitudes.

Letters from the period tell their stories. A letter from my mother while I was in London (1968) contains the following:

> *Another protest yesterday in UCD by the usual crowd led by the usual crowd! This time they attacked the medical profession and the medical students. They were complaining about the high fees being charged by doctors and hospitals etc. D and his friends are very annoyed with these 'hairy mollies' as they have been described.*

A subsequent letter from father:

> *D and eleven other medical students tangled with the rebels in UCD last evening. They found their way barred by the 'sitters in' who tried to intimidate them, and maintaining the old spleen between the Arts and Medical students, referred to them as 'fascist pigs' and 'capitalist spawn' etc. University living in 1969 is a bewildering business!*

Bewildering indeed, and yet many of the societal problems identified at the time are still with us today and continue to evoke passionate debate. In January 1968 at a student conference the topic was 'A Search for Meaning'. A concluding poem read:

The cost we fail to pay
In love and honest courage;
We flinch, we back away,
Kill those we hold the dearest.
And yet we long to soar
Into the sky beyond,
Climb with the sun,
Stand upon the mountain peaks.

That feeling of 'soaring into the sky beyond' is a lasting legacy for me from those heady times.

Una Claffey

Gentle Revolution

I arrived in Earlsfort Terrace in October 1965 to begin my college career as a First Arts student. I didn't really want to be there. I had spent the previous year in the South of France where I did a diploma in French language and literature in Nice. As I had got a good Leaving Cert at age 16, teachers at my school in Beaufort thought it would be a good idea if I studied abroad first. After an initial period of homesickness, caused mainly by ignorance of the language, I had fallen in love with the Côte d'Azur, the French and their lifestyle, the wonderful art galleries, the cut and thrust of French student life — my first exposure to ideological politics. I wanted to continue my studies in Paris. But my parents put the foot down. In their view I was not to be let loose in that cosmopolitan city.

So here I was back in my home town. I knew fewer than a dozen students in UCD. I hated what I perceived to be the smugness of this middle-class institution where virtually all the students had parents who played golf, socialized with each other and were part of a professional network. In 1965 free secondary school education was still a pipe dream, never mind the non-payment of fees at third level. Certainly there were very few printers' daughters in the hallowed halls. I also hated the fact that I didn't know my way around, so much so that on my first day, rather than appear ignorant and ask where the Ladies was, I walked across the Green to the Country Shop, that wonderful establishment of which I was soon to become a devotee. I had yet to become a frequenter of Kirwan's, O'Dwyer's and Hartigan's, the pubs of Leeson Street so beloved of the students of the Terrace. I suppose what really helped me to survive that first year of fundamental alienation was the History Department. To have Hilary Jenkins as a tutor was exciting, to have the support of Sister Benvenuta MacCurtain was wonderful, and to have been present for lectures by Dudley Edwards, Desmond Williams, Donal McCartney, and a very young Art Cosgrove was a privilege. But, confused about what I wanted and torn between socializing and studying, in spite of having a very good academic record up to this, I failed my First Year exams. My parents were horrified and I realized that I needed to pull myself together.

I worked that summer in a canning factory in Norfolk. Maybe it was the pretty grim working conditions that made up my mind, but the following year I threw myself into left-wing politics by joining the Labour Party. Dublin student life was certainly not part of mainstream European political experience. Few students were interested in politics. Both Fianna Fáil and Fine Gael had their small bands of followers. The former tended to be from rural Ireland because of the almost total absence of working-class students, and many had a serious interest in making a career in politics. As for Fine Gael supporters, they just seemed to be born into the party. But there was still very tight control over political activity on the campus and speakers had to be cleared by the College authorities before they could address meetings.

The Terrace was also grossly overcrowded, with library facilities particularly bad, so there were real practical reasons for discontent among a small number of students. And, of course, it was the Sixties. I suppose it was inevitable that the spirit of rebellion sweeping Europe and the US would also infect some of us. I was swept up in the fervour. Life became a whirlwind of meetings, protests and agitation. The Labour Party branch was organized in both Trinity and UCD, and became a powerhouse within the party for radical ideas — much to the irritation of some members of the leadership. But the party too was struggling to change Ireland and these were the heady days of 'The Seventies will be

Socialist'. The Catholic Church too was in the throes of rebellion and that rebellion found its echo in Earlsfort Terrace.

With Basil Millar and Ruairi Quinn I signed a leaflet calling on the student body to march to Trinity in support of students there who were protesting against a visit by the King and Queen of the Belgians. The event took off. Before long UCD was seething with student unrest and the Gentle Revolution was born. It became fashionable to debunk all that went on in earlier halcyon days. A more cynical generation followed, one that was more sensible about education and, more importantly, careers. For me the idea of career was irrelevant. Youthful idealism led us genuinely to believe that we could make the world a better place. Demonstrating in Grosvenor Square against the Vietnam War; in Florence when the Warsaw Pact countries invaded Czechoslovakia; in Vienna when the German revolutionary student, Rudi Dutschke, was shot; taking part in the Burntollet March, not to mention the actions of the Dublin Housing Action Committee: all this created a sense of solidarity which was unique.

And for all that I ended up with just a pass degree in history, politics, and metaphysics. But I wouldn't change any of it. I was lucky in that taking those subjects I was encouraged to question, and benefited greatly from the rigour of Brian Farrell, and the support of men like Dr Patrick Masterson. For those in 'Students for Democratic Action' and other radical organizations, the teach-ins, sit-ins, debates that went on not just for hours but for days, all helped to make us people who said no to a stultifying status quo and, like Oliver Twist, demanded more. For all our protestations at the time, the College actually treated us quite benignly. Far from being punished I got considerable understanding from the academic staff, many of whom, of course, had their own complaints.

Marie Egan-Buffet

Passion Will Out

In the mid-Sixties, young ladies coming up from the country to UCD made the transition from convent to college life via Loreto Hall. There, peering though the flap of the letterbox of the imposing Georgian front door that looked onto St Stephen's Green, Mother Darling (otherwise known as Reverend Mother Eugene) had already screened visiting young UCD gentlemen before they had even rung the doorbell.

Despite its restrictions, the Hall, situated midway between Earlsfort Terrace and Newman House, and possessing a piano in the front parlour that was accessible after the priest's breakfast, was ideal for a music student. The Music Department was housed in Newman House. There, the now famous voices of Bernadette Greevy and Ann Murray already commanded rapt student audiences, notwithstanding a battered upright piano and rattling windowpanes that accompanied the traffic noises coming from the street below. Nor did that same piano conceal the passion in Beethoven's sonatas, or the limpidity of Chopin's nocturnes, at the hands of students such as John O'Conor and Michaeal O'Rourke. It was in the old Aula Maxima that I heard my first symphony concert, the last one to be conducted there by the fiery Tibor Paul. His interpretation of Tchaikovsky's *Romeo and Juliet Overture* remains with me still.

In those days, professors were perceived as awesome figures by most students, but not by the dedicated cleaning lady in Newman House who regularly hailed the Professor of Music from afar with a lusty, 'Mornin', Mistah Hughes'. As we waited for our fugue lecture, greatly impressed, we would watch and listen from the top of the stairs as the professor courteously responded and doffed his hat.

In contrast to the relative intimacy of the Music Department, whose students' recurring nightmare was to be the only one present (out of a possible seven) at the keyboard score-reading class, communications in the French Department were often haphazard and staff–student relations were decidedly remote. It never occurred to me that the professor might even have an office. It was the month of February in my third year before an acquaintance, casually scanning the notice-boards in the foyer of Earlsfort Terrace, noticed that my name featured on a list of prizewinners for Second Year French. Being rather naïve then, I had not realized that in those days nobody bothered to work in Second Year. Perhaps, too, I had not quite recovered from the terror inspired in the First Year female students by the otherwise outstandingly brilliant lecturer Pierre Cognon, to whom I owe eternal gratitude for helping me to bend my mind to the inexorable logic of the French dissertation. I am also indebted to the French Department for pointing me in the direction of postgraduate studies at the Sorbonne, for it was thus that I secured my liberation, far away from Loreto Hall and the all-seeing eyes of Mother Darling.

Olivia O'Leary

Dangerous Enthusiasts

It was so disappointing. I had come from my convent school in Carlow only to find that I had stepped back in time. The convent was run by progressive women, ambitious for their girls. By contrast, UCD in 1966 was as Ruari Quinn has described it: a Catholic boys' academy. Coming from an all-girls school, I was bound to notice how male it all was: the domination of student organizations by the big boys' schools, the absence of any women professors. What startled me though, was how Catholic it was. There were so many priest professors. There was little doubt that His Grace the Archbishop ruled here.

But it wasn't the men, nor indeed the Catholics, who ultimately defeated me. It was the cynicism. It may be that many of the staff despised themselves for accepting an academic regime ruled by John Charles and his henchmen, clerical and lay, and that their loathing extended to the University, to their work, and inevitably to us. Whatever the reason, the cardinal sin, the Cardinal Newman sin in UCD was to take pleasure. English literature was dissected like a body in the morgue. Frozen, it couldn't infect anybody. Miserably, we poked out the innards of seventeenth-century dramatists and nineteenth-century novelists. We didn't stray very far into the twentieth century. Those bodies were a bit too fresh.

When we queried anything, we were referred to F.R. Leavis. I misread the name the first time I saw it and thought he was another priest. In a way he was. His mission was to see that I did not take pleasure in anything I read, but that I search out and if necessary denounce its political purpose. Almost without exception our lecturers referred us to F.R. and Queenie Leavis. It was like digesting great slices of Stalinist suet pudding. It made me feel queasy about literary criticism for years.

There were exceptions to this cynicism, of course. Denis Donoghue's passion for his subject was such that he needed to communicate it, even to us, the scum of the earth. I gather his own view was that he didn't so much lecture, as allow the students to overhear him thinking aloud. Even at that remove he was brilliant. Tom Kilroy was my English tutor for all too short a time. On his first day, he asked us what we thought of a particular set of poems. Trained by now, we regurgitated F.R. Leavis. Yes, he said, but what did *we* think? We were stunned. Nobody ever asked us what we thought. Slowly at first we began to tell him, and by the end of the class he couldn't shut us up. We mourned him when he went to Galway.

There were other dangerous enthusiasts: Mrs Foley and Miss Crowe and Mr Page in the Spanish Department, and in ethics and politics, it was rumoured, a young lecturer called Manning who not only talked to his students but bought them pints. But like all students, I had in my mind an ideal of what a university professor should be: inspiring, benevolent, despotic. There was only one person who fitted that bill: Anthony Hughes, the Professor of Music. In this temple of turgid talk, here was a man who could talk and play and often did both at the same time, or sang a descant over the piano in order to give us a better idea of a choral piece while at the same time banging out a percussion line with his foot. He didn't mind busking if that was what it took to help us grasp the shape of a piece. He just lived the music.

He was also a fine concert performer. He had given a recital in our school, and while he rehearsed in the afternoon my music teacher sneaked me in at the back to listen as he practised difficult parts of a Beethoven sonata. 'Now', she whispered fiercely, 'do you believe me? Even concert pianists have to practise the awkward parts over and over again.' I was impressed.

He'd gone to university on a scholarship, as I did, and he was unapologetically a Dub. I wasn't a music student but I used to go to his extra-curricular lectures in the evening. He talked about musical form, about the way symphonies and concerti were shaped. Every so often, he'd abandon the tape recorder, write up themes and variations on the blackboard and then sing them himself, talking and singing us through the plan of the music. Every so often he'd stop and laugh at himself, but otherwise, he was quite unselfconscious. It was the music that mattered.

I was in his choir, the UCD Choir. He spent hours with us. He knew us all by name. 'What will you do when you leave college, Olivia?' he asked me one day. I told him I wanted to be a journalist, maybe for the *Irish Times*. 'Ah, what'ja want to write for that rag for?' he muttered. I didn't know then that relations between the *Irish Times* music critic and Professor Hughes were not the warmest.

We sang Mozart — he loved Mozart. We sang Bach. We sang Carl Orff. The Christmas Carol concert was always packed to the doors of the Aula Maxima. And everything happened — rehearsals and socials and concerts — in Newman House. Maybe that was partly why I enjoyed it all so much. Unlike the echoing wastes of Earlsfort Terrace, 86 St Stephen's Green was its own little world, shabby and elegant, with the downstairs canteen leading out to Iveagh Gardens. We made endless daisy chains there in the summer term, looking up into the offices of the Department of Foreign Affairs, swearing that whatever else we did, we'd never become civil servants.

When the Gentle Revolution came in 1969, we all joined in. It was my final year and, as a scholarship girl, I had one shot at my Finals, but this was more important. The College authorities and most of the senior staff behaved as though we didn't exist, and junior staff weren't treated much better. We had no representation on the Governing Body. A full church had been built for the move to Belfield that autumn but our educational or other living requirements were ignored. The libraries weren't finished and there was no talk at all of student residences.

These were my concerns. Broadening our agenda to wider social issues was fine, but the workers with whom we were desperate to declare solidarity gave us short shrift. They regarded us as patronizing gits, and I don't blame them. When I expressed my impatience with political grandstanding, our French tutor, herself a veteran of the previous year's Sorbonne riots and therefore with Us and not with Them, replied, '*Mais, la politique, c'est tout.*'

I thought she was being a bit drastic myself, but in any case, we did the sit-ins in the Great Hall and boycotted lectures and brought the place to a halt. When word came in that the UCD Choir was to rehearse for the Easter concert, some of us decided to go and explain why it couldn't go ahead. The Music Department was a little other-worldly at the best of times and just needed to be put in the picture. We mounted the stage in the Aula Max and from our choir positions asked politely that the rehearsal be cancelled. Professor Hughes cut us short. No explanations, he said. Choose. Stay for the rehearsal or go now. Most stayed. The rest of us clattered noisily down off the stage. One or two muttered fiery-sounding things. I just walked miserably to the end of the hall and looked around. Tony Hughes was standing, his back rigid with irritation, impatient for us to be gone.

In a moment, I was heading along Stephen's Green to the Terrace and that night's demonstration. In front of me, Final exams and my first job. Behind me, the friends, the music, and the only part of college life that I had ever really enjoyed. But there was no other choice.

As the woman said: *La politique, c'est tout.*

Dolores MacKenna

A Rich Landscape

My relationship with UCD lasted through three decades. I first entered Earlsfort Terrace as an evening student, that strange species which appeared on the scene at a time when the academic sun had set for a majority of the college. This was the late 1960s and although student revolution was in the air, it did not greatly affect the subculture to which we belonged. Some of us younger ones joined in the demonstrations and sit-ins which were so much part of the times, but on the whole we were interested spectators rather than participants.

Those of us who were in the same age group as the regular students mingled easily in the corridors and libraries. Tired, middle-aged faces could easily be spotted as they passed through the throngs of youngsters leaving for homes, flats, digs or pubs. It was as if the baton were being passed between the two groups in the great academic relay race. Occasionally, retired people ambled in, ready to fulfil long delayed ambitions to study at university. They chatted confidently with lecturers half their age and offered rich experiences at tutorials. I remember listening with fascination as one lady told of her acquaintance with W.B. Yeats. Her reminiscences probably did as much to excite my interest in the poet as did the lectures I attended or the works of criticism I consulted.

Apart from a significant number of primary teachers, most of the evening students worked in offices. They came from insurance companies, banks, and from the Civil Service. There were more men than women. I remember very few housewives. I believe that in order to be admitted to the night course it was necessary to prove that one had a full-time job and therefore was not available to attend college during the day. It is likely that in the late 1960s home making and child rearing were not considered to be full-time employment.

The number of subjects available to evening students was limited. I was fortunate that my areas of interest were well catered for. Even the most senior faculty members stayed late to teach us, and since we had fewer lectures than our counterparts whom they taught during the day, it seemed as if we were treated to their distilled wisdom. Many went out of their way to help. In my first year, when the English Department did not offer tutorials, Gus Martin invited anyone interested to attend his Saturday morning sessions. I was one who availed of his generosity. The following year we all had tutorials.

I graduated on the day after the first men landed on the moon. My younger brother, who had stayed up to watch the event on television, slept through the ceremony. He looks pale and bleary-eyed in the family photographs of the occasion — possibly the way I had often looked as I left the Great Hall at 11 p.m., having read until the sound of the porter's handbell announced the closing of the building. But I don't recall the weariness, although I must have felt it. Instead I remember joining societies, making nervous contributions to the L&H, campaigning against the destruction of Hume Street, dancing at the SRC, the Vets, and the Ags.

I left UCD to begin teaching in a secondary school in the early 1970s. Already some faculties had moved to the new campus at Belfield. To those of us who were used to the city centre, it seemed a remote location, with the atmosphere of a building site. When I decided to pursue postgraduate studies there in the 1980s, I found a different world — busy, modern, cosmopolitan. Once again I felt a little removed from the mainstream, a relic from another time. Now, however, I was the one who had time enough to browse through the rare book collection, to attend lunchtime theatre, to listen to visiting lecturers — and I like to think that I had the maturity to appreciate the experience. I spent four exceptionally happy years at Belfield, taking a rather circuitous route from a B.A. General, then the only arts degree awarded to evening students, to a Ph.D. in English. It was a road of many twists and turns, but through a rich landscape.

Frequently as I sit in the audience of the National Concert Hall, the sound of a bell in the orchestra brings me back to those late nights of reading, when the sound of the porter's handbell echoing through the corridors announced the end of a long day. Even allowing for the unreliability of memory and the clouds of nostalgia, it seems from this vantage point that the late 1960s in Earlsfort Terrace were days of tremendous optimism. Everything, it seemed to us, was about to change — and we presumed that it would be for the better. An old poem, newly learned, captures the moment:

> Bliss was it in that dawn to be alive,
> But to be young was very Heaven!
> (*The Prelude*, XI, 108—9)

Perdita Quinlan (Gusken)

Coming in from the Cold

Belfield 1968–69 was a lonely place. The Commerce Faculty was the first to move out to the new campus. We had spent one year as undergraduates in Earlsfort Terrace and had got to like the city location, the Women's Common Room with its big welcoming fire, the old-fashioned Dining Room in 86, O' Dwyer's pub and the Country Shop. Suddenly there was nothing and nobody. In commerce we had only about sixteen females and several of those were nuns. We did not have the girls from arts or social science to socialize with. Facilities were modern but initially limited. There was no campus feeling.

There were big changes throughout my three years and the most significant was the overturning of the 'No Trousers' rule. One day in the autumn of 1967 all the women wore trousers and that sorted out that problem. Teaching was excellent, with Garrett Fitzgerald, Brian O'Connor, Maurice Kennedy, Helen O'Neill, Pearse Colbert, and Des Hally all leaving a lasting impression.

I graduated and married a fellow commerce student in University Church with Fr Vincent Keaveney officiating. I had four daughters in a relatively short period of time and three of them are now UCD graduates. Luckily, I got the chance to come back to the Belfield campus to study for a Diploma in Career Guidance. A much more settled campus, warm, progressive, and very pleasant.

Áine Gallagher

The Terrace Years

My years at UCD were from 1968–75. The pre-medical year then was spent on the Belfield campus. It passed almost in a haze, and apart from making friends with a few science students and realizing that studies at college required a slightly different orientation from those of school, the year was unremarkable. However, one never forgot Dr Mabel Kane's 'presence', or Dr Tony Scott's lectures.

When you moved to the 'Terrace' — as it was known then — you felt at last that you were a real medical student. My parents were enormously pleased to have one of their five daughters studying medicine, and Mum on many occasions reminded me of how fortunate I was to have this opportunity, as she had never been given the chance, her parents being of the opinion that a woman's place was in the home, married and with a family.

A lot of hard work was done during the pre-clinical years in the Terrace. We were largely then under the capable supervision of Professors Murnaghan and Breathnach, as physiology was the all-important subject. The Coffey Library on many an evening was the place for long conversations and discussions, both inside and outside the main door.

The College itself was starting to undergo change then; the lovely, cozy Coffey Library was altered beyond recognition and turned into a barn-like structure with endless stairs and poor lighting. It had a large central atrium and was altogether quite draughty, and dizzying in its effect. The main entrance and the Main Hall were cut off from the College and were later to become the National Concert Hall — a very fine piece of work. However, the greatest intrusion of all was the loss of the Ladies' Reading

Room, with its lovely coal fires and daily newspaper on supply; one had now to suffer and share this with the opposite sex!

It was during these pre-clinical Terrace years that I met Nance O'Connell (nee Hyland). She was a UCD arts graduate of the 1920s. She had won a scholarship to college and always remained immensely proud of this. Her subjects were French and history, and it was in the latter that we shared a deep interest, for I was an honours history student at school and already had a firmly established love for the subject. UCD's first Rector, Cardinal John Henry Newman, was her particular interest. As a result of our frequent conversations about him at that time, Newman House was especially significant to me. Sausages and chips, coupled with great tea-time chats on cold winter evenings in the dining room, then upstairs afterwards for some meeting or other; to see and appreciate the work of the Lafranchini brothers along the stairway; to be aware that this was once an elegant Georgian home that you were now passing through, and to be familiar with its history: there were times when you were in awe of it all as you looked on up and up the stairwell to the very top.

The run-up to exams in the summer term enabled us to spend some time in Iveagh Gardens, often in small groups, to undertake revision. The warmth of the sun on your back, to be able to breathe the fresh air and to be out of the stuffy lecture theatres for even a short time was wonderful. The fountains and the statuary, some of them headless and others with bits of limbs missing, gave an air of antiquity to the gardens on occasion; at other times it was positively continental. During lunchtime on a fine day the gardens were usually packed with people and it was not unusual to see bodies strewn — in different sorts of positions, one might add — all over the lawns. These were wonderful days with good times. Sadly they were all coming to a close. During the clinical years that followed one was led into the arena; during the Intern year one finally met with the lions!

I remember my UCD Terrace days with fondness and happiness. The medical teaching brought us on quite a bit, but years later one appreciated how basic this all was, for it was not simply with regard to the medical content of one's studies that UCD played such an important role; it also gave the opportunity for the development and broadening of the intellect, added a cultural dimension, and enabled the seeing of and participating in, not only UCD, but Irish history. These were the aspects of UCD life that made it rewarding. Of the friends that one made during those years many are in practice here in this country and others are scattered around the world.

Sir William Osler on talking to medical students about the foundations of habits for life recommended the following:

- to work and to be able to enjoy it
- the art of detachment
- the virtue of method
- the quality of thoroughness
- the grace of humility

Many of us had most of these qualities during our 'Terrace' days.

The 1970s

If any decade can be called the decade of the terrorist, then surely it is the Seventies. The opening years of the decade saw the introduction of internment in Northern Ireland and an escalation of violence. Bloody Sunday in January 1972, when 13 people were killed by British Army, was followed in July of that same year by Bloody Friday, when 26 IRA bombs in Belfast killed 11 and injured many more. This was the scale of the violence throughout the following years, nor was it confined to the North; there were bombs in Dublin, Guilford, and Birmingham in 1974, and at Dublin Airport in 1975.

Terrorism played a leading role on the wider stage also. The 1972 Olympics in Munich are remembered more for the taking and killing of Israeli hostages by Arab guerrillas than for any sporting achievements. Hostage-taking was a major feature of the later years both at home and abroad. In 1975 we prayed at school for the safe release of Dutch businessman, Tiede Herrema, held for prisoner releases. The prayers were answered; the kidnappers surrendered after a month and released their captive unharmed. Not so fortunate were Aldo Moro, killed by the Red Brigade in Italy in 1978, or Lord Mountbatten, killed by the IRA off the coast of Sligo in 1979. In 1976 Israelis freed hostages in a raid on Entebbe. Three years later, in November 1979, one hundred US Embassy staff were held in Tehran.

Two visits that made headlines in the Seventies were Nixon's historic visit to China in 1972 and, in 1979, Pope John Paul II's visit to Ireland. In the middle of the decade unemployment was at its highest point ever in the Republic. However, there was some progress on other fronts. The women's movement had become active in the early years. Thanks in large part to its efforts, the Supreme Court declared in 1973 that the ban on contraception was unconstitutional; two years later it ruled that the exemptions of women from jury service and the property qualification were equally so.

On a lighter front, we sang along to the pearly-toothed Osmonds, the Jackson Five, the Bay City Rollers, Slade. There was Abba too, but it was not until they were re-discovered some twenty or so years later that one could comfortably admit to ever having liked them in the first place. The now-disgraced Gary Glitter asked then did we want to be in his gang, his gang, his gang, and Bowie in the guise of Ziggy Stardust lit the torch for the gender-benders who would follow in the Eighties. We wore dangerously high platforms (though never as high as Elton John's); we wore clogs; we wore flares (which, to be credible, had to cover said platforms or clogs completely); we wore tank tops and cheesecloth; we put studs in everything — shoes, shirts, jackets, jeans, bags, (though not our bodies). In short, we laid the foundation for what look set to be the most embarrassing photo albums of all time.

Looking back with the benefit of hindsight, and taking into account what the dominant themes of the decade seem to have been, perhaps we might suppose that in those tartan braces and that glam rock lamé, we got something we needed at the time.

Anne Macdona

1974   Nixon resigns following Watergate scandal.
1975   Death of Eamon de Valera.
        End of Vietnam War.
        End of internment.
1976   Riots in Soweto.
1979   Margaret Thatcher becomes first woman Prime
            Minister in Britain.

Éilís Ní Dhuibhne

Reader, I Married Him

I came to Belfield in October 1971. What sort of a day was it? Cloudy, I think, but not raining, as I walked up the avenue from the Clonskeagh gate, through the wide, bare football pitches. The shrubs and trees that soften the edges of the avenue now were saplings then, skinny skeletons swaying in the breeze, young and raw, like a lot of things in Belfield. I was wearing a long, white, shiny plastic raincoat, over a long brown skirt and sweater. This was the year of the maxi. All over Belfield, young women in skirts that swept the tiles were scattered like relics of another century among other girls in bell-bottom trousers and tight, scratchy Shetland jumpers in red or green or yellow. What did the boys wear? Jeans and a shirt.

I spent the first day wandering around the upper corridors with a friend, trying to locate rooms called J207 or G319, where lecturers sat behind tables and advised students on which subjects to do, promoting their own. I don't know why we did this since we had already decided, more or less, which subjects we would take. But it was only more or less. And we had until registration day, which seemed ages distant, to make up our minds.

I chose English, which I had always loved and had been planning to do for years. For my second subject I selected philosophy, because I admired a young man who talked a lot about Sartre. And for my third I chose history, because you had to choose a third. Thus I picked the three most popular, over-subscribed subjects in the university. The lecture theatres, when we finally got to them a few days after our first day in college, were packed to the rafters. The lecturer was a minute, gowned figure, half hidden by the lectern, standing far beneath the ranged ranks of students, like a tiny Christian surrounded by about three hundred young lions. It was a situation that created anonymity, but also gave one, as a student, a great sense of power and freedom, deriving from the knowledge that one belonged to the enormous hoard of young, beautiful people. I would love to recapture that feeling, the feeling that life was finally starting, that the world was waiting to be discovered; it was opening out before one, full of delightful possibilities, and starting the same journey were all these hundreds of other people aged seventeen or eighteen. It was almost too good to be true. Maybe that is why everyone counteracted the unbelievably good feeling by complaining, unremittingly, about Belfield. Professing to despise it was de rigueur. It was too new. It was too ugly. It was too far from town. The food was dreadful.

I went along with the complaining although in fact I knew it was marvellous — especially the food, which was much, much better than anything I had got before, particularly during the working day (lunch at Irish schools then, as now, consisting of a sandwich in a plastic box, tasting mainly of plastic box). The campus was undoubtedly not Earlsfort Terrace, but it was beautiful. In those days, much less of it was built upon and there were woods near Fosters Avenue, lovely walled gardens somewhere up in that direction, and a pitch and putt course. It was full of secret places. The architecture of the Arts Block was always obviously stunning on the outside, if a bit bleak within. I loved from the start the flat-roofed, stacked, house-of-cards effect. Surely the Arts Block is among the finer modern buildings of Dublin?

All was not perfect, however. There were disappointments. I had looked forward to college as a place where my soul would sing. I thought I would become Simone de Beauvoir, sit up all night with other students discussing literature and philosophy, with passion and increased learning. A life of intoxicating intellectual liveliness was what I had believed awaited me in college. But alas it did not seem to be there. There were friends aplenty, but we sat in the canteen and discussed clothes, or who was going with whom, or who was a good or a dull lecturer. The conversation never leaped off the ground into the realms I believed a university should inhabit, and I was not the one to take this flying leap to the dreaming spires unaided. Even in tutorials, most students seemed content to sit in subdued silence, while the unfortunate tutor tried to drag out the hour. In school, I had been used to vigorous debate, especially during English class. But in Belfield debate was seldom lively except at the L&H on Friday nights, and then it was conducted by terribly clever young men with very posh accents — past pupils, almost invariably, of Blackrock College or Gonzaga or Clongowes. I can only remember one girl who ever made speeches, and perhaps she was already leaving college as I began. That was Eithne Fitzgerald, a past pupil of my own old school, actually. I remember her pulling a rabbit out of a hat. Can she actually have done this or have I imagined it?

In Second Year, I became a student of Pure English, and a member of the intriguingly named 'Group Four'. This meant belonging to a class of eight rather than three hundred, and attending 'lectures' in small rooms, with life-size lecturers who would quickly get to know your name, and notice whether you attended or not. It meant a lot of translation from Old and Middle English — real disciplined work, in a way, for one who had had a year of fairly free thinking. There were several kind and good teachers, but the star was Terry Dolan, with his deadpan humour and stock of aphorisms. '*Denarius delapsus est*' [the penny has dropped] was a phrase he used when a dim student (usually me) finally managed to understand some obscure or perhaps elementary scrap of the strange texts he specialized in — *Ancrene Wisse*, or the *Agenbite of Inwit*. It is to his eternal credit that he managed to persuade eighteen-year-olds to believe that *The Rule of Anchoresses* was an exciting text. My favourite Terry Dolan gem was the distinction between allegory and symbol: a man running after a departing bus is an allegorical representation of CIE; a symbol for CIE could be a broken wheel.

Halfway through Second Year the most important intellectual and personal choice of my life occurred. I selected as an optional course, from a range of delectable optional courses (which always seem much more interesting than the compulsory ones), a course on 'The Folktale and Medieval Literature'. This was offered by the new Professor of Irish Folklore, Bo Almqvist — an exotic Scandinavian whose claim to fame was that he could actually speak Irish.

The course involved visiting a new part of Belfield, a part as secret, mysterious and astonishing to me as the walled gardens full of delphiniums and peonies and rambling roses. The Department of Irish Folklore was, and is, tucked into the corner of the Arts Block that you pass through on your way to the car park — if you have a car. (As a Second Year student, it was not, then at least, a part you frequented very much.) Behind the smoked glass door was a place unlike any other in the Belfield interior. A cul-de-sac corridor, the walls packed with old rich paintings. A small, cozy library the colour of ripe corn, with a long polished table where students could sit and read in the afternoon sun. Somehow that department managed to look mellow and gracefully old, even in the earliest days of Belfield. It was a place both magical and nurturing. I felt at home there as I could not anywhere else on the big bustling campus.

The subject too was a revelation. I realized that finally I was getting close to where I had wanted to be when I decided, as an idealistic sixteen-year-old, that I would study English because I wanted to know everything about literature. In studying folktales and their connection with medieval literature, I felt I was finally finding out where the roots of the whole enterprise lay. These stories were the precursors of the novel, of the short story, of the plays that we analyzed in the big lecture halls. And the great thing was that this seemed to be a secret. My classmates and I were initiated into a select fellowship of scholars, the folklorists, who know things about literature and life that few others know.

Bo Almqvist was clearly passionate about his subject, and he taught it seriously. He treated us as scholars. 'In scholarship, girls,' he said once, after we had turned in essays of the impressionistic, fanciful kind which were fairly standard stock in English, 'there are no short cuts.' I was tremendously impressed. I had never heard anyone even use the word 'scholarship' before. But folklore *was* about being scholarly. Undergraduate students read manuscript material that in many cases had probably never been studied, or even read, before. We had contact, for the first time ever, with primary sources, and we learned to treat them with respect. Folklore, as taught by Bo, involved a novel mixture of lucid, almost scientific discipline, and the heady content of the stories one investigated.

As a result of my fascination with this subject, I remained in Belfield after my B.A. to take an M.Phil, which allowed me, thanks to its interdisciplinary approach, to combine Middle English with Folklore and to specialize in the latter. Following that, I worked on a doctorate in the same area, which I completed towards the end of 1981.

Thus ended ten years as a student in Belfield. In 1982 I married Bo Almqvist and so have maintained an involvement with the College. Next year, I hope this involvement will take a new form, if our son's hopes are fulfilled and he sets off to Belfield, autumn 2001, exactly thirty years after I first set foot there.

Bernadette Glenn

It's a Learning Thing, Man

When I left home to go to 'Uni' one day in October 1975, I only had to tromp in my black platform boots down the road to Ranelagh. There, slouched with gangs of other smoking, long-haired, bell-bottomed students, I waited at the bus stop with my friend Cora for the 11B to take us out to Belfield. In my mind Belfield was going to be another — though much more modern — form of Trinity (where I would secretly have loved to have gone). But in 1975 that was still a step too far for my imagination, never mind my qualifications. Of course my desire to go to Trinity (or any college for that matter) had little to do with academic aspirations and everything to do with the idea of wafting into town for lectures in ancient historic buildings, and strolling through cobbled squares. The rest of the day would be spent hanging out in Bewley's with fellow students, smoking and stuffing ourselves with cherry buns while viewing the 'talent'. In this dream world we would then retire to our Trinity rooms in the evenings where we would study a little and discuss life while consuming pleasant quantities of wine. I knew Belfield didn't have rooms and it was newer, but I had high hopes of its being a diverting place nonetheless.

Neither Cora nor I had ever been to the Belfield campus before, in spite of living only a few miles from it — I suppose it hadn't ever dawned on us to visit it — but we did know where to get the bus; it was impossible not to, growing up as we did in 'flatland', as Rathmines was then known, a place swarming with students who occupied dingy flats and squalid bedsits.

Now we had joined the ranks of those same students at the bus stop but we studiously avoided eye contact with them for fear of looking new and needy and lost. Especially since we were from Dublin, sophisticates as far as we were concerned, surrounded by 'culchies'. But most of these looked so cool and together; they all seemed to know each other and they were laughing and sprinkling the air with *man*'s and *right on*'s and lots of references to 'the States'. Not only that but most of them were away from home, really living the life, whereas we were expected home to Rathmines for our tea.

Suddenly I felt like we were off to kindergarten, like Cora and I should be holding hands waiting for the bus to take us to 'big school'. So much for my heavily-applied Kohl eyeliner and tasselled velvet bag, intended to serve as armour against these 'first day nerves'. Who did we think we were anyway? Particularly me, since I'd done badly at school. Convinced I was going to fail my Leaving, my mother had tried to talk me into becoming an air hostess. But I'd held out for the Holy Grail; I knew I wanted the life of an arts student. Miraculously I managed to scrape together the few miserable points then needed to squeak into arts at Belfield. What I was actually going to do there wasn't clear, certainly academically — something in English, I thought. Notions of drama societies and student politics and T. S. Eliot soul-mates wafted in the brain. Cora, on the other hand, was a real student, had done brilliantly in her exams and was going to study science. But for both of us 'Uni' was the land of freedom, 'fine things' and who knew what else?

Now that I was being confronted by the reality, however, I was suddenly nervous that I wasn't going to live up to the experience. Before there was enough time to terrify myself into running home, the 11B arrived. It took us in the opposite direction to the city centre, through red-bricked Ranelagh and into the pebble-dashed suburban outpost of Clonskeagh. As the bus drove us through the college gates and down the long, barren Belfield drive, we were surrounded on both sides by empty fields. The only structure was a tall, grey water tower that looked like an overgrown baptismal font. From upstairs in the bus we could see a few miserable saplings planted along the driveway bending away from the relentless damp wind. Further down the drive the bus passed several determined riders, standing on their bike pedals fighting the hurricane force. 'You're not going to catch me doing that!' I whispered to Cora. There was no way I was going to arrive into college with my fur coat matted with rain and my maxi skirt covered in bike oil.

At the end of the driveway, we stood up and got off the bus en masse. This was it. No cobbles, no ivy-covered halls, no rarefied atmosphere. We dashed for the shelter of the covered walkway as we were assaulted by the wind and the driving rain. I remember noticing with surprise a small prefabricated octagonal building with a cross on top, and thinking, 'A church? — Isn't that one of the things we've come here precisely to get away from?' I decided it must be for elderly staff, as no self-respecting student could even think of being caught in there, surely?

But where to now? The last thing we could do was to ask any of the cool dudes we found ourselves blindly following. I suddenly felt homesick. 'I'll follow the anoraks,' Cora whispered, 'it looks like the cool ones are heading for arts.' I saw her disappear in her beaverskin coat as she merged with the throng turning left into the green monstrosity that was the science building. Friendless now, I was going to have to find my own way through this grey, bleak place to the Arts Block.

Nothing I saw as I tramped after the arts crowd into the heart of the campus lifted my spirits. First we passed a murky pond on the left that was lined with concrete steps and was overlooked on the right by a two-storeyed, concrete-slatted building. A sign read 'Library'. Finally, the group I was following began mounting the steps to the right into another grey concrete building. The sign here read 'Arts and Commerce'. My base for the next three years.

In the interior of this building things looked as though they were inside out. Internally, the arts building was even darker and greyer than it was on the outside. The only windows looked out onto a tiny, closed courtyard that was open to the sky and filled with plants. Otherwise no natural light penetrated the gloom. Industrial lights lit the corridors, which, with their cavernous cement walls, offered as much ambience as a bicycle shed. My heart sank. So much for romance, intrigue, or poetry in such a place.

And then a small, curly-headed young woman moved towards me in the gloom and said in a strong Northern accent, 'Excuse me, could you tell me where you register for the English Department?'

I was saved.

Catherine O'Callaghan

If at First You Don't Succeed ...

I qualified with the class of '78, M.B., B.Ch., B.A.O., but I started with the class of '77. I had to repeat First Year Med. One of my fondest memories of UCD and Earlsfort Terrace is the day that I discovered I would be staying back.

I'm sure things have changed now. In 1972, First Med was anatomy, physiology, and microbiology. In the summer exams I failed physiology and microbiology and had to repeat both in the autumn. To help us 'Repeats', as we were known, Doc Daly, our physiology tutor, who was a character and a decent man, gave us tutorials in the summer holidays. I was one of his weakest students. He struggled with me, and coaxed me, and was determined to get me through.

On the day of the results, before they were pinned on the notice-board in the Great Hall, he came out of the Physiology Office, put his arm around me and said, 'You've done it, you've passed physiology!'

I couldn't believe it and replied, 'I hope I haven't failed micro now!'

He said, 'Not at all, only one stupid fool failed micro.'

We looked at the lists together. There was only one name missing from the micro list — mine. He had said it all; he hung his head and walked away.

I always think of Doc Daly very fondly and I wish he could see me now. He would be proud that I made it eventually!

Marie Altzinger

Locker Room Romance

Boys. You didn't admit it of course. And it wasn't the main reason. But as someone recently catapulted from a convent school where the principal concern was how to cross your ankles in polite society, the unisex aspect of Belfield was a distinct advantage. Warning bells should have rung when an older and much wiser female student laughed at the idea that you'd easily find a partner to take to the Debs. No problem, you insisted. Within the first week. Or the second at worst. Two months later the Debs came — and went. You skipped it. Ridiculously expensive. Wouldn't be bothered. Nothing to do with boys. Or absence of same.

Your choice of subjects was partly responsible. History was fifty-fifty male/female, but huge. German and Italian were small and intimate but ninety-nine per cent female. History provided the initial academic shock. The day you were assigned your first history essay and you stayed back after the tutorial. The tutor, whose sherry-coloured eyes exactly matched his jacket, asked politely if there was a problem. You're darned right there was. What books should you read? Four little words struck instant terror. Go to the Library. Had he seen the Library? It took six attempts to make it past the barrier. You missed the history students' Library tour because you had a German lecture. You missed the Language students' Library tour because you had a history lecture. There was only one thing for it. You became a librarian.

But that was much later. Your memories of First Year are by far the most vivid. Jammed theatres, filling jumbo pads, playing noughts and crosses with the student in front. Itching to add your artwork to the graffiti on the desk. Wondering why your new hip friend was spending an age in the toilet only to discover she'd been compelled to air her political views on the wall of the cubicle. (In pencil, so it didn't count.) Mobbing a packed restaurant in the days when 'Finnegan's Break' was a Joycean misquote not a campus coffee shop, and nobody thought to provide facilities for homemade lunches. Watching what the chefs ate so you knew what was safe. It was where you developed the dangerous habit of taking chips from friends' plates as you queued together at the cash desk, which to this day causes problems with strangers in Bewley's. It was where you learned the art of folding paper aeroplanes and firing them with absolute precision from the back row at the L&H. Where you realized that school debating had nothing in common with its college cousin, and that the *Feis* was no preparation for Dramsoc.

The good news was that the boy problem eventually resolved itself, proving the theory that all things come if you are willing to wait. Or forced to. It was a locker romance. His next to yours. The numbers forever chiselled into your brain: 830 and 831. Any excuse to go downstairs. Change your shoes, change your coat (no, you had only the one that was shapeless enough to be worthy of college). Pile books into the locker, ten at a time because you'd learned how to beat the Library's trap system. (They changed it and you never managed to figure out the new one). Take out books again. Still no sign of him. Or was Wednesday his day off? Your female friends rallied gallantly and after a stint of espionage worthy of the KGB you at last became one of the gang. His gang. Heaven on earth. And a radically changed lifestyle.

Goethe and Schiller abandoned in favour of lingering walks around the lake and romantic forays into the hinterland near the tennis courts and the 'Taj Mahal'. Sitting by the running tracks with his stopwatch, knowing that you too should be taking exercise but deciding to think about it tomorrow. Cheering at the restaurant window whenever the phantom 17 bus chugged past.

Dashing back to grab your belongings from the Library in time for the lift home only to discover that you'd exceeded the '15 minute absence' rule by about three hours of dossing, and the diligent student who'd usurped your place had mixed your French Revolution notes with hundreds of pages on Cretan archaeology.

Exams loomed on the horizon. You baked in the RDS, forgot who Parnell was, and muddled your German and Italian past tenses. You went to Hamburg for the summer and brought a trunk full of books because it was common knowledge that sixty per cent of First Year History students had to repeat in the autumn. Otherwise what was the opening lecture all about? The 'Look at the person on either side of you. This time next year, only one of you will still be here' warning. You proved them wrong. You made it to Second Year.

And so the years rolled by. You became so attached to UCD that you did a second degree — and two diplomas. Then you decided to join the staff. And even after you left to pursue a grasshopper career, the pull was so strong that you still spend time in the Library. As an external reader you can borrow six books. But there's still no way around trap.

You're old enough now to be the mother of an undergraduate. You think nobody notices until you peer at your mirror reflection in the Ladies and realize that no amount of anti-wrinkle cream provides adequate coverage for crows' feet. The girl elbowing you aside to apply deep purple lipstick has skin as smooth as a baby's. And she's about to submit her Ph.D.

You once told your mother that UCD was the happiest time of your life. She said it didn't show. Maybe it didn't. But it was. And your husband agrees, although he's forgotten the locker numbers.

The 1980s

The writing was on the wall for the 1980s when a number of UCD social science undergraduates (Class of '86) made a short film entitled *We're on the Road to Nowhere*. It was a difficult time in Ireland. Unemployment had risen to levels previously associated with the 1950s. Emigration was the single option available to thousands of graduates. 'Immigration' was a form you filled out in the American Embassy. Asylum was vaguely associated with issues of mental health. The Refugees were a rock band from Carlow.

This was the decade that brought us shoulder pads and leggings, Spandau Ballet and Nik Kershaw, Political Correctness and AIDS. Quite a line-up.

Full-time politician and part-time UCD lecturer, Maurice Manning, instructed a politics class to write a paper on Northern Ireland under the title, 'The Problem Is that There Is No Solution'. This was the prevailing attitude. And there was no solution.

Amid all this doom and gloom, amid the arrival of the microchip, and the continuing destruction of Dublin, amid a sea of cynicism, life went on at UCD. Belfield was not yet the sylvan campus it has become in the intervening years. Grey was the dominant colour and the dominant mood. The campus was still architecturally suspicious of its transient occupants and provided few suitable focal points for informal meeting and gathering. It is surely no small irony that the Arts Block 'Wall' became a forum for spontaneous social interaction. The image of the wall is central to any overall vision of the 1980s, as brought to us by Pink Floyd, the RUC, and Berlin. Students sat on 'The Wall', or further down the overheated Arts Block corridor on long, low, uncomfortable benches, blissfully unaware that these benches were in fact tables. The scene was appropriately reminiscent of the waiting room at a railway station somewhere in Eastern Europe.

Significantly, the transfer of the Belfield Bar from the original wooden prefab building to its current location represented one of the highlights of the decade for UCD students as well as for the brewing companies of Ireland.

Another central episode in Belfield life during the 1980s was the election of Ulick Stafford as President of the Student's Union. What began as an in-joke among a handful of engineering students snowballed into a national news item. That a relatively unknown, non-political, unambitious and completely inexperienced individual could become the official representative of 10,000 students after a zero-budget campaign lasting just a few weeks showed that all was not entirely lost at UCD. This was 'people power' Belfield-style. The 1980s generation was sending a message. The precise meaning of the message is as yet unclear. But there were signs of life.

Not a lot happened in the 1980s, though quite a lot was about to happen. Environmental questions were beginning to be raised. Food safety issues were tentatively discussed. Ireland's role in Europe was changing. The J1 visa programme was enabling students to travel and experience other cultures and lifestyles. In retrospect, it can be seen to have been a time of relatively calm preparation for the revitalizing storm that was to follow in the 1990s.

Nicola Carroll

1980	John Lennon shot dead in New York.
1981	Forty-eight people die in Stardust dance-hall fire in Dublin.
	Death of hunger-striker, Bobby Sands.
1985	Bob Geldof and Live Aid 'feed the world'.
1986	Chernobyl nuclear power station disaster.
1989	Berlin Wall torn down.

Suzanne Egan

Have J1, Will Travel

I studied law at UCD from 1983 to 1986, and have worked as a lecturer in the Faculty of Law since 1992. It has been an ongoing process for me to compare college life in the 1980s to college life thereafter. At first glance a snapshot of UCD in the 1980s may not appear to be all that different to a snapshot of UCD in the millennium. The fashions have changed and so have the numbers, but the overall impression seems to be the same: corridors full of happy or sometimes hassled-looking students making their way to and from lectures, or hanging out at the various leisure spots offered by the College — the main restaurant, the bar, and even the famous 'Wall' in the Arts Block. A visit to the Library even seems like a déjà vu experience, save for the fact that mounds of rucksacks no longer guide one's path to the Library entrance the way they used to, and there were no notices twenty years ago asking us to turn off mobile phones. But when you scratch the surface of time just that little bit more, some particular memories spring to mind which are unique to the Eighties generation.

Take, for example, the emotional wrench caused to many students by the closing of the old Belfield Bar, located then opposite the main college restaurant. There was no doubt but that that bar was on its last legs by the time it served its last refreshments. But its frayed and torn brown vinyl seats had a charm and character of their own that was hard for the brand new McDonalds-like structure that came in its stead to replace. And despite being enhanced by a bit of a facelift since the 1980s, the college restaurant has lost one vital ingredient: that is, the familiar sound of Alice, heralding us with a cry of, 'Trays, please! Trays, please!' while simultaneously heaving students from 'tables' that were indistinguishable from the 'chairs' on the middle floor of the restaurant, save to her omniscient eye.

From my own perspective of that time, the Friday night debates at the L&H are particularly memorable. In those days, black tie/formal attire was de rigueur and it was donned with unquestioning acquiescence by even the most sartorially challenged committee members. Scores of political figures trundled into Theatre L to put forward their particular platforms, but they rarely emerged unscathed by the persistent heckling from the back rows. On a more serious level, those debates produced many vigorous discussions on the social and political issues that divided the nation at that time. The students of UCD were no exception in their often passionate responses to issues like the abortion and divorce referendums. Those two issues often brought to the fore a fairly dominant theme of debate: the appropriate role of the Church in a functioning democracy. Likewise, the issue of availability of contraceptives was equally divisive, with many students clashing over whether the Students' Union should facilitate the sale of contraceptives in breach of the law at that time. The reaction to the crisis in Northern Ireland amongst the student population at UCD seems to have mirrored the reaction (or lack thereof) throughout the Republic of Ireland: it aroused very fervent responses in some quarters; other students were more apathetic, engaging less with that issue than with issues considered to be more pressing to their immediate environment. The fact that Section 31 of the Broadcasting Act was still in force during that time contributed perhaps to that dichotomous reaction.

When students were not sorting out for themselves the social and political issues of the day, many were simply preoccupied with enjoying the social life college had to offer, as well, of course, as getting through those examinations at the end of the year. Given the economic climate of the times, there was often very little option other than to go abroad to find work in order to finance the following year of college studies. Troops of us headed off on the infamous J1 visa (or without) to the United States to secure work, usually in the service industry as waitresses, waiters, sandwich makers, and the like. Likewise, scores headed over the Irish Sea to the building sites and Pizza Huts of London. For anyone who was lucky enough to find work at home during those summers, Dublin seemed to be a ghost town. The college itself was almost totally depopulated, save for the staff and unfortunate repeat students. The first few weeks back after the summer months were particularly vibrant times. Although the experience of a few months abroad was in many respects a matter of survival, it had also provided us with invaluable experiences, contributed to our life-coping skills, and given many of us a taste of truly independent living. Although many of us had gone abroad in groups of twos and threes, it often transpired that many college friends were met overseas, and many of the friendships developed in that context during those few months matured apace after the arrival back to college in October.

However, the realities of economic recession and unemployment during that time had far more egregious effects when graduation finally rolled around. This was the generation of the so-called 'brain drain' when thousands upon thousands of students went abroad to seek permanent employment outside the State. Emigration was a simple fact of life. It seemed to be accepted almost as a given, a necessary evil, even by the politicians of the time. It was a difficult period for a lot of students and their families. Many did exceptionally well for themselves abroad. Others struggled, socially and/or economically. Fortunately, the birth of the much-hyped 'Celtic Tiger' has ensured that many of those émigrés have had the opportunity to return to Ireland to take up jobs in a market that has changed radically from the one they left behind.

Clare Eager

Age is No Requirement for Maturity

I suppose my journey to becoming a graduate of UCD began in the spring of 1984 when the College announced that it intended to admit mature students. I jumped at the chance, although if asked to say why my application for entry should succeed over other applicants, maturity wasn't exactly the first reason that sprang to mind. Luckily for me, however, apart from the formal procedure for application, the main criterion used by the College at the time was age related. Hark! — age no problem. Once accepted into college life, with the massed bands of seemingly (much) younger (appallingly) more mature men and women, I took my first faltering steps towards obtaining a B.A. by entering the hallowed portals of Theatre L, Arts Block in October 1984.

The years 1984–87 rolled into one another, broken only by the long summer breaks. This was, after all, the pre-semesterization era. During term time, lecture series followed lecture series: history, politics, philosophy. I can still recall, more than a decade later, the sense of awe I experienced as I listened to gifted lecturer upon lecturer develop his or her thesis on subjects as disparate as Heraclitus and his never-ending river, and the reasons why the 1848 revolutions across Europe held historians in thrall like rabbits caught in the glare of oncoming headlights.

The dreaded study was developed into an art form. Attendance at tutorials was simply mandatory, especially if you were borderline between pass and fail. 'T-days', as they became known, and meeting impossible deadlines were the twin peaks upon which I faltered occasionally, as each required precision planning akin to a WW II military campaign worthy of Rommel himself. Unlike the Desert Fox, alas, *my* only certain ally was an ability to balance lectures, work, study and home life, against more lectures, more work and more study — and still have time left for me. All of this study and preparation had one end: namely, the exams. These, I was assured by one in the know, were the absolute highlight of my academic year, an event to be yearned for and mourned over like a long lost love. A pity, then, that that particular informant failed to warn me that examinations in the field of Mills and Boon activities were an optional extra and best kept off campus. During my sojourn in UCD as I waited anxiously on a yearly basis for exam results, I discovered that the only thing that kept me rooted to my seat was, yes, that much vaunted maturity; the very trait that had got me into this educational pickle in the first place.

Ah, those were the days! Group VIIIa, Pass, Honours, the threat of failure. We shared it all with friends and lecturers alike. And, oh, the people I met along the way. The eccentric but brilliant Robert Dudley Edwards; the eminent Professor John Whyte on Church–State relations; Professor Donal McCartney on labour in Irish history — to listen to them was a revelation. Moreover, in an era when (some) Sisters were doing it for themselves, what can I say about Sr 'Ben' (or, for those of us still fortunate enough to claim her as a friend, Dr Margaret MacCurtain)? Hugh Gough, Michael Laffan and Ailbhe Smyth participated in one of the most magical evenings in the history of the History Department, by reconstructing the trial of Citizeness Marie Capet, or Marie Antoinette, Queen of France. Of course, the women in the audience decided that Her Majesty was a victim of a patriarchal society, and by a clear majority she was declared innocent of all charges laid against her. Her case became one of the most hotly debated miscarriages of justice. Bliss was it in that dawn to be alive, but oh, to be in the History Department that evening was very heaven as my interest in the history of women was renewed.

As graduation day dawned in October 1987 I knew that I had been sucked into the system for life. Like all good soldiers, I had volunteered to sign up for another tour of duty by completing a Master's degree in Irish history during the academic year 1987–88. Capped and gowned I waited on that cold and bleak October evening for the conferring ceremony to begin. I whiled away the time by searching the crowded hall for all those friends who three years previously had been strangers to me: Susan, Sophie, Deirdre, Gerry, Collette and Jim, where are you now? There are too many empty chairs and empty tables, my friends, especially the one reserved for my now deceased but hopefully proud mum, Noreen, who was central to my search for personal fulfilment during those years. But of all those I met, Frank springs most readily to mind. He was the epitome of age and dignity, of grace and maturity. A retiree of two days' standing, Frank had enrolled in college and had begun his studies with me in October 1984. He displayed all the qualities the rest of us could only imagine and now aspire to: a sound intellect, keen judgement, and, of course, maturity oozing from his every pore. He was, quite simply, the very best of reasons why UCD opened its doors to mature students in the first place.

With B.A. and M.A. complete I bade adieu to UCD in 1988, but returning as a visitor is like donning a comfortable pair of shoes. My aspirations are modest. I try to live the college-inspired, liberal ideal of life where nothing limits me save those restrictions I place upon myself. Thank you, College! Thank you! *Ad Astra*: look to the stars, students in the new millennium. As a new century dawns, seek and find your star. I know I did.

Susan Towers

From Leg Warmers to Power Suits

Walking into the Arts Block in Belfield recently to visit a friend was a reminder of how things have changed in the thirteen years since I graduated. Mobile phones rang constantly, the students were, for the most part, better dressed than we ever were, and the car parks I'd passed on the way in were jammed with so many cars that they could only belong to students (unless they've started paying the staff better). No doubt some of the vehicles were bought with the proceeds from highly successful 'dot com' businesses said students have been running out of their bedrooms since they were 15.

I was bemused to learn that you can attend college for free these days — maybe that's how they can afford the cars. I remember the angst of having spent my fees (which for some reason had been unwisely deposited in my bank account) and fretting wildly about how in God's name I was going to raise the cash. My dear departed friend, Jonathan (who always maintained that not having money needn't be a problem provided you know someone who has), persuaded me that it was a complete waste of time to feel bad about having enjoyed ourselves, and thus bolstered, I somehow convinced my long-suffering mother to co-sign a loan and managed to complete my education.

And what an education it was. I will provide full disclosure here and state that I graduated in 1987 with a pretty mediocre degree in politics and psychology (with the obligatory year of philosophy thrown in). For some people university is a good excuse to fool around for a few years before going out into the real world and either working or becoming a full-time fool. I did more than my fair share of fooling around — spending long days being chased around the restaurant by Alice, drinking bad coffee and even worse beer, and generally having a good time. But university, and UCD in particular, provided me with an unrivalled opportunity to learn about who I was and what I wanted in life, and also introduced me to some of the best friends a girl could hope for. I also avoided, I hope, becoming a full-time fool and instead managed to find someone to pay me to do something I enjoy.

In Dramsoc, I learned that although I could garner a decent review in the *Evening Herald* for a performance, there is no substitute for being prepared and learning your lines. (I skipped one third of a performance one evening when I forgot where I was — one actor never made it on stage, to his great chagrin and the deep confusion of the audience). At the L&H I watched and learned from the skilled debating performances of some of the best public speakers, many of whom now wage verbal war successfully and to great personal profit in the Four Courts of Dublin. I learned that I had an opinion and that I wasn't afraid to voice it. And having spent two years giving out about the loony left who dominated the Student's Union, I ran for office and learnt a lifetime lesson in politics. Losing the election was a small price to pay for the hours of fun spent plotting and scheming with my campaign team. I won only one constituency and was always very fond of architects after that (but engineers and farmers continued to terrify me). I tried to launch a magazine and spoofed my way into every nightclub in town for free on a bogus press pass. I fell in love in UCD and had my heart broken (not to mention my foot and a few other body parts). I must have experimented with every possible hair colour and fashion, and having arrived dressed from head to toe in black — it must have been my Goth phase — I graduated in a white linen suit and wanted to be a Yuppie. From fluorescent leg warmers to power suit in three years — what a trip.

I also learned to question authority and think for myself after too many years spent in a convent school that discouraged independent thought. Having been hauled over the coals by my politics lecturer in First Year, I was advised by him to consider a more 'feminine' subject like history of art. I realized that his attitude annoyed me and I told him so. But he made me think (if I'm kind I could hope that that was his objective, but I doubt it) and I've never tolerated that sort of put-down since.

The Eighties were an interesting time in the world with large-scale cultural changes and major political events taking place everywhere. We'd missed the student uprisings and sexual revolution of the Sixties, and now we were all becoming obsessed with making money. By the end of the Eighties Communism had all but ceased to exist in eastern Europe, AIDS had killed Rock Hudson, and whilst Ireland was beginning to emerge from an extended economic recession, most of my class still emigrated. I didn't realize when I flew to London two days after my exams finished that I was leaving Ireland permanently, which is probably just as well, as I would have cried like a baby. UCD was kindergarten in my University of Life, and what a great playground Belfield was.

Doreen Finn

Look Back in Envy

My four years as a full-time student in UCD are undeniably among my best. I see them as a whole chunk of my life, rather than four individual years, and most of the time I wonder if they ever really happened.

Just before I started in First Arts there was an open day in the Sports Centre for new students, which I attended with my parents. I remember a speaker advising us to enjoy these years, as they would be the freest times of our lives. In my eighteen-year-old naïveté I laughed at him, but his wise words, uttered and acknowledged only with the gift of experience, are still with me. Many times since I have wished myself back to being a student. Suffice to say that I adored UCD from the start.

On my first day I cycled from home with three schoolfriends, and the thrill of not having to wear a uniform was exhilarating. With our rucksacks and our 1980s clothes — jeans carefully rolled up at the ends, black polos, big hair — anything was possible.

My subjects were English, Spanish, and Greek and Roman Civilization. English was a huge class with over three hundred people. It took me nearly all of my first year to realize that if I did not do my reading no one cared. I remember missing two English lectures given by Dr Docherty because I had not even glanced at the John Donne poems he had told us to read. I was convinced that he would know from my guilty features that I had been drinking coffee and gossiping instead of perusing the loathed work of Donne. My friend Coman assured me that no one had been asked about the poems, but to be on the safe side, I skipped the next lecture as well. My convent school institutionalization had spilled over into my university life. Happily it was to desert me soon afterwards.

With Spanish, it was different. There were only twelve in Mr Cunningham's beginners' class — all girls, much to everyone's disgust. Everyone got on really well in the class, and we all remained friends for the three undergraduate years.

By the time Second Year rolled around friendship patterns had been set, and my closest friends then are still my closest friends. More than school, college made for forming fantastic friendships. Even with people I only see sporadically, it is so easy to slip back into the old familiar ease of established relationships.

Despite summers spent abroad — one, au pairing for a horrendous family in Spain, another working in a grocery store in Martha's Vineyard — going back to college was always brilliant. It was such a secure world, and even though the numbers of students was huge it always seemed as though we knew everyone, and, equally important, everyone knew us.

Even though I was lucky in that I loved the subjects I had chosen to study, it is not the academic aspect of UCD that stands out in my memory. Cheering on teams in bitingly cold weather, dressing up in ridiculous garb to collect money on Arts Day each year, queuing overnight for tickets for the Arts Ball, sangria-soaked gatherings in the Spanish Society — these and more are the fabric of my recollections. The sheer volume of talking I did while a student is also paramount in my memory. Four-hour lunches were regular occurrences in my timetable, as were Friday afternoons spent in that dim and dubious corner of our world known as The Bar.

Of course I look back and think that there are some things I could have done differently — working harder would feature somewhere. I also wish I had had the guts to audition for Dramsoc, instead of just going to hundreds of productions and aching with longing to be on the stage with my fellow students who always seemed so luminous, so talented.

College shaped my life and who I am, possibly to a lesser extent than I would like to believe, but its influence on me was incredible. I feel very lucky, very privileged, to have attended the greatest university in the world, at a time when it was fantastic to be there.

Leaving UCD was probably the hardest thing I've ever had to do. My fourth year, when I did the H.Dip, prepared me somewhat, as many of my friends were no longer around, but making my way in the adult world took me years. At every turn I wanted to run back to Belfield and hide, immersing myself in its concrete and cherry blossoms.

As a postgrad student — yet again — I still get a thrill out of lectures in the Arts Block and walks around the campus. I have to keep my envy of the undergraduates in check. Sometimes when I am going to class, or for a cup of coffee, I am twenty again on my way to the Wall or to the Sports Centre, and I fully expect to see everyone as I knew them. The buildings are full of ghosts.

For those of us who were in UCD then, it was perfection and we were invincible.

Teresa Duggan

A Daring Adventure

My husband was transferred to Dublin in 1985. The following year we sold our house in Ennis and moved to the city of Dublin. Our youngest child was about to begin secondary education. Our other four children either had their degrees or were in the throes of obtaining them. It was time mother got her degree — I 'only' had a diploma. I got all the necessary documentation and enrolled in UCD to do a B.A.

Though a mature student with five grown children — some of whom were the same age as the students in my class — I never felt any older than or different from the students in my year. There were about six hundred of us in First Arts. During the first few days when we were finding our feet we all talked about the same things — what subjects to choose, where to get the books, what societies to join, and so on.

As the days went on, the ten or twelve mature students like myself (some of whom are now amongst my best friends) tended to keep more together. We were told by the staff that the 'Matures' had a stabilizing effect on the class. I wondered about this when little paper arrows came shooting by me directed at a lecturer; or a real live mouse appeared on the platform beside the podium of a female lecturer who had a dread of mice.

The subjects that I chose in First Year were psychology, philosophy, and archaeology. Whilst I loved all three the one I specialized in eventually was psychology. Another student and myself met a psychology lecturer one day and asked him what subject to specialize in. He used the direct approach: 'Whatever you do, don't do psychology.' The two of us went off and did psychology. Later, as I learned about Carl Rogers' non-directive approach, I realized how true it is: you cannot tell someone what or what not to do. People will do what they want at the end of the day.

During term we had the usual lectures and tutorials. Statistics seemed particularly difficult at first, something akin to double Dutch in fact. Dr Delaney wrote points on the board and whilst we did not fully understand on the day we copied them down, later when we put a few heads together we came to grips with it. We eventually grasped enough for exam purposes. The mature students often helped one another and worked together in small groups. We discussed many topics over coffee in the restaurant or met at various places to clarify facts and exchange essays.

Exams were difficult times. The younger students seemed to be able to cram at the last minute and stay up all night. We older ones needed our night's sleep in order to have enough energy to sit through (usually) three-hour exams. The exam hall was mostly the main hall in the RDS. The time was after the Spring Show Week. I can still smell the horse and cow manure that wafted through the air.

Two of the staff that I remember as being especially good and kind, and who even remembered our names, were Dr Ethna Swan and Dr Aidan Moran. They took a great interest in all the students and tried to help in every possible way.

Well, I got my B.A., as did the other mature students. The following year I did a Masters degree in clinical psychology and later a Masters in Counselling. It was all a wonderful learning experience and one which I found very enjoyable too.

Later I joined the Women Graduates' Association. We have meetings, talks and outings. It is a great interest as well as a means of keeping in touch with colleagues. I also joined the UCD Golfing Society. I cannot think of a better way to spend a day than out on a golf course. One of the best things I did in my life was to become a mature student: 'Life is a daring adventure or nothing at all', as Helen Keller said.

Paula Hastings

Meet You at the Blob

I enrolled in UCD in the dark Eighties. It was a decade of unprecedented unemployment and mass emigration not seen since the days of the Famine. Most of my siblings and friends felt forced to leave for America, Canada, Australia or England to have any chance of getting a job. I, on the other hand, had one — and I couldn't wait to get out of it. Madder again, I wanted to do an arts degree, which in those days — as my elders were quick to point out — guaranteed one a place in the long dole queue. But my mind was made up. UCD had offered me a place; I resigned from my job and registered in October 1986 as a First Year Arts student.

An entirely new way of life unfolded there and then. My bike was to become my most revered possession, my trusty steed, as the number 11 bus could always be relied on to arrive at least one hour late, if at all. Fortunately 'The Flat' was annually located within a three-mile radius of the college. Entering Theatre L in a lather of sweat — sorry, perspiration — really wouldn't have done anything for my studied casual image! So every September the *Evening Herald* was bought and the 'Flats to Rent' section circled and crossed from one end of the page to the next. The search might take days, even weeks, but eventually a new abode would be found. Not that any of them were ever likely to feature in *Homes and Gardens*. Ranelagh boasted a regular crop of vegetables in the form of mushrooms, not lovingly cultivated by a kindly landlord, but growing on the bathroom wall. However, the location more than made up for that.

My Second Year abode on the South Circular Road was a wonderful house with the interesting feature of a ground-floor kitchen that was frequently submerged in six inches of water.

Worse again, the only bathroom was conveniently located behind it, so nocturnal visits to the loo were often punctuated by loud and obscene shrieks when the groggy and unsuspecting found their feet soaking wet. But it was a gem of a place, a mixed house of all ages and various souls trying to find their way. The Third Year address was in a tiny street just off the SCR again, and we really struck gold. Our neighbours treated us with a kindness rarely experienced by students — homemade apple tarts and brown bread were dropped in, there were daily exchanges with the locals, but we never had a sense of being monitored or judged. Unusual and unexpected behaviour and definitely appreciated.

College in the early weeks was nerve-racking, lonely, formidable, confusing, and dark. The Arts Block resembled a dingy sprawling nightclub open by day, where the universal meeting point was the 'Blob' and you certainly wouldn't want to have been visually challenged. Darkly dressed figures seemed to lurk in that tomblike space from Theatre Q to Theatre L. In today's world it would have provided the perfect backdrop for Buffy the Vampire Slayer. But I vividly remember the joy and relief at seeing familiar faces collect, as arranged, around the Blob to go for lunch, and the feeling of being saved from the masses of strangers who all seemed so self-assured and at home in this place.

Then there was the dilemma of what subject choice to make. English and French were definites, but what to take for the third? And so the tour began. Economics, a favourite at school, might be interesting. That idea was binned following a brief interview granted by a member of that department. His very tone and demeanour were enough to rid me of my silly feminine whim. Philosophy perhaps? But the crowds, and all those difficult questions and soul-searching — no, I wasn't ready for that yet. Eventually I listened to the wisdom of a very mature young Second Year and plumped for Linguistics. Finally I was ready to begin. Looking back, I am grateful for that time allowed to try and taste the delights on offer. Perhaps today's students are a more directed lot.

Lectures opened up a new world. I remember lunchtime conversations outside J001 where history of art friends animatedly discussed 'colour play', Cubism, and the next slide test. As the years passed the topics changed but the enthusiasm remained. Critical theory became the sexy feature of English and suddenly we were all swept up in the challenge to reread literature. This was the era of change; we were in the middle of a literary revolution. Jane Austen's *Emma* was a pornographic novel, our charismatic Scottish lecturer declared, its plot being contingent on sex and the exchange of money. Heady stuff indeed! That kept us going for the rest of the term. French revealed the works of writers such as Flaubert, Balzac, Hugo, Camus and Fournier. The exotic and decadent lives of Rimbaud and Gide were a marvellous antidote to the drudgery of the essential grammar and Stylistique Comparée classes. The constant patience and genuine enthusiasm of tutors like Joe Long and Johnny Grattan were something to behold. On the flipside, however, I recall one young First Year's wings being brutally clipped when a less kindly tutor advised her to consider hairdressing after she had received yet another poor grade in some assignment. Confidence building 1980s' style.

Social activities were always a hit-and-miss affair. The bar was a misguided imitation of the Pompidou Centre school of design without an ounce of panache or atmosphere. The yellow-and-blue paintwork always reminded me of primary school. Maybe that was the point — to invoke one's inner child. Despite the welcoming staff and the fab decor, it was not a venue for our frolics, although I do recall a brilliant gig by the Hothouse Flowers there.

Sharing a house with a musician meant there was always a chance of a party, usually in a weird location offering the worst homebrew of all time. Then there might be an occasion to crash an art opening or a book launch, which meant free wine and lots of sophisticated arty types — heaven. And 'Risk', that war game that unleashed all the worst military excesses of my male friends. It could last days, and grudges were held and nurtured until the next time. Dramsoc, too, provided some light entertainment, though we were all expected to take ourselves very seriously and fail at least one set of exams to prove our commitment, as it were. The more memorable productions, none of which I was in let me add, had to be Arthur Miller's *A View from the Bridge*, Friel's *Philadelphia, Here I Come!* and of course Shaffer's *Equus*. Each of these would rival any professional production I have seen since. The main point about these various means of entertainment was that none was expensive. One of my friends, a tall, elegant blonde who was constantly strapped for cash, spent her entire college years socializing in chic nightclubs because she had mastered the art of smuggling in her own supply of gin or vodka complete with desired mixers.

All things considered, my memories are rather happy ones. Essay deadlines, lengthy reading lists, horrible machine-coffee, Saturday morning lectures and the grey concrete walls seem to give way to memories of the great friendships made, the fun of learning, and the privilege of waking up on a Monday and deciding to roll over and miss that lecture.

The Wonder Years? Maybe.

Emma Donoghue

A Free Space

Growing up just outside the UCD campus at Belfield, I considered it my vast, private garden. At least once a day I climbed through the hole in the wire fence and lost myself in its winding woods and sodden fields. And when at 17 I made the move from a conservative convent school to First Arts at UCD, I experienced it — for all the dinginess of the buildings, the limp chips and dusty coffee — as heaven. It seemed a free space where anything was possible: I could wear what I liked, say what I thought, and I would never have to take orders from a nun again.

Looking back, ten years after graduation and emigration, I am still fond of Belfield and all it represents — but less impressed. It seems to me now that the friends I made and the books I read during my three years at UCD changed me much more than my formal education did. Teaching standards varied wildly, and when we were taught particularly badly we had no recourse but to skip the lectures. Students were never asked for feedback that I can remember, and a few incompetent lecturers were left to stand before five hundred First Years at a time and drone on inaudibly, year after year.

The English curriculum was highly traditional. We learned to speak Old English in the language lab (in case we ever met an Angle or a Saxon, I presume) and weren't let near any dangerous topics like 'Women's Writing' till Third Year. The only course I remember vividly is Tommy Docherty's eye-opening introduction to critical theory. Significantly, some of my best teachers — Mary Montaut, Lance Pettitt, Eibhear Walshe — had the most junior, least secure positions in the department.

The French Department was much less conservative, and I

benefited from the teaching of Paddy Marsh and Redmond O'Hanlon (on drama and film) and Ailbhe Smyth (on feminism), just a few years before they each split off from French to set up centres for the study of Film, Theatre, and Women respectively.

But my main criticism of UCD, in retrospect, is that its prevailing ethos was not so entirely different from my convent school after all. The student body seemed homogenous — Catholic, middle class, from the country or Dublin South — and generally right wing. I remember the male students, in particular, lining up in great numbers to vote against the Student Union's attempt to provide an abortion information phone number to the many women students impregnated by their male peers. And the Faculty could be just as bad; when on one occasion I objected to a lecturer's homophobic analysis of a Howard Brenton play, he told me that if I didn't like his language I could get out of his class.

The refuges I found and took delight in were Dramsoc — where I got a chance to dip a toe into the playwriting water, as it were — the English Literary Society, and the tiny Women's Group, which attracted vast amounts of resentment because men weren't allowed to join it! I remember the Women's Group lunches as highly entertaining conversational mêlées, an update on 1970s 'consciousness raising'. One friend I made there, Caroline Williams, went on to co-found Glasshouse Productions, a theatre company dedicated to new work by women.

Above all my personal haven was GaySoc, as it was known then. Though it was not recognized by the University — it and Sinn Féin being the two proscribed societies — its unofficial coffee mornings, and the many wonderful people (almost all men) I met there, were what gave me the nerve to finally come out of the closet, halfway through my time at UCD.

Every year for a decade GaySoc had collected signatures and petitioned the Administration for student society status. In 1988 the Registrar, John Kelly, told me in a kindly tone that the

Administration couldn't afford to recognize GaySoc because of the harmful effect this small society might have on innocent Freshers 'whose psychosexual identity wouldn't yet have crystallized'. This baroque phrase lingered in my mind, perhaps because at the time I was the only woman regularly attending the coffee mornings, so presumably would have had to shoulder the responsibility of corrupting the entire intake of female Freshers myself!

Such fears were shared — and more crudely expressed — by the anonymous graffiti artist who scrawled in the women's toilet in the UCD Library, 'Emma Donoghue is an AIDS-spreading bitch'. I remember staring at the words, then going back to my seat, heart hammering, and trying to get on with my essay on the Fool in *King Lear*. (It was in this climate of lethal ignorance about HIV, by the way, that the UCD Administration continued to keep the Student Union's single condom-dispensing machine under lock and key — to protect it from vandalism, it was claimed ...)

I'm sounding bitter, I know. That was the late 1980s, of course, and Ireland was a hellhole of sexual conservatism. But aren't universities meant to be on the cutting edge, a little freer than the countries that surround them? I had some superb times in UCD — especially after I'd found some kindred spirits and come out — but I was often made to feel like an alien there.

Moving to England, I felt like I could take a deep breath for the first time. I found the necessary distance to finish the novel I'd started in Second Year in UCD — *Stir-fry* — and, by putting it in print, put it behind me.

Nowadays, I often stroll through Belfield on my visits home, and feel little but affection for the place. Being invited back to give a reading by the Lesbian/Gay/Bisexual Society (full of confident young women) felt like a milestone. Though the fields have shrunk to make way for new buildings, the atmosphere feels much more breathable these days. And you can even get a proper cup of coffee.

Ciara Considine

Leap into the Unknown

After my first day in UCD, a self-conscious seventeen-year-old hell-bent on looking at ease, I vowed never to return. I hopped on a number 10 bus and walked from Baggot Street to my favourite park at Merrion Square, and there I found an unattended bench and quietly sobbed. Completely overwhelmed by the sheer scale of the campus and the endless sea of assured faces that breezed past me, I was convinced that I would never find a place for myself in this vast institution. I consoled myself with the fact that I could always emigrate. It was 1989 and that seemed to be the inevitable fate of Ireland's young, with or without a piece of paper under their belt.

It didn't take me long to realize that my feelings were shared by the majority of newcomers, and that much of the self-assurance on display was less a reflection of any reality than a part of the communal will to not look lost at all costs, *particularly* if you identified with the emotions of a lone kid in a big supermarket. After hoisting myself back on the number 10 the following morning, things slowly began to look up, and tentative introductions in the days that followed paved the way for firm friendships that would last through my three years there and beyond. Weeks later, and with several late nights in the dingy campus bar behind us, the feelings of bleak isolation had subsided and the atmosphere began to warm.

UCD, with its cold concrete facade, angular lines and airport-style library tunnel, was like Trinity's poor cousin: unadorned, unaffected and living out in the sticks. It was widely held that its design stemmed from State will to suppress anarchy, the primary evidence of this being the presence of a rectangular lake in the only open space on campus large enough for a significant gathering to amass. True or apocryphal, it was good to believe, putting us in touch with a sense of our own danger, the inherent threat that youth and idealism brings. Ironically, this mere impression was often probably enough to settle the vaguest rumblings of true rebellion, but who knows what revolutionary activity could have taken place there if only Ireland had a hotter climate? As it was, the only poor sods to ever enter the murky waters did so not out of choice but at the unfortunate butt-end of another's joke.

There was a certain political apathy amongst the student body of the late 1980s and early 1990s, certainly when compared with the university generation of the 1960s, where agitation went hand in glove with education and the effects of worldwide civil rights' movements eventually trickled down to Dublin 4. But it wasn't a neutral campus, and there was plenty of debate if you wished to get involved. It's hard to believe now, but during my time there it was not legal to sell condoms on campus, a chilling fact in light of a mushrooming AIDS crisis. Educational material on the subject so prominently displayed on the inside of toilet doors provided a stark contrast to an on-campus reality that made following its advice an impossibility. In the meantime, continuing friction between the Students' Union and college authorities resulted in a farcical routine of reinstating and forcibly removing a condom machine in the SU area.

Neither was abortion information available in the country, and a referendum on the issue spawned deeply polarized debate on campus, with all the accompanying fervency. The Gulf War brought cause to protest for some of us, a small minority in reality, and while our slogans and chanting outside RTÉ may not have created the stir we'd hoped for, at least we were raising our voices.

On the surface the Belfield campus might have been hard to warm to but its vibrancy was generated from within, its many societies providing ample opportunities to get involved in the broad canvas of college life. Amnesty International offering free vodka and orange with membership may not have been the most politically correct route towards increasing numbers, but that year a record level of new recruits proved that marketing doesn't judge. From within the confines of a life-size cage built by the father of a committee member, we experimented with new methods of consciousness-raising; attention levels were never so high – a shot of alcohol in return for a lecture on political prisoners or the death penalty the happy pay-off.

The idea of studying psychology had attracted me for years, but the reality of the subject that first year left me empty. More clinical than I had anticipated, the mantle of Arts seemed to sit uncomfortably on its shoulders, a nuisance imposter at odds with its hard-won stake in the world of science. Linguistics, a haphazard 'third choice', turned out to provide all the fascination I had imagined would spring from my first, and an experience in learning I had never before known. At the heart of the subject lay an intriguing mystery, that of how we acquire language, the precise answer to which question lies out of reach. And the structures, the theories, the formulas, the history and perhaps most of all the sheer wonder at this enigma of human expression were imparted to us by the staff of a small, personable department, its intimate structures a haven from the anonymity of the heavily subscribed English department. By second and third year, the linguistics class was small enough that everyone had an identity, and enthusiastic lecturers such as Conn O'Clerigh and Vera Capková encouragingly, if somewhat flatteringly, referred to us as 'linguists', adding to that sense of belonging.

Studying English Lit brought with it a certain surprising ambivalence. This was partially to do with my own naïvety, expectations based not so much on any research on my part, but on the ideas of a fertile imagination: where I thought creativity would abound, instead I found myself challenged by the rigidity of theory; critical thinking was less concerned with your own opinion than the considered opinions of those who had walked this way before you, and got a lot more mud on their boots. Much of it felt for me like tapping a square peg into a round hole, and this, coupled with the clear lethargy which emanated from certain quarters of the department, made for some dull days. Yet there were glimmers of genuine revelation. Younger, newer lecturers such as the Marxist theorist Tommy Docherty, and lecturer in Anglo-Irish literature Declan Kiberd, replete with an unabated and contagious energy, opened new doors of the mind and challenged prejudices. It was welcome relief.

A graduate at twenty, I imagine that if I began again today, I would have a greater appreciation of some of the gems that most likely sailed over my teenage head, intent on more hedonistic pleasures. But when I walked away from UCD after three intense yet in many ways unhurried years, I was glad I'd had the chance for a liberal education, glad for the uncertainty, the leap into the unknown, that being trained 'for nothing in particular' brings.

The 1990s

The 1990s could be regarded as the decade in which secrets of the past were exposed and the land of the proverbial Saints and Scholars did not seem so saintly after all. Political scandals were uncovered involving those who had run the country for years, and the extent of the corruption, exposed by lengthy and expensive tribunals, left a bad taste in our collective mouths. The saints fared no better, with increasingly frequent allegations being made of abuse dating back as far as the 1940s in clergy- and State-run institutions. In 1992 Eamonn Casey resigned as Bishop of Galway following the revelation that he was the father of a teenage son.

Mná na hÉireann had cause to rejoice, however, when in 1990 Mary Robinson donned a power suit to become the first female president of Ireland. Fists were raised in admiration — and possibly some in anger — as she took her place amongst the great men and women in history. A light burned in a window of the *Áras* for returning emigrants, and the word 'diaspora' became forevermore engrained in our minds. She left the office a little short of term to become UN High Commissioner for Human Rights, and was succeeded by another woman, Mary McAleese, the first president of the Republic to hail from Northern Ireland.

Mná (and *fir*) *na hÉireann* had cause to rejoice again when Michelle Smith kept us up late during the 1996 Atlanta Olympics as she won three gold medals and a bronze. Two years later she was banned from competition for allegedly tampering with a drugs test.

The violence in the North continued, but there seemed at last to be some cause for hope. Ceasefires were made and ceasefires were broken; there were bombs in the North and in Warrington, Canary Wharf, and Manchester, but there was also the Hume–Adams Plan, the Downing Street Declaration, the Framework Document, the Mitchell Report, the Belfast Agreement. Elsewhere the news was good too; in South Africa the first multi-racial elections were held in 1994.

The suicide of rock singer Kurt Cobain in 1993 came as quite a shock to those who felt that he was the voice of their generation, the voice of the disillusioned young teenager/adult who did not want to conform and so 'dropped out' of mainstream society.

The students of the late 1990s were children of the technological age for whom the ubiquitous mobile phone was a prerequisite; those of us who did not feel the need to embrace such technology had to endure endless ringing tones in lecture theatres, in the Library, and everywhere else imaginable. It was a far cry from the 1950s when most would have been lucky to have the bus fare home.

To judge from the pieces that form the section following, life in UCD in the 1990s was lived in several very distinct ways. One group of students seems to have experienced college life as an endless party where study was an occasional occurrence; for others, the undergraduate years were years of alienation and unhappiness where it was quite possible to go the distance and make few or no friends at all.

Ironies seem somehow to be a hallmark of a decade which witnessed the birth of the Celtic Tiger, a beast responsible not only for the increased prosperity of the Irish nation, but also for the fact that property consequently became so expensive that those who were forced to emigrate in the previous decade because there were no opportunities at home, can now often not afford to come back.

Emer Horan

1990   Nelson Mandela released from prison in South Africa.

Hostage Brian Keenan released in Beirut.

Margaret Thatcher resigns as Prime Minister and leader of the Conservative Party.

1992   Fourteen-year-old 'X' case rape victim prevented by injunction from travelling to Britain for abortion.

1995   Divorce referendum results in narrow majority in favour.

1998   John Hume and David Trimble receive joint Nobel Peace Prize.

1999   Launch of the Euro.

Anne Cassin

Soldiering On

I studied French and politics at UCD during my late twenties. I was, I suppose, a 'mature' student, but my vanity struggled with the negative connotations such a term conjured up. On the other hand, I was long past seeking out companionship at the UCD bar on a Friday night.

I occupied a role that separated me from most of my fellow students. I was generally older than the majority of students, and younger than the 'matures'. I combined working full-time at night with studying during the day, my working status conveyed by my appearance each morning, suited and fully made-up — a move that didn't lend itself to merging with the crowd.

But my time at UCD nonetheless was utterly positive. Initially it was difficult remembering how to study and asking my mind to open itself again. I enjoyed engaging with new material and the challenges that project work presented. Having spent almost ten years in broadcast journalism, where one dealt with concrete facts and figures, my mind had unconsciously taken a certain course so that when I was presented with philosophical material I struggled. I noticed that the younger students got to grips with Descartes and Nietzsche quite easily whereas I frequently felt as though I was cracking logarithms. I recall an occasion when, with two other equally bamboozled mature students, I decamped up to Dermot Moran's office in the Philosophy Department to ask about Descartes. There and then, he gave us a mini-tutorial.

It was that kind of openness among the lecturers that impressed me again and again in UCD. I was to learn of the reverse situation three years later during an Erasmus year in

Europe: German students got access to their lecturers via appointment on a three-month waiting list.

I didn't take philosophy beyond First Year, but I still count Plato's *Republic* as essential undergraduate reading. I loved politics and French equally. My spoken French wasn't great but I adored the literature. *Madame Bovary* is possibly my favourite book of all time. Flaubert was hugely popular among the students, putting paid to the theory that only 'relevant' literature has any value on a syllabus.

Politics was a wonderful journey of ideas that had, at times, a strong philosophical strain but seemed easy to absorb. Maybe it was because in many cases there was a relevant situation to observe. Certainly it had been some time since the Greek city-states, but the courses in totalitarianism and nationalism were given added urgency as we watched Yugoslavia fall apart.

So you see, university for me was mainly about study: reading books and writing essays. But of course, for most young people university is about life — tasting freedom for the first time, getting to know the opposite sex and generally having experiences outside the lecture hall. University can be hugely enriching on a personal level; one has the time simply to loaf around, taking ages to drink coffee and talk about — whatever. These are years when friendships are formed that last a lifetime. I know this because I have friends from early student days in Rathmines Technical College.

Of course, I did have the odd wobbly when things got on top of me. In my final year, exhaustion and self-pity propelled me to the faculties of French and politics, where I announced that I was giving up. In truth, this arose from the inevitable pressure of combining a full-time job with full-time study.

The French Department was kind. 'Come back in a couple of years. Finish it when you have the time.' But Tom Garvin, Head of Politics, showed no mercy. 'Give up work. Forget it. Pack it in.

Your degree is more important.' Gulp. This wasn't what I had expected. A few days' rest later, I had decided to soldier on. Thanks, Tom.

'Sacrifice' isn't a term that comes to mind when one thinks about doing a degree. Intellectual challenge, personal satisfaction, yes. But to be honest, when I measure up what I had to forego to keep my studies going, it becomes clear that I had to sacrifice certain things. I don't regret that and I still regard my B.A. with deep satisfaction.

I have wonderful memories of UCD, but I won't be enrolling for a Masters.

Anne Simpson

Growing Up

I have always fantasized a great deal as to what I shall be when I grow up. When I go to the theatre I want to be an actress. Just imagine playing Irma in *The Three Sisters* or Pegeen Mike in *The Playboy of the Western World*. I know I have a natural aptitude for treading the boards. Then there's ballet. Oh, to have legs up to my shoulders, to dance in *Swan Lake*, be caught in full flight by Nureyev and transported into a romantic world of make-believe. What about Art you might ask? Well, I can't quite see myself living on brown rice and pulses over an extended period. The fact that I can't draw is also a consideration. I did think seriously about a career in medicine. Doing something for my fellow man is a strong motivation. I also look very well in white. Unfortunately, I have seen too many episodes of *ER* and *Casualty*, which put me right off. The same applies to veterinary. Vets have to do unspeakable things — usually in the middle of the night.

I want something more. You see, deep down I have this recurring ambition to be an academic. It won't go away. Now don't laugh when I say this, but I think it's a vocation. Do you know what I mean? I just see myself in a black gown floating through the corridors of UCD, holding forth on some obscure philosophical theory, or becoming undone with John Donne. Academics are not mundane, practical people. They are ethereal beings. That's what I want to be when I grow up.

However, certain little practicalities have to be attended to on the road to academe. Decisions have to be made, and CAO forms have to be filled in and dispatched. That god-awful wait for acceptance follows, and then bliss — it's all systems go. One of the most important items to be attended to now is getting the right

222

gear. What are students wearing this year? Should I wear jeans or skirts? What sort of bag should I get? Would a purple streak in my hair look cool? You may think I fuss a little about trivialities, but one must have a sense of propriety. Next on the agenda are my books. Fortunately, the all-knowing and ever helpful Cormac Kinsella is at hand. Last but not least I must stock up on writing material and folders. Finally, with the gear, the bag, the folders and, of course, the books, I arrive in UCD.

On Wednesday October 3, 1990 I had my first taste of university life, and the realization of my dream. Hundreds of arts students assembled in Theatre L to be addressed by a host of lecturers from different departments. Erudition just seeped from their pores. One rather mature student leaned across the row in which I was sitting and whispered loudly, 'I wouldn't leave home for any of them.' She didn't stay long. Then Dr Terry Dolan stepped forward and announced to the assembled mass that we belonged to a 'community of scholars'. I knew in my heart that he was talking directly to me. Tables were set up in the concourse where lecturers from different departments advised students on their choice of subjects. There was even a table set up for mature students. One cursory glance at that lot was quite enough. They were all so grown up!

And so to work. I thought it would be a good idea to have some past examination papers, so I inquired at the Information Desk. Armed with my photocopy card and two large tomes of papers I advanced to a photocopying machine. Now, I thought everything in UCD was academic, but when the machine vomited out sixteen copies of the same page when I only wanted one, I became a little suspicious. To add insult to injury it did it a second time. Do you think it was trying to tell me something? The Library posed its own problems. Where to find the relevant books, and then, where to sit that would be conducive to study. I learned very early on that a diary was a must. In my innocence I thought I should remember where to be at a given time. Nine o'clock lectures in First Year may have seemed a drag to some, but to me, skipping down the path towards the canteen and the aroma of Bewley's at half past eight in the morning, they were a sheer joy. The panic of deadlines, the buzz of examinations, and the endless round of discussion, gossip and laughter with intelligent and supportive friends were part and parcel of the euphoria of being there.

In due course I graduated. What a glorious day! At last I could wear that black gown — the stuff of dreams. I had grown up. I was an academic. During the ceremony, however, I noticed that some of the dignitaries were wearing rather smart velvet caps. Now, I wondered, what would I have to do in order to wear one of those? I'm afraid that's another story, for another time ...

If you haven't guessed by now, I have a little confession to make. I did not sit my Leaving Certificate in 1990, or for that matter in 1989. That happened a long time ago. There have been a few little diversions en route to UCD, like marriage, and children, and running a home. Not very academic you might say. But I did use my brain sometimes — for example, when holding the flex of the iron at a particular angle so that the thermostat worked, or kick-starting the washing machine. I read a little, and thought a lot. Some poetry expresses certain sentiments with which I empathize: Miroslav Holub's poem 'The Door', an evocation of the adventurous spirit; or the uncertainties of Robert Frost's 'The Road Not Taken'. On reading Eavan Boland's *Night Feed*, the poem 'A Ballad of Beauty and Time' struck a chord. But I shall pursue that theme when I am really, really grown up.

Anne Mc Gettrick

Following in my Mother's Footsteps

As I walked into the lecture theatre all I saw was a sea of unfamiliar faces. How was I going to get to know all of these people? Would I fit in? Four hundred and fifty people in a lecture theatre is a daunting sight. As I sat down for my orientation meeting, I wanted to make a run for the nearest exit, but I was determined to get through the day because doing a science degree at UCD was a dream come true. I was following in my mother's footsteps. How things had changed since 1960 when she first walked through these doors. They were different doors for a start, because the science building was then situated in Merrion Street.

I mingled freely with girls and guys, and could choose anywhere in the lecture theatres to sit. My class consisted of sixty per cent girls and forty per cent guys. In 1960, when my mum started, there were twenty-five to thirty per cent girls and they had to sit in alphabetical order at the front of the theatres. This caused a lot of embarrassment for a poor French lad called 'Jean' who was placed in the middle of the girls!

As the year went on I met more and more people. Some I never met again, others have become my dearest friends. By the time it came to the fourth year I had specialized in biochemistry, and here the boys were well and truly outnumbered. The honours biochemistry class consisted of five guys and twenty-four girls.

Getting used to the academic side of UCD was hard enough, but getting used to the socializing was even harder. Freshers' Week was an experience I'll never forget. I walked into the Arts Block to be bombarded by people trying to convince me that I should join every society under the sun. I could learn to speak French, Spanish, German, Italian or Japanese. I could try trampolining, archery, rifle shooting, fencing and even caving. I resisted most of the societies but trampolining sounded too weird to miss. I went down to the club and had a go. I was hooked. The society had around fifteen members who practised on a regular basis, fifty-fifty male/female. The one thing that hit me instantly was that the girls had more sense that the guys did. The guys had no inhibitions and no nerves so they learned tricks on the trampoline a lot quicker. The girls would have to make sure that everything was safe before they would do a particular move. All sports in UCD cater for males and females. There are female rugby, football and hockey teams. These teams do not, however, have the prestige of the male teams. All the major sporting competitions in UCD are for males.

Socializing took a lot of time, but there was just about enough left to attend lectures and practicals. Although there were more girls in my class, most of my lecturers were male and no women had top jobs like Head of Department. Women employees do seem to struggle to get the top jobs. Despite this, I believe that males and females are treated equally at undergraduate level, and girls achieved many of the top marks.

I enjoyed my four years at UCD so much that I decided to come back for another three to complete a Ph.D.

Catherine Rossiter

Party Time in the Goldfish Bowl

Life in UCD Merville Residence was often likened to the existence of a goldfish. The parallel sprang from the fact that almost every aspect of each student's life was known (due to large windows) by the other student residents, even if names and identities were not.

Many lounge lizards drank hearty mugs of tea and coffee, munched on biscuits and watched the worlds of the residence go by from their large goldfish-bowl windows. 'Res' really was the University of Life!

Invariably the occupants of girls' apartments and guys' apartments observed each other across squares. Staring would give way to waving. Waving would lead to written signs asking names, and ultimately one party would muster the courage on some future occasion to meet and exchange numbers.

Parties were riotous and enormous fun, especially when organized by mainland Europeans who made such delights as sangria, cocktails and chocolate chip cookies. Despite strict regulations forbidding parties many were organized and were enjoyed by many.

I also remember the scam in my first year with rented TVs that charged £1 for seven hours' viewing. TVs offered RTE 1 and Network 2 only. An American friend of mine endeavoured to disconnect the wires from the meter. He succeeded, and got a small electric shock into the bargain, which made his fringe stand on end like Laurel's of Laurel and Hardy fame. These wires had to be reconnected quickly when the man from the rental company visited the residence to empty the boxes. Luckily such visits were infrequent. Some engineering friends turned their TV upside down while a flatmate dropped the money in, thereby tricking the meter into believing that it had a £1 coin. After the set was upright again the coin would fall out to be used another day. And people say that Engineers aren't creative!

The best night of the year in residence, apart from the end of exams, was the night of the infamous Residence Ball, usually held in Jury's in Ballsbridge in February or March. It was a chance to meet the people you knew to see for months and whose lives you had voyeuristically watched from the comfort of your own apartment since September. The party usually continued well into the wee small hours at somebody's gaff in the res.

I loved my time in Merville. The years I spent there were the best years of my life so far. It offered everything a student could wish for — friends, parties, good times, and fun on tap all the college year.

How could life ever be so good again?

Lynn McGrane

Not Always a Bed of Roses

When my grandfather died, he didn't leave me anything to get to college on except his black 'High Nellie'. It was a great bike that took him around Carrickmacross, and took me to and from UCD every day.

My first trip there was a scouting mission. I had no clue where it was or what it looked like, apart from what I had seen in the brochures I received in the post congratulating me on my entry. I set out from my Ranelagh flat and cycled in the general direction of Clonskeagh. I entered through the back gate, and it was some time before I worked out where the front entrance was. I managed to locate the Arts Block so that I would at least look as though I knew where I was going on enrolment day.

On the offending morning, I got up to a puncture and was panicked enough to blow £4 of my £40 weekly budget on a taxi to get me to enrolment. I had a bit of an affair with French, Greek, and Hebrew, before settling on English, art history, and philosophy. I dropped philosophy in my second year, even though I did well in my exams. It is a powerful subject that leaves no room for anything else. I felt I couldn't have made room in the bed for both it and English, so I bade it farewell.

At that time, I was winning out in a six-year struggle with an eating disorder, but it meant that I was shy of crowds, and especially canteen crowds, who I thought would be watching me eating. For a long time, I pulled my legs up onto the closed lid of a toilet and ate my lunch behind the safety of a locked door, so it is hardly surprising that I made no friends that year.

I did manage to join a society though. Joining the Literary Society was, for me, about assimilating. I attended meetings every week for the first year of college and was directly addressed twice, once to be asked to pass the biscuits.

The very odd thing about all of this was the way my college life was in complete opposition to my 'real' life. I was known as outspoken, confident and funny. I had a lot of friends and was never in the flat, yet I spent my days in college feeling embarrassed for myself.

One of the main reasons we were never in the flat was really because it was much warmer outside, even in the winter. We had no heating, and the walls were mouldy and wet. Every week we scrubbed the mould from the walls — and swept the carpet, as we had not been provided with a vacuum cleaner. In our first year in that flat I got scabies and my flatmate contracted pleurisy. Still, it was cheap.

Things got better in Second Year; I saw the inside of the Library and had people to go to the bar with. My style of writing essays, which had been criticized as 'flowery', was now more of a pared-down twig. I stopped writing poetry and got on with the act of criticism.

I didn't get a locker until my final year (because of the deposit), but one evening I discovered a note stuffed into the steel grill. It was from someone who had been 'watching' me. The next few lines suggested a time and meeting place. When I unchained my bicycle that night, the green ribbon I always kept tied around the handle bars had been loosened and made into a bow ...

I was intrigued, but I didn't go to find out who it was. When I thought about it, it seemed odd. When I think about it now, I can understand how a place like UCD would drive someone to seem desperate to be noticed.

Inside the college building I was an audience member, but in the grounds I found places that were an escape. There is a *faux* Greek temple there, which calmed me, and at the back, near the racetrack, there is a rose garden, quiet and scented.

Before going to college, I would have read a lot anyway, but I am not sure whether I would have understood as much as I did under guidance. Many of the texts that are favourites now — Dostoevsky's *Notes from the Underground*; *The Wife's Lament* (an Old English text); the lyrics of Jilted John (semantics class) — I feel sure I would never have encountered if it weren't for college.

I mentioned my flowery style of writing, which I used to love and which was praised in secondary school. For a while I blamed UCD for making me write differently, for taking my identity away from me, I suppose. I now realize that it was something I would naturally have grown out of anyway. University does teach you a certain type of independence, and ultimately you need a degree of some sort to be considered for work. I am glad I chose the arts degree, but I would like to see the ratio of lecturers to students increased, in the English Department especially. A lot of my friends went to smaller colleges, and when I witnessed the type of support that can give you, I was jealous. Having said that, UCD does do a lot of weeding, and those who make it through generally come out the other end (I make it sound like a sausage factory!) with a good degree. You have to try that little bit harder to make it, however, because it can seem as though no one cares whether you do or not.

Ruth McNamara

Small World

Recently I found myself drinking in the back room of a Jewish bar in Berlin called the *Tabula Rasa*. Ironic name for a bar really — the Clean Slate — given the fact that by the time I left the establishment in the early hours I had managed to acquire that most unclean slate of all: the bar tab.

The reason I was in Berlin in the first place came down to two very good friends, Anika Bardos and Gaby Giwan. I had met both of them at UCD in 1997. Anika and I shared a flat in Merville Residence, and Gaby ended up sleeping on our floor for six weeks. A UCD squatter, so to speak. The favour was returned in December 1999 when I was invited to Berlin for the Millennium celebrations. That night in the Tabula Rasa was day twelve of the festivities, and what a night it turned out to be!

We had just been to a production of Beckett's *Play* and *Catastrophe* at the Friends of the Italian Opera Theatre, and ended up at the actors' local for a couple of after-show drinks (or the premiere party, as the thespians would have it). None of us was feeling the Mae West, and we were intent on an early night. That was until I was confronted by a mass of shocking pink hair — it couldn't be! It was. Una Ní Gabhann.

As undergraduates, Una and I had studied history together at UCD. As a postgrad I often bumped into her and her ever-present tape recorder on the corridors of the Arts Block. Doing her bit for Ulster Irish, as she would put it. As it turned out, her crusade had taken her to Berlin. This was like some sort of mad dream, and any second now I would wake up. But instead I found myself in the company of Mary Schoales, an NCAD graduate who was in the habit of attending English lectures at UCD, and David

LeMasney, a graduate of the School of Architecture. This was a reunion of the Cilla Black *Surprise Surprise* variety! That night our conversation veered from Tom Waits' latest offering in *Mule Variations* to James Joyce's *Ulysses* to the latest results in the UCD Superleague. (Ah, well do I remember traipsing the soccer pitches of Belfield on a Saturday and Sunday morning with my good friend Lorraine Carroll, scouting for talent, so to speak.) For a brief moment, the Tabula Rasa in Kreuzberg, Berlin became the student bar in Belfield, Dublin. It was the first (unofficial) meeting of the UCD Berlin Chapter. All we were missing were the faculty scarves.

I spent four years at UCD, and they were the happiest of my life (so far). For those four years I lived in Merville Residence, and the stories I could tell from that den of debauchery are not suitable for polite ears. But what I'm trying to get at here is that for a number of us, UCD was not only a place of study, it was also home. That may sound like sentimental drivel, but that's just how it was. The student bar was our local, and Art Cosgrove our rich neighbour who came to visit at Christmas. There was a great sense of community out there, and it really encouraged the academic side of things. And believe it or not, I did manage to read the odd book from time to time.

It's difficult to sum up your feelings for a place in a couple of hundred words. But for me at least, that night at the Tabula Rasa where I was surrounded by good people and having a good time, pretty much captured the spirit of UCD.

Katie Long

A Fine Madness

When I first sat down to write these memoirs it was difficult to remember anything that had happened in UCD. My mind drew a complete blank. The entire three years, by this stage, had formed into a single homogenous mass of happy memories. The neck-breaking panic of trying to get essays in on time and the furore of finals had evened out to become an incubator-like bliss. After a time, however, I began to remember more individual details.

I remember arriving, a daft-looking First Year with basically no clothes (being straight from a school with a uniform). I planned to study English, history, and psychology in First Year with the intention of taking my degree in pure psychology. Within the first week, however, I was studying English, philosophy, and Arabic. I think my idealistic reasoning was: 'Why not do something new?' By the time we got past *Allah Akbar* my idealism was spent. One of the abiding memories of my first year was of having a feeling just before Christmas that if I keeled over and died (which incidentally, at the time I felt was imminently possible due to a two-thousand-word essay), Services would come and sweep me up and that would be the end of me.

I was sharing a room in digs with a friend of mine from school. A scientist by trade, she grew bacteria in our room. Between the five Koreans playing their music, a Spaniard who kept trying to convince us that he was a vampire, and a son of the family practising for his band, it has to be the most insane place I ever lived in. It was during this time that I discovered the soothing and medicinal nature of hot whisky.

Second Year is a bit of a blur. One of my main memories is of a day in the week after reading week. It started just like any other. A spectacular hangover lodged in my cranium was made special by the fact of having two tutorials and a class that had to be faced. I dragged my suffering body into college and arrived more or less in one piece to my tutorial — to be asked if I had prepared the material. In my deranged state, I answered no. Of all the fool things to say. But it was ten in the morning and my head hurt. My honesty was of course rewarded with a polite invitation to leave. I tried to soothe my pained noggin with caffeine. Then I attempted my twelve o'clock tutorial — I had the weeks mixed up. The mood was getting decidedly grim at this stage. But it was lunchtime after all and time to moan and gossip and engage in academic disputation, well kind of. Then off to the afternoon class, to discover on arrival a note on the door to the effect that the tutor was — not coming. In an effort to give the day some meaning I tried the Library. A fire alarm drill prevented me entering. Oh, the loss of a day in bed weighs heavily on the lazy.

For the final two months of my second year I was living with a friend from my course and four sweet country boys. They had no sisters and had never lived with girls before. It was very difficult not to exploit the situation. Due to the hedonistic nature of Second Year, when the exams loomed, problems arose. Myself and my roommate decided that the only way to pass was to share a brain. So while she was ploughing her way through *Pamela*, I waded through *Oliver Twist*. Insanity is not the word to describe those two months. Our house was reputed to be haunted, so we played ghost tricks on each other. One time she hid in the wardrobe intending to jump out; instead she fell out with a resounding thud covered in our clothes. I got my revenge with teabags in her boots.

Studying Mode 1 (Pure) English was a strange limbo land to be in. Interdepartmental rivalry seeped down to our level. The Modern English side called us 'Budding Medievalists' with a barely concealed curl of the lip. The Medieval side meanwhile felt that they provided our only reason for being there.

One time I had the same teacher for two medieval classes, one at ten in the morning and another at twelve. That same day I had an essay due in for a tutor on the Other Side. Unfortunately I miscalculated the amount of time it would take me to type up said essay. As 10 a.m. approached I realized that I would miss the class; as noon loomed the tutorial escaped my clutches. Finally at ten to five I was running up to the English Department, *Flight of the Valkyries* ringing in my ears. I had just handed the essay in, when who did I meet but the teacher I had missed twice that morning. Too exhausted to speak, I croaked a 'Hello' and then beat my head off a wall. The next time I met him I babbled a stream of excuses about computers and printers (aliens, etc. — can't recall the details) and he said how inconsiderate it was of the Modern Department to have the essay due in on that day, and that he would have to have a word with them about their deadlines …

The logic behind socializing in Third Year was slightly bizarre. Instead of going into town and thus waking up too tired for the next day, we decided that it would be more sensible to go to the student bar around six or seven. Ah yes, the hedonistic days of can smuggling. My friend still has the beer-smuggling bag, a fine example of craftsmanship if ever there was one.

The Finals came, as they do. I sincerely think that the only reason I sussed them was because myself and a friend spent the whole time quoting Kate Bush lyrics to each other: 'I know you have a little life in you yet / I know you've got a lot of strength left.' It cheered us somehow.

After the Finals, it was pastures new. Now, looking back two years, especially with the perspective of time spent at another university, all I can see is the good. If the picture be false, I care not; I had a fine three years.

Emer Horan

Of Mice and Men

The move from Athlone to Dublin was a transition that was long overdue. Having completed two Leaving Certs, I was beginning to think that I was doomed to remain forever a secondary school student in a wine uniform and knee socks. I had read about the country mouse moving to the city and adapting to its ways and I suppose I too yearned to become that creature — a woman of the city, a woman of the world! I thought that the only way to achieve this would be to move from the valley of the squinting windows to a city where students resided and where debauchery knew no bounds. You would be wrong, however, in thinking that my main reason for moving was for the purposes of debauchery; my main reason for moving all my belongings to a flat in Rathmines to live with two blokes from the Ormeau Road, was to exercise all my faculties in UCD, a sprawling metropolis that didn't look too unlike Lego-land.

I don't remember much about my first day except sitting in Theatre L feeling apprehensive and wondering what the next three years would hold for me. I had decided upon arts as my chosen course, partly because I hadn't a clue what I wanted to pursue long term and thought that it would give me three years to reflect. I picked philosophy as one of my courses, not because I fancied myself as a second Simone de Beauvoir, but because I didn't know what to expect and decided that after six years of being spoon-fed I would try feeding myself. There were moments when I realized that I had never thought for myself before coming here, and although some considered philosophy a subject for pretenders, I, being a country mouse, had no such delusions. I regarded it as a lesson in how to *really* think, and instead of ogling Richard

Kearney as others did, I noted down his most profound phrases. I reckoned that even if I couldn't plagiarize them in an exam, I could at least use them down the pub and impress all my friends. I certainly couldn't use them back in Rathmines, where my two flatmates were more interested in drinking Harp and discussing football than engaging in philosophical conversations about Nietzsche. (How I came to share a flat with two strange blokes on my first year away from home is a long story. Suffice to say that I was desperate, innocent, and sorry afterwards. The only advantage to living with two men is the fact that, unless they have a few skeletons in the closet, so to speak, they won't be interested in borrowing your toiletries, make-up, and the like.) I joined the Philosophy Society thinking it would broaden my horizon and put me in touch with great minds, but it was more like a coffee morning for the bewildered than a forum for superior philosophical debate.

First Year passed quickly and resulted in my having to repeat a Greek and Roman Civilization exam. You could say that it was my Achilles' Heel (excuse the pun) and it caused me two months of grief. I spent the summer in Scotland, surrounded by notes — which I should have been reading all year, of course, but hindsight is a wonderful thing. I got into Second Year by the proverbial skin of my teeth and severed my ties with Homer and his ilk. Having dropped one subject, I thought in my naïve state that things would get easier, but I found that the workload increased and I seemed to be spending most of my time in the confines of the Library. So much for a debauched life.

At this stage, I had moved in with three fellow country mice and life back at the ranch was once again restored to normal. We all became familiar with each other's idiosyncrasies, and the fact that we all did different courses made for a varied life. Business, medicine, occupational therapy, and arts; one managed our financial affairs, the other two dealt with hangovers and sickness, and I cast a philosophical glance over the whole lot.

I enjoyed Second Year but it was neither a beginning nor an end and I wondered if I had chosen the right course after all. I hadn't time for real doubts, however, as the summer passed rapidly and I returned to the autumnal campus of Belfield for the last time as a student. I was determined to beat the rush and start studying early to avoid the last minute panic, but my shadow did not darken the library door until early spring. Essays were a constant feature in my life, so much time was spent at home willing on the creative juices. I had trouble grasping the concept of word count so my unfortunate tutors were sure to get some hundred words fewer than the requirement in most of my essays. Only one tutor had a word in my ear about it and I was glad she did, if only to bring me to my senses.

Throughout the three years in UCD I had entertained the idea of getting involved in some sort of sporting activity, as I had been very active in school playing basketball, volleyball and badminton. As soon as I entered third level, however, those days were forgotten and I was no longer worthy of the name Sporty — Lazy Spice was more the thing. I decided to change my ways and visited the gym for a preliminary warm-up, hoping that it would invigorate mind and body. I vowed never to go back after spending two hours thrashing the equipment, an endeavour following which my body felt like it had been steam-rolled, but it did provide a means of releasing stress and the gym eventually became a sort of haven. Leading up to the final exams my visits got fewer, and the Library instead became my second home.

The exams dawned and I felt a great sense of melancholy as the end drew near. I remember sitting on the steps outside the Sports Centre on the morning of my last exam — Old and Middle English. It was warm and everyone looked tired and relieved, and all I could hear was the sound of voices drifting off into the summer air. It felt like an era had come to an end, and at home two large sacks of revision notes were waiting to be discarded. I rose from the steps, like a phoenix from the flames, and went through the doors for the final round-up, catching as I did so the eye of the tutor who had commented on the length of my essays, and I had a feeling that the essay I was about to write wouldn't be any longer but would have more meaning than any that had gone before because it signified the end of one life and the beginning of another. Three years had come to a close and the country mouse was going back home for the summer.

University College Dublin Women Graduates' Association: Now

The main aim of our founders, as discussed in the introductory pages (xviii–xxiv above), was to secure for Irish women the full advantages of university education. The inequalities and injustices that have faced women graduates (and indeed women in general) in the labour market and in the workplace, have also been addressed by the women graduates' movement since its foundation. At national level, women graduates' associations were represented on the Ad Hoc Committee that was set up in 1968 to investigate all forms of discrimination against women. This was followed in 1970 by the establishment of the Commission on the Status of Women, for which the UCD Women Graduates' Association conducted important research on women in employment. The Association takes an active part in the National Women's Council of Ireland, helping to shape policies on education, health, social affairs and work.

At local level, the Association runs a very successful annual Public Speaking Competition for girls under fifteen years of age, and awards a bursary to the highest placed woman graduate in the examinations for the Higher Diploma in Education.

The Association forms part of the Irish Federation of University Women (IrFUW), which comprises Queen's University Belfast, University College Galway, Dublin University (Trinity College), University College Cork, and University College Dublin. An annual weekend conference is hosted by one of these universities each year.

Through University Women of Europe (UWE) and the International Federation of University Women (IFUW) we reach out to the wider world of women graduates. UWE holds a colloquium each year; in 1995 it was held in Dublin. The International Federation holds a triennial conference, which provides another opportunity to renew friendships and join in challenging and stimulating programmes.

Friendship is one of the most important elements in the fabric of the women graduates' movement. The UCD Women Graduates' Association organizes a programme of lectures and cultural and social events that provide opportunities for members to meet one another; the activities of the Irish Federation, University Women of Europe, and the International Federation extend the web of friendship over an even wider field.

Joyce Andrews

UCD Women Graduates' Association
Chronology of Activities and Events

1879   Royal University Act. Women could be examined
        and obtain degrees.

1901   Establishment of Robertson Commission.

1902   Foundation of Irish Association of Women
        Graduates and Candidate Graduates. Witness
        Evidence Presentation to the Robertson
        Commission.

1904   Trinity College opened to women.

1906   Witness Evidence Presentation to Fry Commission.

1908   Foundation of National University of Ireland.
        Statutes enshrined equality of education for
        women and men in all positions in the Colleges.

1914   Association of Women Graduates divided into three:
        Association of NUI, Dublin University, and Queen's
        University Belfast.

1916   Proclamation of Equality between Men and Women
        proposed equal rights and opportunities for all
        citizens.

1924   Irish Federation joined International Federation of
        University Women.

1925   Foundation United: UCC, UCD, UCG, DU and
        QUB.

1925   Civil Service Amendment Act. Passed in Dáil,
        defeated in Senate, following women graduates'
        canvassing of University representatives.

1935   Conditions of Employment Bill. Women's security of
        employment threatened. Ministerial powers to
        prohibit employment of women in certain industries.
        Challenged unsuccessfully.

1937	Certain Articles of the Constitution challenged. Some amendments obtained. Constitution passed by nine per cent majority.
1968	Two Women Graduate representatives among ten on Ad Hoc Committee to investigate and research discrimination against women in Ireland. Memorandum to Government. Research conducted on Graduate Employment.
1970	Commission on Status of Women established. Research Report published 1972. Women Graduates' contribution acknowledged.
1972	Graduates represented on Council for the Status of Women, formed to campaign for full implementation of the report recommendations.
1978	Council for Status of Women officially assigned task of monitoring implementation of recommendations.
1978–97	Women Graduates are affiliated to Council for the Status of Women/National Women's Council of Ireland.
1990	Submissions to Green Paper and White Paper on Education.
1992	Submissions to Second Commission for the Status of Women.
1995–97	Submissions to committees/commissions on Education, Women's Health, Anti-Poverty Strategy, Safety and Security of Older People, Violence Against Women.
1996	Submission to Minister for Education on Universities Bill (1996).

Presidents

Professor Mary Hayden, D.Litt.	1913–42
Professor Agnes O'Farrelly, D.Litt.	1943–47
Professor Mary Macken, D.Litt.	1947–49
Miss Kathleen Phelan, M.Sc., Barrister-at-Law	1949–51
Mrs Maureen Beaumont, M.A.	1951–52
Dr Annie Keelan, M.A., B.Mus.	1953–55
Miss Nora Stuart, M.A.	1955–57
Miss Geraldine Roche, M.Sc.	1957–59
Dr Neans de Paor (N. Wyse Power)	1959–62
HE Mrs Josephine MacNeill, B.A.	1962–65
Dr M. P. Fanty O'Dwyer	1965–67
Mrs Kathleen Garvin, M.A.	1967–69
Mrs Rosemary Muldoon, B.Comm.	1969–71
Mrs Sheila MacDonagh, B.Comm.	1971–73
Mrs Peig Roche, B.A., B.Comm.	1973–75
Miss Mary Ena Walsh, M.A.	1975–78
Mrs Helen Griffin, B.A.	1978–80
Mrs Caitlin Ó Ceallaigh, B.A.	1980–82
Mrs Maeve Carroll, B.A., B.Soc. Sc.	1982–84
Dr Vera Randles	1984–86
Mrs Eilish Ellis, M.A., H.Dip.Ed.	1986–88
Mrs Toni Phelan, M.A., H.Dip.Ed.	1988–90
Mrs Marguerite O'Sullivan, M.Sc.	1990–92
Mrs Mary Horkan, M.Soc.Sc.	1992–94
Mrs Joyce Andrews, B.A., H.DipEd., M.Ed.	1994–96
Miss Mary Tinney, B.A.	1996–98
Mrs Ita Kirwan, M.A.	1998–2000
Mrs Eithne White, B.Comm.	2000–

Vice–Presidents

Mrs Eithne Tighe, B.A.	1973–75
Mrs Helen Griffin, B.A.	1975–78
Mrs Maeve Carroll, B.A., B.Soc.Sc.	1980–82
Dr Vera Randles	1982–84
Mrs Eilish Ellis, MA. H.Dip.Ed.	1984–86
Mrs Toni Phelan, M.A., H.Dip.Ed.	1986–88
Mrs Marguerite O'Sullivan, M.Sc.	1988–90
Mrs Mary Horkan, M.Soc.Sc.	1990–92
Mrs Joyce Andrews, B.A., H.Dip.Ed., M.Ed.	1992–94
Miss Mary Tinney, B.A.	1994–96
Mrs Ita Kirwan, M.A.	1996–98
Mrs Eithne White, B.Comm.	1998–2000
Ms Joy Wheeler, B.A.	2000–

Hon. Secretaries

Miss Ellen Hartnett, M.A.	date uncertain
Miss Ellen Power, M.A.	1929–33
Miss A.M. Barrett, M.A.	1933–37
Miss Mary J. Hogan, B.A.	1937–39
Miss Isabella Carey, M.Sc. (Mrs Farrell)	1939–42
Mrs May Conan, B.Sc.	1942–45
Miss Ita Malone, M.A., B.L.	1945–46
Miss Mary J. Hogan, B.A.	1946–48
Miss Mary Davoren, M.A.	1948–52
Dr Carmel Humphries	1953–57
Mrs Kathleen Garvin, M.A.	1957–59
Mrs M. Kearney, B.Comm.	1959–62
Miss Phyllis Purcell, B.Comm.	1962–64
Mrs Joan O'Callaghan, B.A., B.Mus.	1964–68

Mrs M. Kearney. B.Comm. (Records Secretary)	1964–68
Mrs Sheila MacDonagh, B.Comm.	1968–71
Mrs Peig Roche, B.A., B.Comm.	1971–73
Mrs Eithne Tighe, B.A. (Records Secretary)	1971–73
Miss Mary Ena Walsh, M.A.	1973–75
Mrs Olive McNally, M.Sc.	1975–77
Mrs Minna Ryan, B.Comm.	1977–79
Miss Ursula Leonard, B.Comm. (Mrs Corrigan)	1979–81
Mrs E. Gilligan, B.A.	1981–82
Mrs Toni Phelan, M.A., H.Dip.Ed.	1982–85
Miss Clare Dwyer, B.Comm., B.A., H.Dip.Ed	1985–88
Miss Gabrielle Doyle	1988–90
Mrs Maureen Murphy, B.A., Dip.Soc.Sc.	1990–92
Mrs Audrey Woods, M.Soc.Sc.	1992–94
Miss Niamh Hynes, B.Sc.	1994–96
Mrs Eithne White, B.Comm.	1996–98
Miss Joy Wheeler, B.A.	1998–2000
Miss Sally O'Donnell, B.A., D.P.A.	2000–

Hon. Treasurers

Miss Margaret Bowler, M.A.	1929–43
Miss Mary Semple, B.A.	1943–47
Dr Carmel Humphries, B.Sc.	1947–49
Miss Maura Belton, B.Comm, A.C.A.	1952–59
Miss B. Flynn, B.Comm.	1959–62
Dr M. P. Fanty O'Dwyer	1962–65
Mrs Maura O'Higgins, B.Comm.	1965–66
Mrs Helen Griffin, B.A.	1966–69
Miss Eileen Bourke, B.A., B.L.	1969–71
Miss Brid Cotter, B.Sc., B.L.	1971–74
Miss Mairead MacParland, B.Sc.	1974–77

Mrs Olive McNally, M.Sc.	1977–79
Dr Vera Randles	1979–82
Miss Carina Doyle, B.A.	1982–83
Mrs Pat McDermott	1983–86
Dr Caroline Hussey	1986–87
Miss Maura Belton, B.Comm., A.C.A.	1987–91
Mrs Nell Brady, B.A., B.Comm.	1991–93
Mrs Olive McNally, M.Sc.	1993–96
Mrs Catherine Wood, B.Sc.	1996–98
Mrs Olive O'Neill, B.Comm., A.C.A.	1998–

UCD Women Graduates' Association contact address:

The President
UCDWGA
c/o Services Desk
UCD
Earlsfort Terrace
Dublin 2